Our Mother's Messages to Michael

"Our Mother's Messages to Michael," by Kenneth Heck. ISBN 978-1-63868-043-7.

Published 2022 by Virtualbookworm.com Publishing Inc., P.O. Box 9949, College Station, TX 77842, US. ©2022, Kenneth Heck. All rights reserved. No part of this publication may be reproduced, stored in a retrieval system, or transmitted in any form or by any means, electronic, mechanical, recording or otherwise, without the prior written permission of Kenneth Heck.

.

Email: kennethmheck@gmail.com

Since Articles 1399 and 2318 of Canon Law were abrogated by Pope Paul VI in 1966, no ecclesiastical permission is required, neither can anyone incur censure, for the publication of information dealing with revelations, visions or miracles, provided these do not endanger faith or morals.

In conformity with the Decrees of Pope Urban VIII and the Second Vatican Council, without wanting to anticipate it in an undue manner, we accept gladly the judgments of the Holy Mother Church concerning these Messages.

THIS BOOK

IS DEDICATED

TO

The Most Holy Trinity,

the Father, the Son and the Holy Spirit,

and to the Mother of All, the Blessed Virgin Mary.

Contents

Messages

1982 and Prior 9
1983, First Quarter 19
1983, Second quarter 40
1983, Third Quarter 59
1983 Fourth Quarter 88
1984 96
1985 112
1986 119
1987 132
1988 137
1989 145

Litanies and Prayers

St. George 150
St. Anthony 151
St. Joseph 152
For a Happy Death 153
St. Michael 154

St. Patrick 155
St. Sharbel 156
The Blessed Virgin 157
St. Ann… 158
The Mercy of God 159

Our Lady of La Salette 160
The Miraculous Infant 161
St. Benedict 162
Our Lady, Queen of the Holy Innocents 163
The Holy Angels… 164

St. Philomena 165
The Three Patrons 166
The Saints 167
Our Lady of Mount Carmel 169
The Holy Childhood of Jesus 170

The Holy Spirit 172
Our Lady of Sorrows 173
Our Lady of Good Counsel 174
The Souls in Purgatory 175
Shorter Souls in Purgatory 177

The Faithful Departed 178
Short Prayers… 180

PREFACE

The twentieth century has witnessed an astonishing number (nearly 400 at latest count) reported Apparitions of Our Blessed Mother. These apparitions have been reported on every continent on our globe. The seers, men, women, and children, have been people from many walks of life. A spiritual outpouring of this kind has never before occurred in the nearly 2,000 years of the Christian religion. The vast majority of these claimed apparitions have yet to be investigated and approved or condemned by the Roman Catholic Church.

The apparitions are typically accompanied by communications which have displayed a remarkable similarity in content. They normally warn of very dark days ahead and future catastrophes. They appeal for a return to God, with renewed emphasis on prayer, the Rosary, Mass attendance, Penance, Confession, Bible reading, and distributing the Messages widely to save those able to believe.

Michael, a young, teen-age Seer, experienced visions of the Blessed Virgin Mary and other saints, but did not seem to develop further as a Seer beyond his twenties. His cause was never investigated. It was during this time, the decade of the 1980's when the Cold War had reached its peak and international tensions were quite high (threatening nuclear war), that Michael's Messages were being released to the public. Subsequently, the Berlin Wall fell in 1989, and both the Soviet Union and Yugoslavia disintegrated in the early 1990's, relaxing the previous tensions. I have no doubt that the activities of Michael and many other Seers, known and unknown, contributed greatly to these positive developments.

Now, nearly thirty years later, we see international tensions rising again, combined with an economic downturn and a complex pandemic of worldwide proportions. It would be well to revisit the Messages of the past for what guidance they can provide, since true Messages from Heaven concern both the short-term and long-term future. Unsurprisingly, comparatively little has been published concerning most seers. This volume is derived from the original typed pages mailed out in the 1980's. There is no guarantee they are the complete set.

Since certain selected Litanies and Prayers were also included with Michael's Messages, they are also provided in the second section of this work.

WORKERS OF OUR LADY OF ALL HOLY TITLES

Dear Fellow Servants of Mary:

I first would like to tell you of the fact that my last name must not be revealed publicly. I am a Seer of the Blessed Virgin Mary. The Virgin does not exactly speak through me - but rather She writes through me. I will tell you now how this Mission from Heaven came to me.

On December 7, 1982, I was just an ordinary person. I say ordinary in the manner of a person who was a member of the unapproved Catholic Bayside Shrine at which site the Mother of God appears to another Seer. I had had a few small 'visons in the past prior to this prodigy of which I now speak. I had never thought the Mother of God would come to me, a lowly sinful teenager.

On December 7, 1982, the date is to be recorded as the first date She came to me. I went into almost what might be called a trance - and I would add that I did not know what had happened until I awoke and I found myself praying for the Holy Father in Rome, Pope John Paul II. Then I noticed the Message that was in front of me. I must admit that when I first read the Message I did not believe that it was the Most Holy Virgin Mother. I had thought that a demon had caused me to write, but this was changed the second time I received a Message.

On December 21, 1982, our Mother of all Sacred Titles spoke to the word (and me) through my hands via an ability called telesthesia. During this mind contact I was permitted to view from Her mind, the unearthly beauty of which She alone possesses. I was able to see how She truly looks.

On December 24, 1982, The Virgin came to me and caused my hands to again begin to write Her Message to the world.

On December 26, 1982, St. Theresa came to me with a poem Message to the world. She did not even awaken me from sleep. The poem was from when she had been upon earth herself. It had never been published when she was upon earth during her own earthly life.

On December 28, 1982, Mary spoke and Jesus. I was very tired, I might add, when this Message was given to me.

There have been other Messages which have not been set to type as yet. If you are interested in what I am sending to you, then please remit to me a letter to let me know. I will continue to send them to you if you will help spread the Message without my address or telephone number on them,

Sincerely yours in Jesus, Mary, Joseph
and my Guardian Angel,

On Friday, December 7, 1979, The Eve of the Immaculate Conception of Mary, I was upon the Sacred Vigil grounds of our Holy Mother's Shrine at Flushing Meadows Park in Flushing, Long Island, New York. The night was to be listed as my first attendance of a vigil upon those Sacred Grounds, as well as the first vision ever of a Heavenly Figure. At that time it was a very cold night. I, at that time had been only previously by three years (1977 in October till December 7, 1979) been awakened from my slumber of an untaught Catholic. I had previous to this been only 12 years old and had hated God for the death of my grandmother.

As I have already stated, I was not very knowledgeable yet of the ways of the Catholic Church and of God. Thus, you can see why that it became easy to hate God for the death of a loved one - not only one but 3 grandparents. I knew not at that time that death was only a rebirth to the afterlife. I also was saved from the clutches of Luciel, the Prince of Darkness, as I was involved in a coven before this awakening. I was one of a group of 13. I was to be trained for a future as a high priest within the coven, called Blackfoot. I narrowly escaped being caused to do a human sacrifice to Satan. Well enough of the past when I was not spiritually alive.

When attending this Shrine Site Vigil of Prayer at New York. I took some pornographic pictures in my wallet (sad as of yet I was still into pornography's snares at that time) these I did not think would bother Heaven. Little did I know, that I would soon think, differently as Jesus would convince me not only of it but that Bayside (Bayside is one of the titles of the Shrine) was true.

The vision began in this way. I was kneeling amongst the crowd and reciting the Rosary with the crowd when I began to cry for no reason (or so I thought). Every time we would come to the name of Jesus during the Hail Mary and the O My Jesus Prayer, I would let loose a trickle of a tear, but only during His name. I looked up to the sky and saw a beam of wood seemingly stretching into infinity, directly across the sky, and yet nothing was holding it up there (at least nothing I could see). Next after looking down, I then looked back up and saw only a complete wooden cross, crucifix without the nails or the corpus. I again looked down, thinking maybe I was going crazy. Then I saw blood falling upon the crowd from nails which appeared upon the Cross. The blood did not stain the crowd as it fell only above the crowd (it never actually hit). Next the body of Christ appeared upon the Crucifix and I heard an ear shattering yell from Jesus - He said, "Why"?

He was referring that my pornography was cause for Him to suffer the cross again in his Mystical Body. Next I looked down and pulled my hat over my eyes. The hat was immediately flung off of my head by Heaven so that I might continue to view. When I again looked upwards in the sky the head of Jesus was bowed and His heart most Sacred was pierced and He was dead, while blood, the Precious Blood of Jesus, was still falling over the crowd. This vision then vanished (December 7, 1979).

****

Monday, December 31, 1979, Eve of the Solemnity of Mary. On that day, I viewed a large wing-like image across a huge area of the sky. It was that of St. Michael the Archangel. This wing was the size of a wide oak tree in the crown.

****

This is the Message of the Blessed Virgin Mary to the world through a privileged soul on December 7, 1982, the Eve of the Feast of the Immaculate Conception.

"This day has lived in the annals of your world, and your nation as the Second World War's beginning. This day brings both joy and sorrow to my Immaculate Heart. You cannot see the thorns. Although you cannot see Me, nor realize that you are writing this, till after I have left from you, I wish for you to know that I am the Immaculate Mother of He who is creation. I am the Queen of Poland - the Sorrowful Virgin of La Salette and all apparitions, and Patroness of your country - as well as the Queen of Heaven and I have many more

Blessed Titles.

"Pray much for your Holy Father, he needs many prayers because of those about him who wish to remove him from among mankind. You when you read this will long to pray for him as you wish him to live. You wanted at one time to see him, when he came to your country, but you were unable to. I promise you if you heed the directions I gave all at Fatima, Lourdes and many other places you will see not only him, but all the popes someday with My Son and I.

"There are many errors in the Church of today. Your angels of your Churches have not reported good activities to the Padre of Heaven. St. Michael's prayer must be returned after Mass. The Holy Hours are made by too few (but they are blessed who make these). The Rosary must be allowed for recitation in your Churches or those Churches will fall and crack from within, spiritually, not physically. When any guild honoring my name is rebuked, calumniated, or chastised for something done or said justly these groups shall be doubly blessed. When you tell only the complete truth and no lies as well as not withholding any truth - and are not believed, a ray of grace shall come and fall upon you.

"Not enough concentration is given upon the Blessed Eucharist and the Crucifix of my Son. My Son was crucified for your sins, all of you, yet many of you are forgetting this: Honor my Son, kneel before Him. Pray to Him, He will hear and bless you, for all your prayers. My Son bleeds for all your sins my son, turn back now so you may come to me as a Beloved Son. My Son, he is recrucified by the sins of all of mankind.

"As you pray for the souls in Purgatory, do not forget to beg that they pray back for you on earth in your earthly mortal plane of existence. One drop of holy water is, if sprinkled in the air anywhere, in honor of an unnamed soul in Purgatory, is a glass of water to the parched mouth of a man in the hottest of your earth's deserts. Only if you pray while on earth, for the souls in Purgatory will any prayers be allowed to reach you when you are there in the Spiritual Life.

"Communism is the scourge of mankind. As you know, Czechoslovakia, Poland, Hungary, Tibet, East Germany, Vietnam, Cuba, Lithuania, Laos, Burma, Bulgaria, Khmer, North Korea, Malaysia, Bhutan, Chad, Siberia, Mozambique, Mongolia, Russia, and many other countries have fallen to the communistic regimes. In Yugoslavia, I have built a source of grace for the communist countries; I repeat: in this manner, a source of Hope for them.

"In 1982, the following received Great Grace from Heaven for their part in Pro Life... Senators Heflin, Deconcini, Armstrong, Biden, Roth, McClure, Lugar, Jepsen, Dole, Ford, Huddleston, Johnson, Long, Durenberger, Boschwitz, Stennis, Eagleton, Danforth, Melcher, Exon, Laxalt, Humphrey, Domenici, Helms of North Carolina, Boren, Hatfield, Thurmond, Garn of Utah, Hatch of Utah, Randolph of West Virginia, Proxmire of Wisconsin, and Wallop of Wyoming. Abortion is Murder, and shortly you must all weed out the weeds in the Senate, and help these good Senators to pass a law forbidding this murdering of the Holy Innocents of your time era upon this earth. Tell all to join on January 22, 1983, in the March for Life in your country.

"Your country and many others soon face great war, World War III. We sent you a warning Aurora Borealis display, which followed the time zones on Palm Sunday of 1981, April 12th. This was sighted in the sky from Canada to Mexico. In 1938 we sent Lucia the sight as well to the rest of the world January 25th as a warning, a foreboding of the Second World War. In 1939 war began. Your country joined in 1941. Wars are punishment for mankind's sins. Turn back all of you and pray. Remember long ago when Lenin stated this statement: "What does it matter if ¾ of the world should perish, as long as the remaining ¼ is Communist?" And, "It is inconceivable that communism and democracy can exist side by side in the world; one must perish."

"Soon in your U. S.A. many crops will rot or dry in waters or parched land. There will be a great tremor in the near future – eruptions of volcanos in the West. Floods and rains in the East. Cattle will starve and famine will be set upon your once rich and plentiful nation. Japan will sink below the sea. West California will sink to the waves, but many will be forewarned in time. I will tell you this much only, you are close to the dates of all this in your guessed date, but you must not reveal this date until that time as it may be a cause of fearful conversions. This close date may also change.

"I have appeared to many in all parts of the globe and have shown unto them many visions of the near and coming future. I have made myself known and present in every nation and country on your earth. All Messages and Visions pertain to a general area, but are for some of other areas as well. My Messages must be read and reread by all, until my counsels are heeded. Go and read all Messages and counsels of the past. Beware of the unjust Seers who not receiving my counsel or direction, will go about claiming of visions to everyone. At Palmar, I and my Son, gave three true Messages; the rest have now been fabricated by Clemente Dominquez Gomez, the Seer of that area. Heed to find and obey my true Seers in New York, Yugoslavia, Mexico, and Italy. These I have appeared to for many years and they have been weathering life's storms very well."

****

This is the Message of the Blessed Virgin Mary to the world through a privileged soul on December 21, 1982.

"Mankind seeks a great chastisement from his God. You must all help in the battle ahead of us, and even now raging about you, in the unseen world of the spirit. Your men of California heritage who are entitled as scientists have many a warning about them. Some realize the potential danger of the Balls of Fire. To envision these through the scopes used upon your earth to view the Heavens may cause one to go insanely crazy for a short time. These balls must be viewed indirectly. Atlantis was once such a city, as well as a continent-wide city like today North America is slowing becoming. Their men of science sought not the ways of God. Instead they sought only the ways of man which are as the ways of Luciel. They had technology as great as you have today in your country and Russia and Japan as well as China and Malaysia and many other countries. They even had gotten to the point of a bomb close to the inter-continental ballistic missile, but they were not used to war with other nations – no, only to war with themselves between North and South Lemuria - (Atlantis). This continent was four times the size of America, but it fell below the waters of a thousand melted caps of Polar Ice and the Sea. This was all during the time of the warning of Noe and his continent before the deluge of his time.

"Great balls of fire hundreds of miles wide cut the Polar Ice and melted both caps of the North and South Poles. Soon a war broke out between North and South Lemuria. The continental city being pagan yet containing many just was forewarned, and those who believed the warning fled the continent. Noe was not, along with his family and the animals, the only survivor. He was the only recorded survivor along with his family because no continent knew of the other continents, except Lemuria, which considered the other continental people uncivilized.

"The gods and goddesses of Egypt were really Lemurian men and women of great medical knowledge as well as many other scientific advancements beyond the Egyptian's understandings. It took 20 days for the continent to be totally wiped off the visible face of the earth in the deepest sea (ocean) of those times. 20 days as well it took for the seas to recede over Ararat for Noe. The other unrecorded survivors from a city of 7,000,000,000 people numbered at exactly 32 in each Ark and there were five Arks. All remained unseen by Noe's people for 700 years and then began to integrate with them. Beware of the future – remember also the fate of Sodom and of Gomorrah. So it will be upon your nation a total combination of the three destructions from a just and all loving God.

"This time, I speak in word via telesthesia -- a telepathic impression upon your mind from Heaven. You also will remember almost clearly how I truly look.

"Amen till next I call upon your hands, My son. Now you understand the fishhooks in your photo from the Shrine in New York where I visited Mrs. Veronica L."

(he was interrupted here).

****

This is the Message given to a privileged soul on the Eve of Christmas, 1982, by the Blessed Virgin Mary.

"I have given Warning after Warning to mankind. Does he heed Me? No. Accept and learn by these Warnings from Heaven. Your country, the United States of America, and many other countries of your earth that were consecrated to My Immaculate Heart, have in the past been spared these most grievous trials that have been upon mankind for many years now.

"There shall be tremors in areas such as that have never had the tremors before, never seeing such great destruction. There will be many great accidents - many of these which will not really be accidents, and you will know it comes but from the Hand of God, the Father Almighty. He is a Just God, but He is also an angry God, this being because mankind has gone too far; he does not listen - he is too conceited - too stiff necked - and too proud.

"O Pastors of the World, O Ministers of the World, heed Me now or face the Heavy Hand of My Son, alone, without My Grace to protect you. You have changed the Church of My Son so that no longer is the Mass of now a days the same Mass that My Son instituted upon your earth when He was among you. I warned you. I warned you many times in the past, to beware of changes which served no purpose, and now you even persecute those We send to you who tell of Our Commanding Wish for the Church to, again, be made the Church of My Son. I tell you now, O religious leaders of the world, you have become unfaithful to Heaven's Providence.

"At Lourdes, I gave the name of the 'Immaculate Conception' to Myself as a title, in realization that the Pope of those days had just released a 'Bull' on My life, calling Me by this new title of the Immaculate Conception. A few months earlier, in that area, the Priest heard of this Bull, only a few days before My visits began, but did not say anything; this initially led to My Message being heard world-wide; this and the cures of the water - the waters' powers.

"At Fatima, I gave the sight of the sun whirling, and falling down upon the people and was then believed in, but at some of My Apparitions upon your earth, My miracles were for those attending, who would fall away if they did not see anything - such a case is My New York Shrine of Our Lady of the Roses. None of Important Theological Stature were upon the Sacred Grounds on that night.

"Faith must be used to see the truth of the Messages I bring to My Seers, Voice Boxes, Mystics, and Stigmatists upon your earth. To deny My Seers, when they speak My Messages, is to deny the Message - and this is just short of denying Me. To deny Me is to deny My Son. To deny My Son is to deny your God, and thus deny yourself and evoke the wrath of a Just but angry God. You shall bring the Heavens down upon yourselves and be Planet-Struck - but the U.S. of A., being My nation has a chance to avoid this, if you will all turn back now; if not, your nation shall be the first struck, and worst damaged, of all - almost no living flesh will be left. Many Shrines will be given approval - those that were denied truth, and that were called Liars by My Pastors, will be revered soon after the Great Warning to come upon mankind, but before the Great Miracle.

(Break in Message - Continued at 4:25 A.M., 12/25/82)

"To all who condone abortion, hear Me now, for I tell you of your future; if you do not turn back now. Mankind seeks a terrible Chastisement from His God. Abortion is strictly murder. Remember the times of Herod the King, and of the Murder of the Holy Innocents. So it is today in your world; mankind is murdering the Holy Innocents of today. Murders, Killings, Rapings, these things will increase upon your earth unless you all pray. God, the Father, gave the Command long ago - **Thou Shalt Not Kill**. So then, why does mankind seek the Wrath of the Father and My Son upon your earth? I tell you now why mankind does not believe Me when I warn him; it is because mankind has become debased to the point of being worse than during the times of the cities of sin: Sodom, Gomorrah and Atlantis.

"Because of this, a Great World War shall soon be upon mankind. This war, being World War III, it shall begin, or start, in these countries: Jerusalem, Egypt, Arabia, Africa, French Morocco. And Syria, sadly, is not bringing enough help to peace. The Key of Syria is being used for war promotion more than for World

Peace. Heed My Messages of Fatima, 1917 and the Message of June 13, 1981 at Bayside, New York.

The following is a Poem to the Lukewarm of the world's Catholic population:

"Why do you not honor Jesus, Our Lord?
Is it because when you try to be good, you're bored?

Have you obeyed Me, Jesus' Mother, and said many Rosaries?
Or are you still picking the Flowers of the Neighbor's Posies?

When you are in Church, do you pay any heed to thy Pastor?
Do you find yourself wishing the Priest would 'Sacrifice' faster?

Does your concentration fade and wander when you kneel to pray?
When in Confession, do you always tell that Sin you did yesterday?

Do you always visit Jesus in the Blessed Altar Sacrament?
Or is it reserved only for Easter, Christmas and during Lent?

"These things mean you are prideful and hurting Jesus My Son, if you have answered 'yes' to even one of these Questions."

"My son, you may give the Message without your name, if you wish, but you must be sure the Message is complete. My son, you may use the help of a small number of people to spread the Message, but beware, Satan is almost everywhere now a days, upon your earth. Your first worker is true at this time, but watch, in the future, and pray for her because Satan will seek to stop the Message. Inform her that I will guard her with My Immaculate Heart from the attacks of Satan if she will say a Hail Mary aloud when she feels troubled or uneasy or nervous. She has been blessed upon this Eve and will be again, by Heaven, by Jesus, when she attends Mass.

"Our Christmas Present to you and your worker, My son, is this; 30 souls have entered Heaven by your acceptance of My Message, and 30 more will enter tomorrow. There will be many heavy thick thorns on the shallow, narrow road to Heaven. Only upon the wide open deep road are there no thorns present. The open road leads to the Abyss.

"Remember, My son seeks for souls to enter into His Kingdom. This means all must remember to pray for the dead - all people of all religions - not just the Catholics, Protestants, Baptists and Christian Religions - but mankind must pray for all of his fellow mankind who have become deceased. Pray for all be they Black, White, Red or Yellow. Pray for the living as well. Great graces are obtained in this manner.

"More people should pray to My spouse St. Joseph. He is not prayed to often enough. Examples of this are clearly seen in the fathers and sons throughout your land -------and the mothers and daughters also the families are divided. There no longer is unity within the families. Pray to your Guardian Angels - they are besides you always. Pray to them for guidance and protection from the evil spirits which are all about you my children.

"Not enough pray the Rosary. There must be a complete reversal of the new trends in the Church, in which the weapon I gave mankind, the Most Holy Rosary, is being ignored. It must be prayed every day. Not only one Rosary must be said - no but all three mysteries consisting of 15 decades because there are many upon your earth who may make up for those who refuse to pray the Rosary. I do not attempt to brag of what has been granted to me by my Son, but everything I say is of importance to all Heaven and Earth. A writer of long ago once coined the phrase – "All Hell must shake and tremor every time the names Jesus or Mary are spoken."

"Thus you see the importance of the Hail Mary and there are 53 Hail Mary's in the Rosary.

(Break until Vigil Shrine 9:30 PM, Friday)

"You will kneel for the Sorrowful Mysteries of the Rosary upon all of My Shrine Site Vigil Grounds. You shall either pray during this set of five Sorrowful Mysteries - in total concentration - or leave My Sacred

Vigil Grounds upon your earth in various countries. The dishonor given Me upon earth I can take - but you will not dishonor My Son. He died for your sins, O mankind, so you will either honor Him or you will suffer the consequences of not remembering the Passion, Agony and Death of My Son, the Lord Jesus On High. He died for you, now remember Him.

(Skip till 1-1-83, 4:00 AM Saturday)

"The Mass of the modern Roman Catholic Church is valid. The consecration is true. It is not done in a pleasing manner to Heaven, but it is true. You must kneel from the time of which in the modern Church is called the Preparation of the Gifts, until what is known as the Consummation or Communion being over. When you receive My Son, which you should do daily, do not chew Him or take Him in your hands. Only take Him from a priest and on the tongue while in a kneeling position.

(Interruption)

****

This is the Message of Heaven given to a privileged soul on December 26, 1982, The Feast of the Holy Family.

"I am Theresa. I will be with you till you have written out a poem of the Passion of the Walk and of the Robin all in one. You will find I did a beautiful job while upon earth in writing poetry.

THE PASSION OF THE ROBIN RED BREAST AND JESUS

The Savior, bowed beneath his cross, climbed up the dreary hill
While from the agonizing wreath ran many a crimson rill.

The brawny Roman thrust Him on with unrelenting hand,
Till staggering slowly mid the crowd, he fell upon the sand.

A little bird that warbled near, that memorable day,
Flitted about and strove to wrench one single thorn away;

The cruel spike impaled his breast and thus tis lightly said
The robin wears his silver vest, Incarnadined with red.

"This poem is your Message of today for one and all. This is how all should try to be as the little meek Robin who tried to help his Master the Lord Jesus.

****

This is the Message given to a priviledged soul on December 28, 1982, The Feast of the Holy Innocents by the Blessed Virgin Mary and Jesus.

"My son, despair not your present situation. While you wish I would wait and come back tomorrow, it is my decision that you write today on the Feast of the Holy Innocents. Yes, it is true that Theresa came to you and had you write, while you slept, [the] last Message. It was not a demon. Write the following next few thoughts that come to your mind. They will not be your own, they will be My Son's words. Remember the voice in your mind. You will hear it in the future when it may be needed.

(Jesus speaks mentally to me).

"Write the following for My Priest sons upon earth."

"O Pastors, awaken from your slumber - you have fallen asleep. You who mock me and say when is He coming. I tell you this now - I shall come to you without your knowing. I shall slip in upon you as a thief in the night. Amen, I say to you the Pages of John are turning fast. These are the last days - the latter days. All that is written in the Book of Life must come to pass. It is not the wish of the Eternal Father that you flee the battle, O Pastors. You must not desert the Barque of Peter. It may flounder, but you must not desert it - you will remain - or face your punishment when you pass beyond the veil. O My Pastors, if you continue to allow the immodesty of mankind to enter upon My house, I shall come among you all with My angelic warriors and fling the heretics from among My house's people. I shall chastise you too, O Pastors, not just those heretics who you allow within My house - I shall chastise you for your silence. To be silent means you condone these sinful evil ways.

"A demon of Hell sat beside your past Holy Father, three back, Paul VI. I warned you of this through all my Seers, but you did not see what was going on about you. You have become blinded O My Pastors. Go back to My Mother and obey her. Do not run from the wishes of My Mother. She is a Mediatrix between Me, My Father and the Spirit. Listen to her, do not continue to ignore her, because if you do then My Hand will come down upon you and the chastisement to your nation will be great.

"Your Holy Father is a just man and the demons fear him. But although the demons fear him, they still seek to dethrone him and remove him from among you. Your Pope of today fears the wolves about him and this is the reason the Latin Mass of the yesteryears is not being brought back, although the Holy Father does wish that the Mass of Today was still the Mass my Son instituted.

"Soon your Holy Father will be caused to flee for another country. Rome will go under great strife, and be caused to lose the ruling power of the Papacy for a short time. The red forces will come close to dominating Rome for a short time - but this time will be short.

(Now towards me He spoke after a brief pause at about 3:15 AM)

"My son, think not thou the thoughts that thou are thinking. The Father has chosen you for an instrument and you will be used by Heaven whenever we call upon you. Your stubbornness has caused that only seven souls were saved by your final acceptance of today's Message. There would have been more but you chose to try to stop the Message yourself today. This will not be tolerated in the future. My son, you are still very temporal in nature, this is not good. My son, please accept your fate. Do not try My will upon you. You thought that thinking a sinful thought might make the Message cease, this cannot happen in your case because you were not given a choice to give the Message, you are chosen by Heaven from the stubborn teenage race of mankind to give My/Our Message. You will not give your name upon Our Messages in the future - you will do as you have been.

"You will not do the interview with the newspaper reporter that you thought about doing this evening. Remember the Message We give is not yours, it is Heaven's to mankind. We place you under these rules and guidelines because you are proud and sinful. You must not disobey these rules because all that your name on a Message would do is boost your ego. This we will not permit for you to do, without a punishment to the one who names you in print or vocally to the wrong person or persons. My son, again heed My Mother's lovely Message to you."

(Our Lady then continued with Her part of the Message)

"Pray the Rosary, men of Earth. Your playtime is filled with the perverse pictures of an audio tube known to you as the television. Many, I know, could not pray the fifteen decades of My Rosary every day, but five decades is a necessary thing for all to try to do."

"Heed the following poem on abortion - see what is about you.

PRO LIFE LAW - OR ABORTION LAW

>The rose symbolizes the Immortal Soul,
>The Pro-Lifers know it has Heaven as its goal.

Many religious should make the trip on January 21, 1983,
For the Pro Life Law you may then be able to see.

March for the Holy Innocents of today - his life,
You must not allow it to be cut by the knife.

O women of the world - because of your own promiscuous fault,
You seek to destroy the life we gave your child, with the salt.

The little ones from your own wombs you are giving over to abduction,
This all being done by the accursed machine which does the suction.

(The Poem is done - a brief one minute rest)

"Abortion is murder, My child and My children. You must fight the abortions in your country until it is again illegal. Do this all of you if you wish ever to have peace in the world again. Your country will seek to be the Peace Maker in the Wars which are happening all about your world now, but peace will elude mankind until abortion ceases.

"Soon a Great Warning is to come upon Mankind. In this Warning Time first the sky shall roll back; the sky will then become as white as snow, while the ground around about mankind will remain dark for a great time. Mankind will be fearful of what is happening round about him and then he will see the scroll of his life revealed and unfolded before him. All of the sins he has committed will be revealed to him to each person within his own soul. After this Great Warning many scientists will try to explain it off and will be able to do just that.

"A Great Miracle will happen in the near future. This will happen at Garabandal in Spain's mountainous country area, but will be viewed around the world, but unfortunately mankind will try to explain this off as well; even the millions of cures will not cause the scientists to believe We are present there. A Great War will break out when the Miracle is happening, but the war will cease during the period of the Miracle, then continue when the Miracle is over. Mankind will hold the key to the severity of the war.

"Prayer, my children, Prayer only, this is the key to peace. Once the war begins only its severity will be able to be controlled. Already the Roman Communist Parties of the United States are beginning to plan the takeover of the country of the USA. The party within the USA has not been sleeping, O My children, please I beg of you now, Heed My Call. Pray My Beads of Prayer, the Rosary! This is the only weapon you have against all that is planned for your nation. All this will come to pass soon. The time between events is in you, O sinful mankind, in your hands.

"The Chastising Comet has been viewed by your scientists, the men of earth, who are ever seeking but never finding the truth - it is because the truth is too simple for them. The comet has already been sent heading towards your earth. It will strike when My Son Jesus - and the Father drop it upon you. The Comet is light years long. It shall burn ¾'s of mankind off of your earth. The skin shall dry and peel from the bones of mankind who has become sinful and disregards Our Warnings of the past to him. There will be many skeleton-charred and dead lying about after the Comet. Then the Father will remake the earth as it was in Eden. At this point these in the rapture will return to a purified earth.

"I warned of floodings on the East Coast - this will happen in the future. You may view in the West what the East will soon be like - only prayer has held this in check. Sadly the prayers are-not enough - mankind's sins tip the scale heavily to the left. Soon your East Coast shall experience the monsoons that the seas to the south - Deep South experience. You are forewarned. Remember I have warned you."

****

This is the Message of the Blessed Virgin Mary to a privileged soul on The Eve of the Feast of St. Catherine Laboure, Eve of New Year's Eve - of the Solemnity of Mary, December 31, 1982 - January 1, 1983, Friday PM - Saturday AM.

"My son, soon your Holy Father will suffer much unless there are many victim souls who are willing to suffer for him. Many in the past have said aloud: "I will gladly suffer for the Pope to help him in his Mission from Heaven." But what has become of the Spirit of these Victim Souls? Once We begin to put a heavy cross on a soul, the person then begins to think that the cross is too heavy. And what of the cross that every person carries every now and then? Why do you despair it? There is always a great joy in Heaven when a person accepts their Cross. Do you, O mankind, think that life should always be a bundle of roses? Well then if life is a bundle of roses, why does mankind not accept the thorns?"

****

1983, First Quarter Messages

Message of the Blessed Virgin Mary to a privileged soul January 1, 1983 - Feast of the Solemnity of Mary

"My son, there will be Messages on the following dates in January for sure - Be Prepared."

January 2, 1983 – Feast of Epiphany – Feast of St. Seraphim, Eve of St. Genevieve, - In Honor of St. Anne Seton.

January 6, 1983 - In Honor of St. John Neumann – Eve of St. Raymond Pennafort.

January 9, 1983 – Feast of our Lord's Baptism – Eve of the Feast of St. Stella.

January 16, 1983 – Feast of St. Priscilla of Rome – In honor of Sts. Habakkuk and Michael – Eve of St, Anthony the Abbot.

January 20, 1983 – Note: This day is mentioned as only a possible day for a Message depending upon the need from mankind to perceive Her warnings. Eve of the legalization of Abortion – Feast of St. Fabian– Eve of St. Agnes – Feast of St. Sebastian – Eve of St. Michael.

January 25, 1983 – Note: This day is mentioned as only a possible day for a Message depending upon the need from mankind to perceive Her warnings. Feast of St. Elvira – Feast of St. Paul's conversion – Eve of Sts. Timothy and Titus – Eve of St. Margaret of Hungary and St. Paul.

January 27, 1983 – Note: This day is mentioned as only a possible day for a Message depending upon the need from mankind to perceive Her warnings. Feast of St. Angela Merici – Eve of St. Thomas Aquinas.

"Remember to remind your assistant in the Mission from Heaven to call upon the Holy Ghost when type setting our Message to the World. It is important as when she is tired she may make many mistakes. Please send our Message to the World - out to the people about you but beware of the Dark Ones - they are all about you, My child and My son, as well they are about you, all My sons and daughters upon earth.

"You all must beware of the ones who shine forth with radiant faces but have the hearts of the Ravenous Wolves. All about you there are dead bodies with dead souls moving about your earth. Beware of all that is a cause of drawing the demons to you. Destroy the agents of Satan, which are made of plastic and other such materials that have recorded upon them the Music of Hell - the music of the Prince of Darkness, Luciel. This music is called Rock and Roll – Acid Rock – Light Rock. It has all been consecrated to Satan. Destroy it. This so called music from the Abyss is truthfully leading souls down the road to Hell.

"Parents do you not care of the State of your child's soul? You allow the children of earth to slowly deteriorate until now sadly, there is not a large number who are truth carriers - who are true Christians. Not only Catholics, but all Christians.

"You have condoned the use of drugs - pornography - allowed your children to join the witches of earth by the use of the Devil Boards. I do not say the name that they are known by on earth because in Hebrew the language of my day, this name was a sinful swear word. I warn you now all parents do not allow your children to play the Tarot Cards. These cards come from the Devil. They will sooner or later bring death upon many in your family through the demonical influence of the Demon within each card. O parents, if your child has these do not throw them in your rubbish barrels, burn them with the face of every card facing towards the earth. Do not allow your children to listen to the Evil Music. I am warning you again.

"My son, 77 souls were released this Eve and Feast day. More will be released next Message. As we pray together next time as well. Now join me in a Rosary. I thank you for obeying the second part of the first part of the Message and kneeling, My son, now join Me in the Sorrowful Mysteries.

1st – [The] Agony of Agonies is suffered by Jesus in the Garden. He sees before him all who will not follow him and all who even in ·spite of sufferings will be damned. Then he sees all who He will save. He asks the Father to take the cup of Wrath and Agony away from Him, but immediately falls back upon the Father's

Will. Then He sweats blood. -1 Pater, 10 Aves and 1 Gloria.

2nd - Jesus is brought before Pontius Pilate. He is stripped of his outer garments and is whipped leaving very little flesh that was not cut open and bleeding. Then he is put into a robe which is matted against His open wounds and the Blood most precious begins to coagulate upon the robe and it sticks to His Flesh. This is then removed and the wounds thus reopened. Pilate brings Jesus and Barabbas before the crowd and Jesus is turned over to the tribunal and is ordered to be crucified as Pilate washes his hands of Jesus' Most Precious Blood and the guilt of His death - 1 Pater, 10 Aves and 1 Gloria.

3rd - Jesus is forced to sit in a chair after again being made to wear the Robe of Red. A roman soldier-guard goes without the building to the brambles and briars and comes to the Hawthorn and removes some small branches. He finds he is unable to make a crown shape from them because they prick his hands, so he takes a soup bowl and puts the branches within it in a circular shape. After it began to resemble a crown the soldier put the bowl upside down upon His Sacred Head and hammered the thorns into his Sacred Head with a stick of wood. Jesus' face immediately took on the expression of deep pain as his eyes were filled with Tears and Blood, but he did not cry out in pain. He suffered inwardly. The executioners and soldiers began to mock him and they spat upon him and took turns beating him as they said "All hail Jesus King of the Jews" - 1 Pater, 10 Aves and 1 Gloria.

Mankind by this passion from the scourging to the death was gaining the Kingdom of Heaven. The sins of the flesh are what Jesus was suffering for, the sins committed by mankind who gave no repentance before My son came among them to show you how.

4th - Walking on the Road to Golgotha (skull place) Jesus met the women who believed whom he truly was. They were weeping profusely. Jesus spoke to them saying "Weep not upon Me, but rather upon yourselves and your children. I go to the Father." At this He also meets His mother's gaze and from that time She (I) had a sword of sorrow in the Heart Most Pure. He was prodded on by the soldier and began to again walk. He fell three times enroute to Golgotha, and Simon, a Cyrenian, helped Him unwillingly to carry His cross. - 1 Pater, 10 Aves and 1 Gloria.

5th - At Calvary, the skull place Jesus was thrown down upon the ground back on the cross and he was stretched cruelly in both directions on his arms, then tied to the cross. Next the long spikes were positioned at his palms and he was then wracked with more pain than before as they were hammered these spikes through his hands - then they positioned his feet and the spike went the bone and made a cracking noise. Then the inscription which read "Jesus Nazarenus Rex Judaorum - Jesus of Nazarus King Of The Jews" was nailed above his Sacred Thorn Crowned Head. He was offered Wine and he refused - He knew that it was mingled with Myrrh, a Nerve Depressing Pain Killing Perfume. The cross was then placed into the ground with a thud. From the Sixth Hour of the Day Darkness covered the Land and Silence until the Ninth Hour - Jesus spoke "Eloi, Eloi, Lamma Sabacthane - My God, My God why has thou forsaken Me?" Before this He said to His Mother: "Woman, behold thy Son;" to St. John: "Son behold thy Mother." Jesus soon gave Us His body to death. Let us remember His Agony. 1 Pater, 10 Aves and 1 Gloria - 1 Hail Holy Queen, l Our Father, 3 Hail Mary's, 7 Glory Be's.

(I heard a voice, feminine and sweet during the recitation and writing.)

****

This is the Message of the Blessed Virgin Mary to the world through a· privileged soul on January 9, 1983 - Feast of the Epiphany - Feast of St. Stephanie - Eve of St. Genevieve - In Honor of St.. Anne Seton.

"My child, sons of earth, repeating My Messages of the past you will find that I have said many times before - but I will repeat it again for all mankind. What God has joined in Holy Matrimony, let no man place asunder. The dissolvement of many marriages in your State and in country is leading many down the Road to [the] Abyss. My children, recognize that it is the Hand of Satan reaching in and capturing many. In the marriages which are separated, man or woman usually becomes an adulterer and remarries another man or woman. If you are given by your husband or wife that your marriage be set asunder, do not seek another man or woman - because then you are accursed - and sinful before the Eyes of the Father.

"For 35 years in Wisconsin I pleaded unto all mankind. I pleaded that the religious teach the young children. I gave warning after countless warning that the homosexuality will lead many down the road into the Abyss.

"The sins of the flesh lead many down the road to Hell, and the souls fall faster than the snows in the cold winter. I warned [of] this - was I heeded? No, My children on earth. I tell you now I was not heeded. Oh yes, My shrines people usually heeded Me and a few small groups of others as well, but not nearly as many as We expected to have heed Us. I say Us because [of] the saints [who] pleaded with Me also - specifically I speak of Little Joanie, Theresa and Francis.

"They were the major patrons of the Shrines' Seers. I still choose on occasion a visit publicly with her for a Message. She has become confused with modernistic ways and her own workers are trying to lay her low, especially the top official of the shrine who does not send My Message free - he charges. This is not good. They do not seek to remove her; they only laid her low. I am with her always. She views Me at every Vigil she attends and will until she joins me, but she only gives a Message when I tell her what to say.

"I repeat much of what I have given to mankind in Warning in the past. Soon My words to all mankind will become weak and be few. Go back, O children of earth. Read all these Warnings given in the past. Act upon them before My Son's avenging hand must descend.

"Shall a great warning be given to all mankind no matter where they be? I say yes, O children of earth. There were many warnings in the past; all that were unnoticed by an unwitting mankind. Those warnings that [The} Eternal Father sent to awaken you, O mankind. These will be, I tell you now, there will be earthquakes and tremors in places never known or the possibility of these quakes existing.

"Cities shall fall below the sea under huge tidal waves. The Ball of Redemption hovers near now to your earth. It is no ordinary celestial star, but it is a star, while also being a Supernatural Manifestation - performed by the Father. Many will die in the Great Flame of the Ball of Redemption. This ball far outsizes your earthly sun or star called Sol, My children. Believe me when I say it has been hard to stay the Hand of My son from coming down upon you, and soon I shall be forced by the Eternal Father to allow the Hand of My son to come down upon mankind and the Chastisement will be Great. Prayer is now your meter - The Rosary - Peace - Light - Love to all Mankind. Amen."

****

This is the Message given to a privileged soul by the Blessed Virgin Mary on the Feast of our Lord's Baptism, Eve on the Feast of St. Stella, January 9, 1983.

"My son, write now as I tell you to write. I will tell you word for word the words My Son wished me to tell you so you may repeat them on paper and spread them to the world. (Words of Jesus brought by Mary)

"Every day I am, being again tortured by mankind. Was not my death enough for you, O mankind? You seek to recrucify Me again. Every blasphemy against is a blow to My back with the whips - a thorn both in My Heart Most Sacred and My Head Most Sacred to Heaven [and] you, O mankind. Soon I shall no longer suffer for you, O mankind, who have become perverse. Soon My hand shall come down upon you all - a sinful generation which must be punished. Look at My figure upon the cross more often. Kiss the image of My Corpus when you say My Name during the Rosary. The cross must be kept the same as it was given to you - with my body upon it. The body must not be removed. Remember, honor My Body upon the cross. I died for you all - now remember Me, O mankind."

"My son, Jesus is not the only one, O my little son, who suffers in Heaven. No, I tell you, I too suffer. I suffer pains which are very excruciating within My Heart. View My Heart. (I see a heart covered with thorns.)

"The thorns of mankind's blasphemies, My son of earth, that is what they are (the heart I see is bleeding and is drop by drop draining of blood. You view the cause now in your mind (I see pastors who are not setting complete concentration upon the Eucharist as they are at the altar and doing the sacrifice). Now our Lady and the vision of the priests have both vanished.

12:55 A.M. Our Lady has returned.

"I ask this of you all on the earth, My children:

1. - Tell all the peoples of the earth to recite at least 5 decades of the Rosary a day.

2. - Tell all that only through Me may one obtain Heaven and Jesus,

3. - Through Me Jesus came to earth and through Me must come His Reign.

4. - Accept My love with faith and charity.

5. - Tell the world of My goodness to all mankind.

6. - All must wear the Brown Scapular and the Rosary.

7. - Do not be afraid to approach Me with many requests for favors. Some I will grant.

8. – Console Me often with good works and by going to give Honor to My Son at Church.

9. - Make Me a place to dwell within your hearts, minds and souls. I wish to dwell with you.

10. - Work with Me to form the salvation of at least a soul every day.

11. - Honor Me by the name of Our Lady of All Holy Titles.

12. Honor Me as the Queen of the Universe and of Mankind and you will gain (if you follow My other requests from here and Fatima) the Kingdom of the Father, the Son, and the Spirit of Life for Eternity.

"I now tell you of the knowledge of Satan, some of which is powerful but permitted. Remember he too was an angelic warrior of one time. Then he was cast from the Choir of Archangels for his arrogance. Satan carries great knowledge of the sins of each and every person, but only those which have not been confessed. Satan will attempt to tempt a person who has sinned and he knows he has under his evil wing, but he will try to tempt more a person who is the State of Grace of the Church. He will work his hardest against the person in the State of Grace.

"Do not think that you are free from this temptation for all will be tempted as the metals are hammered and tested within the Fires. (1:30 A.M. Our Lady is silent for a time and is standing motionless as a statuette - a figurine but She has a smile upon her face which fills me with joy).

"My little son, I tell you now a secret of the past. The Antichrist is born now. He is alive and well. There must be much prayer or he will come out among you all. He is alive but lives in the war zones of Palestine.

"The Antichrist is young at this time, he is unable to be harmed by conventional weapons used upon earth. He (unlike the movies used and made upon your earth) knows who he is even at his young age. The movie Our Lady refers to is Damien - Omen 2.

"Without prayer the Antichrist will soon be of age to come forth (allowed by Heaven) to bring destruction among you all.

When he comes forth the Great War to End all Wars will begin - World War III.

"Pray the Rosary every day, not only with lip service, but with your mind, heart and soul and he will not enter upon your country first as he had planned to do. The United Nations is his first target.

"If you only knew how soon, My children, you would be upon your knees for all your free moments of the day.

"I do not indicate that the Antichrist is only one man - he is the Legion of Hell, working by one man. 33

souls, My son, were sent to Heaven by your willingness this morning. I will see you again on the 13th. "Goodbye for now, My son, tell your workers that this Blessing is for them as well as for you."

(Our Lady is lifting a large wooden Rosary from Her belting sash and Blessing in the sign of the Trinity). "In the Name of the Father, and of the Son and of the Holy Ghost. Amen."

(End of Message)

Our Lady today as I viewed her, had upon her feet a pair of sandals alike the kind the Roman women wear. They were long extending high above what was visible from the golden hem upon her robes. The robes were of a fine material - almost a silk like material. The color of the gown was constantly changed as it was alike something shimmering one minute blue, next purple and then pink - then white then blue again, perhaps not in this order but the colors were all present. The mantle was blue and trimmed in fine gold with jewels among the gold trim. The hair of Our Lady was mostly tucked behind the mantel upon her head, but a small amount hung forward so I could clearly see it. Her hair is a light brown, or actually a medium brown. Her eyes were a blue that resembled the sky. Her sash was all of a golden weave of material. The sash as I viewed it was actually miniature links of gold all entwined together in a way such as I don't think we upon earth could ever duplicate. Her Rosary was all of wood.

****

This is the Message of the Blessed Virgin Mary to the world through a privileged soul on January 13, 1983, 11:25 AM, the Feast of St. Hillary, Eve of the Feast of St. Malachias.

"My son, we realize the trials you have this day undergone, for remember we are the ones who warned you in the past of such devils about you all. A well-meant good deed could always be turned around upon you. Any ideas for this Mission from Heaven (to spread the Message) must be prayed upon. You know, My son, the instance I am referring to - the priest and the Message which was given unto him. I warn you now, My son, you tell the others as well what I am about to tell you The words I give to you, My son, Satan would love to remove them from among mankind. He will seek to send the Pastors-Priests of the world against you. Even the person least suspected of being so - he or she may be an Agent of Satan. Some people question if you are to carry on the Mission of My New York Seer. No, I tell you now this is not true. You will see her again very soon. She will be back for a Vigil this year of 1983.

"In the bloom of a plant there are many seeds, some seeds stay to mature to a full size and some fall to the ground immature and die off. So it is with your Mission, My son. Many will die off. Pray for the fallen away Catholics as they will be tempted by Satan not to come back to the fold.

"Mankind today shows much vanity and pride. This is always present before a fall and helps for the downfall of the nations. Too much time is spent amusing the human body - Lust, Sexuality, especially Homosexuality, these are sins of great offense to the Father.

"Protect your children from the exploitation of sex and from the horrid magazines and movies sweeping your land: Pornography. The eyes are the mirror of the soul; not what goes in but rather what comes out is the sin, but what goes in most often comes out of a mind and is then a sin. The Child Pornography, My children, this is the worst kind, sadly is selling more than any other kind.

"If a man looks upon a woman and even thinks to himself of how he wished she was his sexual concubine he has committed a sin. This sin is greater if he is already a husband of another woman. This same woman if she be wearing very tight clothes of a very skimpy material, she then has led this man's fantasy on and is immoral and committing a sin before God.

"She may not realize this fact, but if this man turns upon her and commits sexual acts with her, it is only because she led him to do such an act by showing too much flesh. If you women of the world wish to be like the saints and come to Heaven, then dress like Me; dress in the non-clinging clothes. Long skirts will help greatly. A woman should be decent and ladylike because she is the example for all children. The man who is put into temptation by a woman is alike a wild beast. He must be tamed and kept like a decent man by a decent woman. Thus you can see why I speak of the woman's role in life this day, My child, because many of the women of the world need my counsel. Farewell."

****

This is the Message given to a privileged soul by the Blessed Virgin Mary on January 16, 1983, Feast of St. Priscilla of Rome, Eve of St. Anthony the Abbot, In Honor of St. Habakkuk and Micheas.

"My son, I see you have awaited me and are seeking to receive My Message. I came to remind mankind of a need for prayer. The deadly blade of the death angel is still among you all.

"I refer to he who goes by the title of Apollyon in Greece and Abaddon in the Holy Lands while called in all countries not therein included - Exterminatus.

"This death angel wanders about your earth now. He has taken many human bodies for his habitat in the past and will continue to move about in the future without a constant vigil of prayer. Prayer only can stop him. My Rosary and Scapular are your greatest weapons against him. He moves about now seeking to pit death against so much of society as he can.

"Babylon, the great evil city of Babylon: This city in New York causes all of New York to take the title of Babylon the Great. Not only Babylon, New York causes this title upon the whole city, but also the area of New York entitled The strip. The area where Satanism is rampant. The city of Babylon within the Great State We in Heaven call Babylon shall be, along with the strip, the first and hardest struck when the comet comes.

"I have not ceased pleading unto mankind since 1884 in Nevers, France and in many other places throughout the world. Of all My many Messages to the world very few have been heeded, and acted upon.

"You must heed me now as I, the Queen of the Universe, Our Lady of all Holy Titles, your Mother, request the Rosary and Peace. I leave this up to you. It's your world. You have a choice men of the world.

"You can have the Rosary and Peace - or you can have the ICBM with the Laser Satellite and the War - World War III. Pray. Pray."

****

This is the Message given to a privileged soul on January 27, 1983, Feast of St. Angela Merici - Eve of St. Thomas Aquinas.

"My son, please listen closely to me now. Look in your Bible and find where you placed what I had you write on January 25, while you were subconscious - asleep. This and today's Message will be placed together along with what will be spoken to you on Saturday. My son, you do not have to even ask of Me the question you have in mind, for I tell you now, I am Mary Immaculate of the Immaculate Conception. I produced the Son of God, Jesus, the Savior, your God. You were to ask Me this since the last time when you had remembered having a Message from Me. You had prior to that been visited by Luciel, the Prince of Darkness. My son, I leave up to you the choice of going to the priest, or not going to him. I would say that your faith and the faith of those that assist you is weak if you do not go and pray on your way for assistance from the Holy Ghost, in speaking to the priest. Now place the Message of January 25, 1983 after this part of the Message. I will be back soon."

****

January 25, 1983 was the Feast of St. Elvira - Feast of St. Paul's Conversion - In Honor of St. Francis de Sales - Eve of St. Timothy and Titus - Eve of Margaret of Hungary and of St. Paula.

"My son, tell the world that the medal of My Immaculate Conception, the Miraculous Medal, and the St.

Benedict Medal are the most powerful medals after the cloth of the Brown Scapular. A few of these should be purchased by all, because soon they will be unavailable.

"Tell your assistant that has an M in her name that soon Satan will try to attack that which is dear to her at this time unless she prays enough. Tell her also that St. Pio, the Saint of modern times, may help her if she prays through him to the Father for the souls in Purgatory. Many souls there which have suffered 500 - 700 years may find relief through her prayers and they in turn would be very happy to pray to God for her and that which she holds most dear. With enough of their prayers Satan could be easily thwarted and stopped from his plans. Tell her as well to pray to the Little Flower St. Therese and to pray to St. Gerard.

"My children, Jesus is always alone. Go to His feet at the cross and pray to Him. He is an all-loving God. He has many favors to grant you. The soul who daily recites My Rosary all 15 decades - I will one day before his or her death come to that soul and embrace that soul in my arms. This soul will also have thus a chance for Confession and a last Communion before death.

"You must all love your neighbors and all mankind as brothers and sisters. You must love a person even if they kill your wife or husband, mother or father, daughter or son and brother or sister. You must of course hate the sin, but I tell you - you must love the sinner. This I tell to you all, for hatred is a tool of the devil for getting inside of a soul. Many, too many souls have fallen to Satan through hatred of another of their fellow mankind. So I say again love your fellow mankind as brothers and sisters. Heed not the sin of the person as being the person, because in many cases Luciel will cause a person to sin without their consent and then they must still be loved, only the sin must be hated no matter how great a sin committed, remember hate only the sin."

****

This is a Message given to a privileged soul on January 27, 1983.

Our Lady appeared misty as if She was not solid, but almost in a split second She was there solidly again in her blue robe with golden trim on the edges of it. She had golden colored wooden roses on her feet, at least they looked like wood, but her shoes were of wooden texture like shoes worn in the Mt. Carmel visions, or more like the Dutch Shoes of 1800 - carved out of wood. She removed them as she stood beside them on a pillow. The Rosary - well she had two of them - one of all wood which glowed, the other of Aurora Borealis Beads which took tones like I've never seen; the colors were multiple, but the beads themselves were white (see through almost). Her crown was gold imbedded with five rare jewels and it too shone with light from within them. Her dress or tunic was white, Her belt was blue, Her mantle was a lighter blue than Her robe was by about one shade of blue.

"Patience, Humility, Pardon, and Love and Charity, what has become of these in all of mankind's countries of earth? Patience is had in the manner of waiting for God to grant a thing which you have prayed for if it be a Holy thing. Humility is had by one who does not fear to go before a crowd showing My Messages about, and not having many be accepted while that this same person is made fun of for his or her cause, this is Holy Humility. Pardon is best described by not holding a man to an evil he may have committed years before if he is no longer evil today. Love is giving, love is caring, but' above all love is God, for God is love.

"Charity is in giving not of one's own excess wealth, but rather in giving until it begins to hurt. Charity is also had by this example - A person who is elderly and unable to mow their lawn or shovel their sidewalks or driveways, even if they can afford to pay you to do it for them, you say yes to money only every other time, then when you do not accept money you have given charity. Yes, not only charity but Love, Humility, and Patience as well in one of these two cases. Charity also is had by praying for mercy upon the poor souls in Purgatory who suffer incredibly."

****

Saturday, January 29, 1983, in Honor of St. John Bosco.

"My children, when it is time for war many will be the men and women in the U.S. of A who will be martyred. What will become of many of you? I know, and therefore, I am now going to counsel you on it, this topic.

"Satan's troops will seek out all Christians and ask them each and everyone this the following question:

"Who do you believe in, God or the Devil?"

"Do you wish death for saying God or a job as a solider of Lucifer and life eternal?"

Our Lady "My children, learn now what this means. Satan troops will mean life eternal in damnation in Hell as a demon soldier for not choosing God before you are killed, for Lucifer always kills those who join him. He has been notorious for this for all of times as ever since he was cast from Heaven. If you say yes to God, you will die but you will gain direct admittance to Heaven before My Son and the Father, with the Holy Ghost, forever. You in this case would not even touch the Fires of Purgatory. Many souls will be lost because of Luciel's way of asking trick questions which say one thing but that mean another. My son, I must leave you now. Please do not forget to pray your Rosary. Amen."

****

This is the Message given to a privileged soul on February 1, 1983, Eve of the Presentation of Jesus.

Our Lady is coming, I sense it. It is now 3:28 in the afternoon. I have been waiting for her this day, because She gave me this date as a definite date for a Message from Her. The feeling I could not really describe. The feeling is almost like when you have many hours of rest and are really refreshed, yet also an inner peace, joy and tranquility, such as you do not normally in everyday life feel. It's like you are with a lot of nothingness all about you, yet there is beauty in all of it. A beauty within everything about you. It's like almost having the infinite of knowledge right in front of you, but not quite being able .to grasp a hold of it, yet you can sense it is there.

I have a way of knowing if it is truthfully Mary appearing to me. Only the Saints of Heaven and Mary, Jesus, the Father and the Holy Ghost along with the angels can read a man's mind accurately. The devil cannot know what Mary, the Virgin Mother, must tell me this time before I will know it is Her. I have told no one, nor have I spoken it aloud. I must now stop my own words for Our Lady is beginning to materialize within a light blue mist. She has nothing upon Her feet. She has a long blue and white mantle with a long blue robe underneath. She has a long billowing, soft but heavy, material dress or tunic on which is white. She is holding out now Her hands and the Scapular and Rosary are in Her hands.

Our Lady: "My son, instruct all to wear the Scapular and the Rosary every day and night. You have mentally requested to know what My favorite color is. I will answer Blue, of course, this must be very obvious to you already.

"My little son of earth, listen well to my instructions now even as you write this, for this part you must remember and do immediately as soon as I leave you. You must (for your own sake as well as the Mission) destroy all of your original copies of the Holy Messages I have given to you. You will keep only the typed copies. I tell you now the reason for this. It is because if your earthly mother found them she would have you committed to an institution for a check of your psychiatric profile. You must not allow her to find out that I am coming to you for Satan, Luciel, the Prince of Darkness, can get to you through your mother who is easy prey for him. In his snares she has the potential to cause a failure in the Mission.

My son, look in the corner behind you. See he who is the most despicable angel ever. See how he truthfully looks. No, be not afraid, am I not here. I have brought him here for a reason which you will soon learn. Watch his face now as you see those whose faces, bodies and souls he has both possessed and claimed in the past and throughout history. I screamed out – that's Amy and that's Tony and that's Ursula.

"You will not, in a short time know in your memory anything about these three people who you recognized from the fifty thousand who Satan, Lucifer, has claimed in possession in earth's time. These three were the three faces you knew who were already dead bodies within dead souls in the coven you were once a part of. I tell you now that you almost became alike them. I intervened and sent someone to meet you upon a street one night and set you straight about the Catholic Church, and to remove you from the coven successfully, but without his ever knowing. Lucifer, while you were in the coven, used one of either of the three bodies whenever he felt like it, but made it impossible for you to know that those bodies were long dead already.

"The other nine members you knew were human like yourself, but they all sadly went where you would have gone had it not been for the prayers which your grandmother alone in your family has recited for since she was a little girl.

"Because of her prayers I sent one to you who could help you turn back as you, as well could then help him make Rosaries for Me. I took pity upon your case also because of the unstructured childhood you led with only one parent and sister available to talk to you, to teach you and to guide you.

"Your father, We realized, was not available for you when you were a small child, your case was saved for this, and because of the Rosary of your grandmother, all 15 decades.

"I cry tears for My children, because how many will not listen to me. How many would I willingly attempt to save if they would only be ones who would remain true to Us in Heaven.

"I tell you even Luciel, Satan, would be accepted back by Us if he were to turn from his ways, but alas he never will and that is why he was condemned in the first place, condemned to Hell. The Eternal Father is all merciful and forgiving but this must be granted only by merit. Upon earth you will be punished by God, if not then, then it will happen in the afterlife. If you are not truthfully sorry for a sin, then do not attempt to confess it until you are, for it will not be forgiven until you are sorry for it. I do not say to stay away from Confession, I only mean that you should examine your conscience before Confession.

Our Lady: "Look, My little son, out your window and view Michael, Our Golden Warrior of Heaven. I am now leaving you so heed him and then you may go about your regular daily activities which you normally do at 5:15 in the afternoon."

St. Michael is as if there was a huge ball of light in my backyard. I cannot make out his features. I only know this, his wings take up the whole backyard. He even seems to stand right in the middle of the clothesline. but he seems unaffected by it. He says in a deep booming, reverberating voice:

"Heed the words of the High Queen of Heaven, O Mankind, or you shall be lost as a nation, as a country and as a world. WOE, WOE, WOE; WOE, WOE, WOE to the inhabitants of the earth!"

He has vanished.

****

Message given to a privileged soul.

I am sitting now on my bed looking out the window and now I'm writing this here. I have seen two things now, a sky filled with both blue and purple color, the thing I had mentally in prayer requested of Our Lady to show me, to signify when She was coming to me. She is now here.

Our Lady: "My son, I have much to tell you, but I know not where to start, since mankind does not listen to Me. There is assembled within your nation a great spirit of evil. Public opinions have become perverted by propaganda of sex initiations. I speak of the horrid sex education classes which have widespread effect upon your land. All of this is done under your eyes, O parents of the nation. Even under the eyes of the educated married couples. My son, you are unable to finish as you will have a call on the telephone. I will, therefore, call upon you on Saturday. February 5. 1983."

****

Message of February 5, 1983, Feast of St. Agatha.

A light blue mist is coming into the room about me. Our Lady is beginning to appear and She is radiant and more beautiful than I even remembered Her ever looking. She looks about 14 or 15 years old and She said:

"Be not at all frightened today. I am the Immaculate Conception, Queen of Heaven and Earth, Queen of the Holy Rosary and Peace. Yes, My son, I will bless you and your workers when you pray your Rosary. When you go to meet each other and stay together for a few hours at a time, I request now that during those times you all recite the Rosary - in as much as at least the 1st Sorrowful Mystery. If you so choose you may then recite the 2nd through the 5th decade of the Rosary. The Mystery that I want you all to use is that of the Sorrowful:

        1. Agony in the Garden
        2. Scourging at the Pillar
        3. Crowning with Thorns
        4. Walk to Calvary – Carrying the Cross
        5. Crucifixion, Agony and Death

"Across the American Nation, the Rosary should be recited at 7:30 PM by all people. I say 7:30 for two reasons:

    1. Most of mankind's evils happen between 7:30 PM and 2:00 AM

    2. At 7:30 you will be united with hundreds of thousands around your nation to recite the Rosary. It will be as if you said that many if you but say "I unite now with all everywhere who are reciting the Rosary," when you begin.

"Pray, My little one of earth, pray for all your fellow mankind, your brothers and sisters of earth. If only half of America's people would pray the Rosary all at one time for the conversion of Russia, I would plead unto the Father and He would grant Me this great miracle of the Conversion of Russia. Pray - Pray - Pray Hard and Devoutly. Pray the Rosary wholeheartedly for the conversion of sinners. My Son's heart is heavy because for worldly desires and greed. Man has forgotten the Ten Commandments - My Warnings of Fatima, My Warnings of La Salette, and My Warnings of Lipa.

"Wake up America - the enemy of God is creeping all over America. Yes, I know you all think He can't do this, but He can and He is. O Mankind of the United States, you read the most perverse of literature, printed material. You are committing great sin by reading this material. I speak of the evils of pornography widespread throughout your land.

"Children are removed from the streets of your land and they are forced into doing all manners of perverse and evil sexuality. I speak of children ages almost from the cradle and they range to as old as 16 and 17 years of age. These children are brought into many private studios throughout your land and forced into sex before the cameras. I tell you it would be better that the ones forcing this never were born for they already have both feet into the Abyss.

"The children are threatened with no food, or death, if they do not comply with the sex that is demanded of them. I tell you now that the flesh of the adults who are forcing this sex upon these little innocents I speak of, will burn in both the Ball of Redemption and in Hell.

"Pray much for these little innocent ones. It is true that all children are born pure and holy. It is what is shown as an example to them and what is made of these lives that is hastening the Ball of Fiery Redemption.

"I will return, My son, on February 9th and 10th to complete this same Message with Part II on My Message about pornography."

                                        ****

This is the Message given to a privileged soul by the Blessed Virgin Mary on February 10, 1983, Feast of St. Scholastica, Eve of Our Lady of Lourdes.

I am waiting for the Holy Mother at this moment and I feel inner peace; yes peace within but not so that I would be able to say outward peace only inner peace. Our Mother has come before me now, and I must now repeat in print what She has to say:

"My little son of earth, in My last counsel with you, I said I would come and continue My Message on pornography to the world. Before I begin, you wish to know if your grandmother and two grandfathers are in Heaven or Purgatory. This I am not permitted to tell you. However, the Father Eternal has permitted Me the permission to say this much - pray for your grandfather on your father's side. He had obtained Purgatory by only the prayers of his wife, your Grammy Antoinette. He would sadly have otherwise been lost. He is still in the second stage from the lowest stage in Purgatory.

"Dear children, I now speak My Message to you all. My faithful children, tell all to pray, pray especially for the purity of your children's souls for cleaner lives. Clean out the schools. Put clean thoughts into the minds of your children's teachers. Put devotion to My Son into at least some of their hearts.

"How many priests and bishops among the Hierarchy are reading now the filth in print that I speak of in this Message? They are hypocrites dressed in sheep's clothing. You must live clean lives. Live the 10 commandments, for I tell you now God does not make laws that cannot be followed and obeyed. For I tell you now what law you break when you break the 9th commandment given by the Eternal Father on the Mountain to Moses.

"The Ninth Commandment states **"Thou shalt not covet thy neighbor's wife."** This forbids any unchaste thoughts, desires or passions of another's wife and even in many cases, with your modern age of society, of another's husband. All unlawful or impure thoughts are, as well by this law, forbidden.

"I ask you now to heed what I next am about to say, as it will clarify what I have already spoken. When you, O mankind, look upon a pornography object, be it a photo, movie, or book - when you realize that, you then begin to lust for it. These things may to some, help their passions, but then again they are usually what causes the passion, sin, in the first place. I tell you there are so many souls who have fallen into Hell because of pornography that it is amazing. Souls have fallen faster than the snows of your cold winters.

"I tell you now that the war is soon to come - it hovers over you all now (the black cloud of war); when it settles in, you will all scream, but it will be too late. You were warned at Fatima, you were warned at La Salette, you were warned at San Damiano, Necedah, Bayside, and many other places throughout your world.

"Earthquakes are a sign of volcanic activity in the area of Mammoth Lakes, California. Volcanic activity which flows down to the San Andreas Fault Line - California, as I in the past have warned you, My child and My children.

"Homosexuality is rampant about your land, My children. Homosexuality - this day lesbians, bisexuals, homosexuals, I speak now to any of you who hear Me in this written copy of My words. I bring you the command now: Change your lifestyle. Do you not know that I am the Mediatrix between God, Heaven, the Saints, and the Angels, and you, mankind? I come to earth only speaking what the Father Eternal has given in command to Me.

"I will see you again on February 14, 1983"

****

This is the Message given to a privileged soul by the Blessed Virgin Mary on the Feasts of St. Valentine, Feasts of Sts. Cyril and Methodius, Eve of St. Georgia of France, February 14, 1983.

I have a feeling of peace and any moment now She will be here with me. I wish to wish Her a happy heart on this day, for the Feast of St. Valentine. Oh, She is here now.

"My son, I thank you for your kind wish. May your heart be happy too. In the future We will use the instrument known as a tape for the Message. Tell My children of earth I love them all and I will bless them all. Tell all who can be trusted not to reveal who you are, that I have blessed their Rosaries, all who are close to you, as they pray the Rosary with you, be it one decade or a whole of five or fifteen decades. Continue, My son, making Rosaries for people. Thank you. These Rosaries will grant many miracles in these latter days for many people. For I tell you now, We in Heaven have placed five special blessings upon these Rosaries. These blessings will be revealed in the future in other Messages.

"This short Message is your Message for today, My son.

"Good-bye for now."

****

This is the Message given by a privileged soul on February 16, 1983, the Feast of Ash Wednesday, in Honor of St. Bernadette of Lourdes.

A voice I recognize as St. Michael's is booming in the sky, "Woe, Woe, Woe to the inhabitants of the earth! Guard your children in the near future, for many shall be removed from the face of earth in the near future, this being in the realms of Satan's choice for what will be removed from your earth."

"I give you this much in knowledge, keep the Sacramentals upon your children, or they will have not have them upon their side to keep Lucie1, the Prince of Darkness, who is among you, from choosing them.

"The rest of what must be revealed in Warning from Heaven upon this day will be revealed by the Queen of Heaven, Earth and the Universe. Heed Her Message or you will hasten the Chastisement upon yourselves."

St. Michael now has left and I now see the blue shimmering lights in the sky which always appear before She will appear before me in my bedroom. Now the light which is like a radioactive glowing blue mist is filtering through the trees and as well now through the window panes. Now the peace-giving blue mist is beginning to take up a shape and Our Lady is now materializing before me. She has on today a beautiful crown, it is so regal looking upon Her head. Under this She has a white mantle which almost completely covers Her hair, only a little shows on the sides in the front.

Upon Her body she is wearing a medium to dark brown tunic or dress of a materials such as we upon earth have not ever seen. Covering over this is a tan or yellowish cloth which is wrapped over about the tunic to form almost a robe. She looks so beautiful. The brown of the tunic is as that of what the Franciscans or Capuchins wear. Around the edges of the cloth wrapped around Her is an interwoven trim of gold which sparkles and blue which glows.

There are many star sapphires, rubies, emeralds and diamonds in the crown she wears and they are reflecting the light coming from within her. Upon her feet she has a pair of shoes that look almost like the clogs that women today wear, but they are carved out of wood completely. Now she is beginning to get ready to speak - this I know because she has said.

"My son, listen now as I have been well described already now by you and now I wish to speak. I have just come from the Dutch Amish Hills of Holland where I now am establishing a Shrine. These shoes are for the people of that area, My son, as that is what they expect to see Me wearing. I am converting many of them in that area. Many have come to My Son at the Catholic altar rails of the Church in that area. I now, My son, will take these shoes off and stand upon the pillow at My side. I thank you, My son, for leaving it here, it is very comfortable upon My feet. My son, the stamp you are now mentally thinking of, it is good. Please use it to distribute the Message.

"As Michael told you, I will give counsel for the Lenten Season concerning what must be done to protect your children from becoming victims of Satan. You must put the Medal of My Immaculate Conception and the Medal of St. Benedict upon your children before sending them to school in the morning. Satan's own cohorts are all about you, some are in the spirit world and some are in the physical world heading some, or actually most, of the covens on earth.

"These coven leaders are now walking your earth seeking victims and holding them until Holy Thursday, Good Friday, Holy Saturday and Easter Sunday.

"Upon these days, they would and will be murdered in Satanic Ritual, which is supposed to make a mockery of the Agony, Death, Descent and the Ascension from Hell to His tomb. Many of the children who will be killed will not be ready to go into Heaven or Purgatory, and sadly because of the ritual which is used by the covens, many will fall into Hell because they will submit to many of the ritualistic abominations which the coven does. They will submit to this in the hope that they would be released to go home, or if they do, it is not truly them who returns home, but rather a demon in human form.

"Goodbye for now, I will see you and be with you again soon."

****

This is the Message given by Our Lady on March 9, 1983.

St. John of the Cross is before me, upon his cross, and he says to tell all to remember Our Dear Lord Jesus and how he suffered. "Know also that the Mother of God will not be here with you for any Message today. You will only try to describe what you see as I am luminous in body upon a wooden cross. Goodbye now. Blessings upon all of our followers of the Queen and a special one to your workers and yourself, My son. Goodbye now."

****

Message of March 14, Eve of Feast of St. Louise of France, Feast of St. Matilda and in honor of St. Geralda and St. Gerard.

Our Lady has come forth wearing the usual semi-sandal that she wears upon her feet in most visions throughout the world. She's wearing a blue robe with a white sort of dress or tunic, with a golden colored trim on her cape and her robe. The question that is put before Her has not yet been answered by Her. She is just standing there in a radiant form of light. There is a sort of peace given by Her presence. But, the presence is not exactly one that would be seen upon earth in the normal state, not a normal state at all. She now wishes for me to speak in response to Her and in reply to what She says.

"My child, the questions you have put before Me this day, I cannot give the answer. You have asked Me to respond to where the state of a certain soul is, I cannot reveal that information for that is not to be known, but I must give you a Message that must be given to the world:

"Sorcery and mind control are what are practiced by many of the covens. My son, My child, My children, the greatest anguish of heart that We suffer now is because of the sorcery that has come into the lives of many of the children. We call this sorcery, My children, because of the great combination of the practices of the Occult, Witchcraft, and Drugs. The minds of your children are being destroyed and distorted by the use of mind controlling drugs from Hell. I say from Hell, My children, because it is a diabolical plan from Satan to control the minds of your children.

"O parents, if I could only allow you to see into your near future. I say near future, because your future is not counted by weeks but days now. You will find that sin is true insanity.

"Children shall rise up against their parents and truly many of them (parents) will be put to death. Murder shall be rampant in your streets, My children. Why? Because you now have setup another God to worship. A god of materialism and atheism. My children, arrogance and pride have reached even into the hearts of the clergymen. In the plan of the Eternal Father you are permitted to be blinded by sin. Avarice, [and] Pride.

"My children, you must use the exorcism of St. Michael constantly, daily in your lives, for those who knock upon your door now may be evil. Many are human bodies that are dead but with live diabolical spirits within them.

"My children, gather all of the past books of knowledge given by your God to you. Do not allow the Satanic Agents to destroy them. There are only two forces upon earth, My children, Good and Evil. You cannot at this time walk the middle course, for if you become lukewarm you shall fall.

"Satan, the man of perdition, the Prince of Darkness, now walks among all of you on earth. Yes, he walks the earth. Satan, not his consorts as humans, but Satan is loosed now from Hell and walks the earth. He has been permitted to send unto you the test, My children. He has entered among you and upon you all to claim his own.

"Pray, My children, for your brothers and sisters, for many are fast falling into Hell. Satan was always a murderer, and that, My children and My child, shall be his greatest vantage point. You will understand soon.

"Because of the major role of the City of New York and what it plays in the world's government and the governing of your nation, the United States; My children, it is for this reason that Satan chose that area for his fight, to bring into your country a full overthrow of the Christian Belief. It is his endeavor now to replace the Church of My Son, with the Church of Satan.

"Already because too few listened to, and acted upon My counsel, in the past, already MY children, your nation is covered now by secret societies, a Church of Satan, being founded by the master of deceit and the father of all liars.

"My son, I do not have to explain to you the evils that he will create and manifest through your children, as all of those who have given themselves to the hands of the classroom of your nation, your schools, for Satan has planned his role well.

"It has taken many years for him to reach this point, My child. You understand the knowledge of the supernatural has been stilled and has been placed in the minds of man as a myth, to be laughed at and met with derision.

"Many of you cannot understand in your human nature now, his role which is being played now among men. I assure you, My children, you must not cast aside the supernatural, for I told you in the past, and I repeat it anew that Satan now is loosed from Hell. He is walking the earth. He is going about now searching for an abode in the body, the shell of a human being and any man, woman or child of conscionable age can be his abode. Satan is one person, but there are many of his followers. He will use individuals, places, this being one of the highest intelligences next to God the Father. He (Lucifer) and they have a great knowledge to promote accidents that are not accidents. He has control of nature. Understand, My children, you must not test him, but accept in belief. You must understand, My\children, this counsel is not given lightly.

"While man has cast aside the knowledge and belief in the supernatural, Satan and his agents have had the time now to take a firm hold upon your children. O My children, all manner of foul and debased acts shall be created by your children. The future is now. Many of them are agents of Hell (teachers, the teachers of your schools).

"My children, you must now act upon My counsel. Each and every one who hears My voice must act. It is too late now to sit back and expect your neighbors, your brothers, your sisters to go forward as a solitary agent. You must now gather together and fight this evil along with your brothers, your sisters, the world.

"My children, I have promised you always that I will be with you. You shall not be abandoned in the days ahead. The greatest lesson man will learn in the days ahead is, should he place his trust in another, he will be doomed to disappointment and sorrow. You must always keep your eyes turned upward and say: "MY JESUS, MY CONFIDENCE" for My Son is always your confidence. He is always there.

"Man has created an abomination where he has created this false life, the test tube baby. It is not true; it is a monster from the Abyss direct. You are bringing demons into your world, not a child. You seek your Armageddon sooner than it would come and Satan is laughing as you create these abominations. You are bringing forms for him to enter into this world. You do not realize, O mankind, that when these forms are grown full, that they shall be entered and they shall be used by Satan (Lucifer). He knows his time is short and these forms shall be used. They must never be allowed to govern your nation, though they will in the future.

"Man was created in the image of the Eternal Father. Should He make him now the head of sorrow, as he bows His head in sorrow, as he (man) defies Him now? Do you think with all this scientific knowledge and endeavoring that you can escape eventual death from your body? I say unto you that is one measure of knowledge that man shall never find. I watch my children run to and fro marrying and giving in marriage.

"The commandment of the Eternal Father will not be changed to suit the basic carnal natures of the human mankind. My children, many latter day saints have come out of the crises, and shall come.

"The Eternal Father knows full well the outcome. He watches with a heavy heart. We ask for many victim souls in the days ahead. All in good spirit and heart will now make a concerted effort to soothe the injured Heart of My Son Jesus at the tabernacles of the World. Communion in the hand is promoted by Satan because of the rise of the Satanist in your country and in the world. They are conducting Black Mass secretly and openly. The children are the greatest victims of the evil.

"The Sacred Species, the Host, is being used during these rituals of the Black Mass and Satanism. It is in the most abominable way.

"Do not accept the Host in your hand, I beg of you as your Mother, as your Queen and as your Mediatrix from God. Do not allow this to be done without an outcry. No man is worthy to accept My son's body in his hand.

"Yes, My children, Our Hearts are torn as We see many are falling into the Abyss, lost forever to Heaven.

"You wonder why I am crying; I tell you now why I am crying. You must repeat exactly what I say. Repeat: My children, Our Hearts are torn, for there are many priests now who are falling into the Abyss. Pray for your priests who have not received enough of your prayers to enlighten their hearts.

"Pray for your brothers and sisters, extend your charity to the sinner. Do not condemn him but pray for him. And, My children, you must retain tradition! You must retain [a] firm foundation of your faith by keeping all of the good publications. Do not accept the changes that have been made by Satan to seduce your soul. Come every chance given. Pray, My children, as a constant vigilance of prayers. Whenever you feel despair or discouragement, remember to pray to go unto My Son for confidence. Keep your eyes upon the sky, My children. Search through the darkness; the Ball is coming. Pray for your brothers and sisters that have gone astray.

****

This Message [was] given to a privileged soul by the Blessed Virgin at 11:15-12:00 PM, March 20, 1983.

Our Lady has come and has been before me counseling me for an hour now, and she is now going to speak to me and, through me, to the world.

"My child, today you have record of yet another statement which I made in prophecy to you. I told you and all who read My Messages to you that soon the waters would rise upon the East Coast in various parts because of man's sins in those Eastern areas. Check, O unbelieving mankind, the area of the township of Methuen for an example and the area of the Merrimac River and other parts of New Jersey.

"In this We of Heaven include many parts of the State of Connecticut, as well as the Royal River of Yarmouth, Maine.

"I do not seek to brag of what I know, but rather I seek that mankind shall heed My Messages to all our true and just Seers. I also tell you now of the fact that there must be much more prayer, as the beast is running rampant. This year, now especially among the young, does he roam. The just and those under My mantle, yes, many of those will be taken by him and caused to fall under his wings.

"Always, My children, you must wear your Sacramentals. My children, heed this request, because with them on, Satan cannot cause any harm to you in [your] mental/physical or spiritual state.

"He may throw you, but he could hardly harm you when I had you under My blue mantle and My Scapulars brown and green. Also, the red scapular of My Son's Sacred Heart, this should be worn. It too has many mystical favors to grant unto mankind by My Son. You, My child, will now repeat the poem which Therese gave you only but a few days ago. Take this from your subconscious mind. Now you will put it on the paper that is before you. It will be called:

SATAN'S PLANS FOR JOHN PAUL II - POPE

Your Holy Father must not come or go,
The danger before him - He does not know.

He must not right now in another country show,
Planned is an ambush from the forces below.

Your Holy Father will deal with the anger never greater in any earth age,
The head Luciel shall attempt to turn his page.

Not only him but all of the forces of Hell
But with prayers we will cause them to quell.

That day for him will begin as just any other
Except for the entity that attempts to smother.

Everywhere along his travel will follow the forces of Hell
They shall attempt to attack him wherever he may dwell.

The attack may be by day among a big crowd
Or by night in a dwelling of which he'll be proud.

Daily now you must all remember to pray
that on the throne your Holy Father will stay.

Upon this Son our graces now all do fall
But you all must help him stand up real tall.

Unless you wish him under Satan to now fall.
Send all your prayers to Heaven to call.

Jesus will hear them with all Heaven too
Your prayers may save him as well as you.

****

March 21, 1983 Monday Evening 11:00-12:00 PM

Our Lady: "My child awaken" (me) O My God, there are many blue beams of light now that are falling unto my bed from her hands.

Explanation of beams: Now the beams lasted only but a short time before they came as graces instead, that is little slivers of glass in all shades and tints of blue. How beautiful it was, imagine light beams above you, then slivers of multi-tinted blue shaded glass of spiritual existence which filter right into you and do not harm you, but rather produce a feeling of pure happiness, with peace and joy. This feeling [is] only existing when She is present (meaning Our Lady).

Our Lady now speaks: "Now, My child, you must not ever disobey Me again and you must remember to write exactly what I am about to show you, as it will be of great importance. View, My child."

I see before me a great land mass, narrowing slowly, the image is coming in of a boot shaped area of land, jutting out from this area. This land mass is, I think it is Italy. Yes, She said, "yes it is Italy." Now She is taking me in closer to view. Oh, the Dome of St. Peters, She says, at the Vatican. I don't know what kind of rock that the stairs of St. Peter's are made of, but I think it is cemented or mortared marble and granite. But I can see a sign or plaque which says something in the language of Italy and Rome, especially Italian. Oh, now Our Lady is saying "The Church of St. Peter and, and, Oh, She says "The second name will not be revealed to you. Observe."

Oh, Oh, No, now the scene is changing and now I see many dead bodies and blood all over the place. There is even a number of cardinals with their tiaras on top of their heads among the crowd of dead people, or I should say dead bodies.

Ugh, it's horrible like someone or something made everyone go crazy and become killers all at once. Not a person is moving, some even look like they were burned or charred from radiation. Now I see planes landing nearby and a tank moving in the street heading towards me as I now stand at the Vatican.

The driver does not seem to see Our Lady and myself. Now there is a small group of people - they all have on Cardinal's tiaras, also oh, oh, also they have on, Our Lady, is now pointing to them - Nazi Swastikas armbands. These are on or near the fatty muscular part of the arm the upper arm. Also, they have the Illuminati's symbol of Luciel's Evil Eye on the Pyramids on the armbands.

Our Lady: "My child, the whole vision is now over. You have much to suffer now. I will not alleviate it, but rather you must offer it up for your Holy Father."

****

March 22, 1983 Evening 11:00 - 12:00 P.M. A Voice and Face Only.

Our Lady is before me now and her thoughts are being transmitted directly to me.

Our Lady: "Courage, My child, courage. Your next day will be depressing and you must be willing to accept it as it happens. Otherwise people will think you are in danger, but I tell you now the only danger is that which now is in your mind. You must not allow yourself to wish to stay in your confinement,"

(Me) "I did not allow myself to follow this small Directive."

Our Lady: "I say this because if you do not, you will be placed into a worse situation and you will find it quite unbearable"

"Your Holy Father is in much danger now and in his near future. Rome is to undergo a great siege, much of China, Russia, and the USA will be at war in the near future. I say very near future. The warning is at hand, very soon and preceded by a small but full scale war between Russia and the United States of America. O, mankind, if only you knew how soon."

The rest of the Message was to be for me alone so I do not include it here at all.

****

March 23, 1983, Wednesday 11:00-12:00 Complete Visage.

Our Lady has come down and is in a purple light which is now being emitted from her purple gown which she is wearing. I have wondered if she could explain why purple and or if she would repeat the Message that had been given which was lost or destroyed.

Oh, She is now placing her finger to her lips. I am to repeat:

Our Lady: "My child it will not be replaced for reasons not to be revealed to you at this time. The gown is purple for all My children who will soon die and all of the Holy Innocents now dead.

"My child, what I am about to say to you is of great importance, supreme to the health of your nation as a general body. Russia, Red China, Germany, and all of the Communist Nations and Countries are the scourges of mankind. Your President, he constantly speaks of S.A.L.T. II and the Geneva Arms Talks, But ask, does he know of who or what seeks to remove him soon from his job as National Leader of the United States? Does he know that Russia, the Big Ugly Scourge of man all over the world, lies in wait for the attack upon his White House in Washington, D.C.? I tell you no, he does not know. Yes, Russia lies very near and at this time the American Communist Parties know of this and rejoice. They are secretly planning to remove him and place this country under Russian communist authority and control."

"Many children of ages just out of the cradle are being now constantly defamed and desecrated. Majorly the abortion murders have increased. This all calls for a well-deserved punishment upon you, O mankind of the United States. It will come in months, weeks, and then soon in days.

"In Europe (the Western Area) the communist parties all laugh because America is going to go to War with Russia over an attack by Russia on American Shores. Without prayer, America is doomed soon to a great major war.

"Since you of America do not know what it is like to see your family and/or friends dead before your eyes in the streets you will have only one chance.

"My child, do not write what I am about to say until I tell you to do so. Repeat now:

"My children, there will be charred bodies which will be totally unidentifiable on earth in your country if you do not all pray. I say all. Remember or all of you will soon die in the streets and sidewalks. You must not allow yourself to see the horrors of this kind of war."

****

March 24, 1983, Thursday, Eve of the Annunciation of Mary, 12:30 to 1:00 AM

Our Lady came to me directly by going as a beam of bright light through my picture window towards me. She is all in white and is bare footed. She has on a long flowing green cape or robe without any arms in it. By this I mean sleeves. It is a robe, but it flows long like a cape to her feet. Her Rosary is heavy-looking brown wooden beads. Her mantle is trimmed in a ½ inch border of fine gold. Oh, now she is smiling; what a happy looking smile. It is very radiant.

Our Lady: "My child, I am happy for you only. I am not happy for anyone other, at this time anyway. But you, My son, will still have a great depressed feeling at times, given being semi-free. You must now accept and utilize the help offered here, for you may go to a worse place if you do not. I, in the past warned you about your anger. Now you may work on that. I also warned you about your freeness and sexuality, now you must pay the price.

"Instruct those who hear this Message to read Ezechiel 1:1 thru 1:28, so thus that they may learn more about angels - they must be brought back.

"The Church must teach now of the angel guardians which are about you constantly. You can send them away, but is it not more beneficial to have them with you always? Tell your bishops that the only true Bibles are those printed prior to the year 1964 or 1965, or the Modern Day Douay-Rheims Bible. My child, I must leave you now but I will return on 3-25-83 tomorrow."

****

March 25, 1983, - Friday, 12:30-01:00 Feast of the Annunciation

Our Lady came about 5 minutes ago and requested I not write until now. She is wearing all blue for clothing except the white gown. It is also trimmed in gold. She now says:

"The United States spends much time on anti-ballistic missiles. This is that they waste much time in an attempt to build a missile which can destroy an intercontinental ballistic missile or a submarine launched ballistic missile. For now, I tell you of fact. Your next war with Russia will not be a war on foreign soil. The Russians will land on American Shores. The big communist parties of your land are heading America for Great War. War is a punishment for man's sins.

"My child, abortion is murder. View now the image upon your window. The father sends you an image of abortion. My child, do not only view but describe it as well."

I see an office - a patient is now lying down. I cannot see her face. The doctor who has a face I cannot see either, is now - he is reaching below the table to grab the straps to strap her down so she will not move. He says: "Now her legs are strapped down spread eagle and her thighs are open for the abortion." She now sees the vacuum suction machine. I now can hear it - it is very noisy. But now, oh, the woman is now screaming out in pain: "I changed my mind, I want my baby. Please let me up, let me go!" Now the doctor is saying: "No, it is too late now, I won't let you go, I need the money. That's why you should not have come if you were still indecisive about your abortion."

Now the horrid doctor is shoving this tube shaped device up into the woman's thighs. She is now screaming out in pain: "My God what have I done - please forgive me. Don't let me die." The woman's chest has now sunk in about 2" since the machine was inserted. Now in a clear disc, which collects the remains of the baby, I can see floating, oh it's horrible. I can see floating an eye and a finger. This is all that is identifiable.

Now the scene is changing; I see yet another woman and doctor. This time she has skin of Asian type descent. This woman is drugged, but still strapped down. Now the doctor is putting a forceps type of devise into the woman's canal to hold the vagina open for a long tube in which he is now slowly inserting into the woman. The tube is now passing through a small hole between a muscle which I believe is called the cervix. I can see now inside the woman and the pole is at the edge of the area where the womb is. "Blessed Mother, please don't make me continue to view."

"My child, you must. Please have faith in Me."

I now see, oh the doctor is now cutting the baby into distinct little pieces and is pulling them out through the tube. The pieces now are removed, yet when the tube is also removed she is still bleeding. Now I am noticing that Our Lady is not going to make me view the salt abortion. "Thank you, Blessed Mother."

Our Lady: "My child, both of these women you have just viewed will never bear any children ever again, as will none of the women who these two doctors worked abortions on. My child, since you are tired, I will now grant you a rest period until tomorrow morning or evening. Child, which would you prefer?"

"Evening, Blessed Mother, evening." "Yes, My child, I will see you on March 26th in the evening."

****

March 26, 1983, Saturday Evening - Eve of Palm Sunday 12:30-1:00 AM

I did not notice Our Lady coming, but She is here and she says:

"My child you see My feet. My robe is white, My mantle white, and My tunic white. Now I have a fast and important Message for the United States of America. Should the USA not resist, they (the huge communist party) will take over the USA. Andropov now lies in wait. He uses the Plan of Stalin and Lenin (peace until you can pounce upon the peaceful). Your nation faces a major war soon. Goodbye until tomorrow, My son."

****

March 27, 1983, Sunday (Palm Sunday)

I have been awaiting Mary for a while, but now I hear angels and I see before me a most strange sight. Many little cherubs or that is miniature angels ... blobs of brilliant light, piercing light which have wings emanating from them. They are of a high glossy white, and are made of a feathery down-like substance.

Now they are all going around me on the walls in my room and are now singing:

"Ave Maria gratia plena. Maria gratia plena, Maria gratia plena. Ave, Ave, dominus, dominus tecum. Benedicta tu in muliaribus - et benedictus, benedictus fructus ventris-ventris tui. Jesu. Ave Maria. Sancta Maria mater Dei. Ora ora pro nobis-ora ora pronobis peca toribus nunc et in hora mortis in hora mortis nostria In ora mortis nostria Ave Maria." (Latin spelling is as it sounded.)

Now an angel who looks human with added wings and brilliance is now before me. He is saying to me "Come forward little weak one. The Son wishes you to come and kneel down here, now beside me." Now, Oh, I see a bright light in the room either, yet still I am surrounded by angels. The sky about me now is all purple and bright pink, a tone such as I have never seen upon earth, by me or anyone.

Now Jesus is coming forward to me. He has on a deep red or scarlet cape with a hood. It looks to be made of fine plush velvet with a satin trim on it. Jesus says now "See My wounds, My son. See how they bleed raw with mankind who does not heed Me. Tell, O won't you please tell, mankind to heed the Holy Father, John Paul II.

"Your Holy Father, the Father of Rome, has at Heaven's request to him directly via My Mother ordered a year entitled as a Holy Year. This Jubilee Year, if you go to the Holy City of Rome to John Paul's Mass, you will receive, O Mankind who do go, the blessings of having your sins forgiven.

"My son, I chose this chance to ask you to give Me a vow of celibacy. I do not deny you feminine company, but you must stay out of any sexual promiscuity with a woman or you will break the vow. You are not being requested to the Holy Roman Priesthood, but you are being asked for this vow, which will make your life much easier."

I have thought for a moment and do not know if I could carry the burden of that load. As I went to respond to Him, The Lord then said unto me "Since you are not able to make this vow right out, it shows that you wish to be truthful. I now only ask you to vow to make an attempt at least to resist the lures of sexual urges, but I will ask you for celibacy in the future. At this time you are still too immature for that vow."

Oh, Our Lady is also here now dressed all in blue, all is blue that is, except for her gold belt. "My child, lie down now. Jesus has said all there is to say. Go to sleep. Tell us now that you vow. Goodbye, My child, rest well. Tomorrow We will be with you."

"You will allow the doctor to give you the medication for it will not have any effect on you. I will see to that. Blessed are the nurses you are thinking of. My Son did not make all beautiful outwardly because then vanity and pride of Satan might take over a man's soul or a woman's soul. A small secret, My son; seek that which is ugly and then console it for unto it is easily found the Kingdom of your God. Sleep now my child."

I note here I awoke on March 28, 1983 today which is Monday and found that I did not remember at all having written this; yet while receiving the Message I must have done so. Maybe I wrote it while sleeping or on my way to sleep.

****

March 28, 1983, Monday 12:00-12:08

Our Lady has been here for five minutes and now is finding me quite depressed.

She says: "Tomorrow you will awaken very late, My child, due to lack of sleep. Thus, I will cut this short. I say short because I have today also a blessing for you and your questioning, wondering workers. I will give you all this blessing while you all sleep tonight. I give you counsel, My child, on your Mission for Me. It may be halted in some details, but it will not be totally stopped. I will be always here with you to help you, to console you. I say, I will always be with you, that is unless you disavow My aid and My holy right to intercede for you.

"I will seek to aid you where there is any physical danger to you if you are at that moment just in actions. I guarded you with My blue mantle and guided you from Koulbourn in New Marlborough, Massachusetts to the very steps of St. Mary's Apartments. The teens I sent along when the man was going to shoot you, picked you up at My mystical mental request. Thus, you were saved from a fatality.

"My child, and My three little ones, you must seek harder the means and ways to spread this Mission Message. The time is short. The first worker has questions on the Message from [the] tape. Thus tapes must no longer, My child, in the future be used. They are no longer a practical idea. My son, on Tuesday, at 10:00 on March 29, 1983 I will see you again."

****

March 29, Tuesday, 10:00 – 10:15 PM

I await at 10:00 the Celestial Mama of the ages, Queen of the Universe, of all hearts of all men and of Heaven. A voice I recognize as Our Lady's is saying. "My child, patience, in one moment, I shall be with you. Now do you see Me coming? "Yes, Mother, yes."

"I am the light of the world, but you are not always heeding what I say. Many times you, O mankind, all attempt to ruin yourselves in sin and abominations. Should man not turn about and pray, now a great comet shall strike and three quarters of earth shall be obliterated. The remaining will envy the dead. The U.S. shall experience, in a short time, a great major war. The Warning and the Miracle are also far sooner than the Ball of Fire.

"But all three are within your own lifetime now, My son. You now are allowed visitors, but be cautious in your talk, especially with the three, and I mean the workers. I say be careful because of the doctors, there are eyes and ears in every place in the hospital.

"Goodbye for now, My child."

****

March 31, 1983, Thursday

The first part of the Message [is] private - only this part is public.

"My children, in Popayan I came at 7:45 and warned to a girl age 14, by the name of Mary that she was to warn the cathedral that at 8:15 there would be a quake in Popayan and parts of Piendamo and Cajibio.

"I warned that the cathedral would fall. She told the Father, whose name I will not say, but he refused to believe her. Thus, he did not tell the crowd of about 24 other people. Before leaving the cathedral, she yelled aloud: "This cathedral will fall in a 5.5 Richter scale earthquake." All laughed at her in unbelief. The cathedral fell and only the girl survived. I tried to warn them but it was impossible for Me to save them. My children, learn a lesson from this for also to another I predicted the quake in that area 3 days prior to event of destruction. I was not heeded. Thus the quake happened."

"Good night, My son. Peace be with you."

****

1983, Second Quarter Messages

April 3, 1983, Easter Sunday – (Beginning was private)

Our Lady: "My son, you question the wishes of the Father. It is not well and befitting of you, as one of My Seers to question what is revealed to you. You have been given the grace of great knowledge and now you still, My child, question the Father's wishes."

"My children, do not torment yourselves in mind. If you are calumniated, insulted or ridiculed, think, My child, [of] your God, Jesus, who walked the way of Calvary. He was the King of Kings, and He was insulted, beaten, and always on the way to Calvary each passing moment more insulted, beaten and calumniated than before."

"I do not say to forget these mockings, ridicule and pains of torment, but rather I say to offer them up unto the Father. It is so now with mankind that you do not wish to endure anything for Jesus, who did everything to save you and who died on the cross for you. Always, My children, must you now offer all your pains, sorrows up unto My Son. Be humble, always act with great love and patience, gentleness and serenity. If you have great enough of a love for Me and for My Son, you most assuredly will find the way unto the Kingdom.

"You all, all My beloved children, cannot understand the feeling that I have for you all, the love I have for you all. We seek to give you many consolations and joys, but the Father demands that in every bed of roses, must lie many thorns. The hours you all spend at the Holy Sites of My appearances upon earth, if done in love, will be removed from your stay in the fires of Purgatory, especially the hours spent in the summer's great heats and the winter's great colds. I tell you now of fact, one minute upon earth may be one year in Purgatory.

"St. Michael is ever present beside Me. Pray your Rosary at every time that you find yourself being attacked by Lucifer, for then I will send Michael to use his sword to defend you all. Pray, My children and My child, for those in the prisons and concentration camps.

"Pray for the Holy Souls in Purgatory. I told you in the past that I did not want you to forget them. What has become of My counsel? Many have sat in the same spots in lower Purgatory in the hottest flames for 500-700 years, all because they have been forgotten. You must pray now, My children, and always for them.

"You will pray:

> (1) Five times the Apostles' Creed
> (2) One Hail Holy Queen
> (3) One Our Father
> (4) One Hail Mary
> (5) One Glory Be to the Father
> (6) One Requiem: Eternal Rest Grant...

"By these prayers you will release many from the deepest recesses of Purgatory, let alone all who will be saved from the highest part of Purgatory. They will be in the multus (great many)

"You who have the Bibles dated in print prior to 1964-1965, or the Douay-Rheims version, read the second book of Maccabees, Chapter 12, Verse 46.

"The Maple Leaf and the Eagle (Canada and the USA) are now surrounded by the Bear of Communism. It shall be a major war that will bring great bloodshed. (Russia) Pray. My children, the Rosary. Send it as missiles to Heaven. It will make you feel at ease and peaceful. It will bring a quick end to the semi-long war soon to begin. I say soon to begin. I say soon to begin because now it is too late to avoid. Now it will happen.

"You were warned of this in the year 1630. You were warned in the year 1780. You were warned in the year 1838. You were warned in 1926 at Philadelphia. You were warned in 1947 and 1949 at Lipa, [the] Philippines.

"You were warned from 1950 to 1969 at Necedah, in Wisconsin. You were also warned at Garabandal in

Spain. You were warned in San Damiano 1961-1971. You were warned at Fatima and Lourdes. You were warned at Bayside, New York prior to the move of Bayside to Flushing. You still had a chance to avoid a war.

"Now you will face this war in full force. But I give you this much consolation. If man goes down upon his knees, your nation will be spared from the throes of a full communistic regime.

"My Son, Jesus now is here; heed His words, My children,"

"My little sons of earth, fight with (alongside) My Mother. Pray the Holy Rosary. It will conquer all, I repeat all, [in] the battle.

"My sons in the priesthood, put St. Michael back into the Church. Recite the prayer, put his statutes back or else he shall soon cease in aiding your parish Churches, out of lack of your prayer.

"Goodbye, My son."

****

Message of the Week after Easter from Our Lady to the world, 1983

"My child, you will disregard what I have said to you in the past in regard to using this cassette. You will record everything that I tell you until I tell you to pause. At this point you will pause the cassette, for parts of what I am to say will not be recorded on this cassette. My child, it is important, My son, that this cassette is being made.

"My child and My children of God, I have come to warn you that the cup is overflowing and has overflowed. The abominations of the world shall bring upon mankind great suffering.

"Man in the creation of God has cast aside his Mission to do honor and glory to his God. Man has given himself up to all manner of abominations and sin. Slowly the cup has been filling up and now it flows over because of your sins, because you have cast aside the way mankind has been cleansed by trial.

"The major sins being committed in your world in offense far above any sin committed in such a majority in the past is the sin of heresy. You have committed the great sin of heresy. You, O My children, have opened the doors of the Eternal City, the home of your Vicar, to all manners of heretics and non-believers.

"You violated the sacred trust, you have taken the body of your Creator, the Son of your God in the Trinity and violated Him. You must do your eating at home. When you come to the great sacrifice, the Holy Sacrifice of the Mass, you must come in reverence. You must sacrifice by going down upon your knees. Do penance now for the offenses to your God.

"During the Holy Sacrifice of the Mass there is a change of the bread and a change of the wine and it is the Real Presence of the Body and Blood of your God. As in the past, cannot you recognize the mystery of Heaven and earth? Did not the staff of Moses turn into a serpent in the will of God? Did not the river in Egypt turn to blood in the will of God? Cannot God in His Will come to you changing the bread and the wine into actual presence, His Real Presence, the actual presence [of] His Body and Blood? But no, mankind you do not pray enough, because you lack humility because you have given yourselves to the world and pleasures of the flesh. You have lost the way. You have gone into darkness.

"A Church, a house in darkness wears a band of death about it. All that is rotten shall fall. The Heavens and the earth shall shake. There shall be great earthquakes. Many shall die in the great flame of the Ball of Redemption.

"My children, Heaven and the way does not change. It does not need improving. It is the simple way given to you from the beginning of time by the Eternal Father and made known to you by the visit of My Son to earth. Read, My children, your books that I have pleaded with you to gather before they are destroyed. Do not give yourselves over to the publications of the Anti-Christ in your world. As you pray, you will seek out the Spirit of Light to enlighten your knowledge and you may know when there is error. Then you may recognize the truth. Then you shall not fall victim to the errors of your world.

"Use the prayer of St. Michael, the exorcism, for I tell you now why you must. For St. Michael will cast out Satan, and Satan was a murderer and liar from the beginning. Satan was then allowed upon your earth to separate the sheep from the goats. My children, he is a master of deceit.

"I must tell you as your Mother, that unless you remain in the State of Grace you cannot recognize him. He is a man of a thousand faces. He has great power. He can throw his voice, My children, into animals and even into the air. Unless you give your children a firm foundation of knowledge of their faith, they will fall to his subtleties, My children.

"You will pray a constant vigilance of prayer in your homes and in your world and pray for those who are fast falling into Hell, victims of cruelty of Satan, victims of the deceit of the Prince of Darkness. He was a murderer from the beginning and he is a murderer now. He has many disciples in human form. I have begged you in the past to recognize faces of evil about you. You must constantly, when you are out in the world, say the exorcism given to you by the good Pope.

"The greatest defense which you will have against the evil now walking the earth: You will say: "St. Michael the Archangel, defend us in battle. Be our protection against the wickedness and snares of the devil. May God rebuke him we humbly pray, and do you O Prince of the Heavenly Host, by the divine power of God cast into Hell Satan and all the evil spirits who wander throughout the world seeking the ruin of souls. Amen."

"If you do not recite this prayer, your children, your streets will run with blood because you have not listened. Pastors, a great attack is being planned against the priesthood and has been planned against the priesthood. Many of you will be shot down like targets within the streets. Prepare now and pray, wear your Sacramentals. Protect your sheep now the battle is raging.

"The lives of many are filled with degradation and corruption. The knowledge of God in Heaven [is] being uprooted and supplanted with knowledge of Satan being glorified all over and upon your earth. Satan is one of the destruction with evil. Every city, every state, every country throughout the world will now feel the test.

"You shall be tried like metals within the fires. When you come out of this test, My children, all that is rotten will have fallen. You will be cleansed by trial. It is truly now a battle of the supernatural. If you remain close to My Heart, My Son's Heart in the Eucharist, you will nourish your souls with My Body and My Blood. Yes, for I too have given My Body and My Blood through the Trinity and through My Son.

"I assure you, My children, you will not fall into darkness. This will be a glory of a time for many. For many will be given the light to see Lucifer and his army of ogres. The entire forces of Satan are known as 666. He will eventually, with his army, be destroyed.

"However, it is the plan of the Eternal Father that the world proceed now upon this test. There will be much gnashing of teeth and woe set upon the earth by the evil one. He will seek out souls to vanquish in dark places, for as he is the Prince of Darkness, he must live in darkness. My children, those that are within the light have nothing in common with darkness. Put on your armor of grace. Fight now against the Prince of Darkness and his consorts.

"Do not be fooled by their outward appearance of piousness and holiness, for many of them will come as angels of light, but they have ravenous hearts of wolves. They are the wolves in sheep's garments and sad to say, My children, I find that many of these are within My house, My Son's house, the Church upon earth. Throughout the earth's years of time, I have given much direction through the Holy Spirit. My Son has given this direction for Me, for it is the course of the Church, but man in much time has joined with Lucifer who was kicked out from Heaven. Man in power has decided to take it upon himself to go above his Creator, seeking to create life, seeking to accept the knowledge of life and using it to destroy until the world has created a force of executioners from Hell.

"My children, sin has become a way of life, and your children shall turn upon you. It will be Father against Son, Mother against Daughter - division in the household, all because you did not prepare your houses and your homes for these times. Recognize now the signs of your times.

"You will all keep in your hearts the prayer of St. Michael. You will use it for consolation and direction. If you come upon a questionable soul you will be inwardly awakened and you will say this exorcism to St. Michael and your eyes will be opened to the truth.

"Many shall receive the gift of discernment of spirit. It is necessary now for in this fight, the battle against the spirits, it is necessary that you see against the unseen forces of the supernatural, a force of your own... You see a force to beat them by knowing that they are there.

"Keep a constant vigilance of prayer going in your country and throughout your world. The time, time and a half is here. The time has passed and the 'time' is past. The half is now here."

Our Lady is now slowly dissipating and she says:

"My child, your Rosaries have been blessed. I will be back to see you soon.

"You are depressed at this time, but worry thou not. Do not commit what you were believing you would want to commit, for it is Satan who has tempted your heart...

"Amen, Amen, Amen. Goodbye now, My son."

****

This is the Message given to a privileged soul by the Blessed Virgin on April 22, 1983.

She is coming forward now.

She says: "You will listen, My child, very carefully and you will repeat all the words with exactness.

"You are coming on the road of a great chastisement. Man has set fast the pace for his own destruction. My child, you will please ask your leaders to continue now the fight for the Message to be spread.

"You must not stop, the Message will go through the world, through the channels I have given you, My child. Out in the world beyond the farthest star visible to man's eyes is an instrument planned by the Father for your chastisement. Pray, pray My child and My children. Pray a constant vigilance of prayer now until the moment of darkness.

"I have wandered throughout the world for countless earth years warning and preparing you for the great chastisement. Many warnings have been given to man but they have passed by unnoticed by most. You will repeat this, My child: rigid-discipline and self-control and self-denial must be exercised by men of God in the houses of God. Can you not sacrifice for the souls in your care and for your own souls? Men of God, return now to your rightful way of life, make right the house of God. Rigid discipline must now be restored in the houses of God. The leadership in the house of God is much in need.

"My child, My children, you must now shout from the roofs, for the time grows short. Repeat now, repeat now, My child, this list of the kinds of sins which you must make atonement and restitution for. Not only you, My child, but all of My children must make restitution for the sins that all the people are making this day on this list and all those of this list:

Infamy, Blasphemy, Immodesty, Worship of False Idols, Disrespect of Authority, Infidelity in the Family, Disrespectful Dress, Rewriting of the Words of the Prophets, Arrogance among the Men of God, Intellectual Pride among the Men of God, Lack of the True Vocations, and lastly, Chastity.

"There must be a sacred Mission for all of the priesthood, sacredness for the nuns; yet why are many marrying and engaging in sexual activity? They were supposed to remain chaste. The nuns were to be the Brides of Christ. The priests were to be ambassadors in carrying on the duty of Jesus upon earth. They were supposed to recommit the sacrifice of Jesus at every Mass. They appear chaste, but many of them are no longer pure and chaste again in the married state. Many have abandoned this for the pleasures of the flesh.

Damnation follows this course for all.

"Let alone the priesthood and the nuns, also married life, all three. Do not think, O mankind, that just because you are married to a woman or man that you are free to commit any sexual activity that you wish with that person. Yes, you are free to that person; but it is also true that it is sinful if it is continued and continued and continued with no real purpose.

"You must restore within the houses of God true discipline of life and procedure. Return to sacrifices and self-denial. You must starve your bodies of the demons which you have allowed to enter upon you. You cannot partake of the full pleasures of earth, all created for soul destruction, and take you also then to their kingdom.

"There is no middle road, the left side is into darkness and the straight road to the light. My child, how weary I grow as I wander throughout your world shedding many tears."

Our Lady now is crying before me, she is crying. Big tears are rolling down her cheeks. Many out there do not believe that she really cries. Many out there do not believe that she really appears, that she really cares. She does care folks! She does. If you could only see the tears upon her face. It is a really depressing scene to see her in this manner.

She continues: "Your Father plans a great chastisement for your earth's nation, for your earth's nation! It is for you that I now cry; it is for your return that I beg. What more can I do but give you our Hearts? See, My child, the Hearts are torn asunder by the sins of ungrateful man."

Now, before me I see a great heart. The heart is surrounded by thorns, thorns of which I have never seen any so big before; except possibly at the time of the crucifixion in the vision I saw of the crucifixion. The thorns which Jesus had on His head were the same kind, I'm almost certain. They surround the head and there are now, two swords through the heart. And now, below the heart there is a chalice and there's blood dripping into this chalice. I didn't notice the chalice before, but now I've noticed the chalice and it's almost full, and now it is full. Now the whole scene, except for the chalice, is vanishing and the chalice is pouring out. It is pouring out and there is blood spilling down all over the place, but it is not, it is not appearing here, it is not sticking here, it is vanishing as it falls.

Our Lady says: "We have shed Our blood for mankind. We have shed it upon mankind. It has cleansed many souls and it has saved many souls, My child, My children, but many souls have fallen, many souls shall fall. The Abyss is wide open now and many are falling. Satan is walking the earth.

"He walks among mankind and he seeks the souls of mankind. Many shall fall, many shall fall. Graces in abundance, My children, are given to you to strengthen you in the battle ahead. You must now choose the allegiance of Christ. Do not expect comfort upon earth. Do not expect Glory.

"No, you will scratch the earth and burrow into the dirt. Your glory shall be in the life everlasting with the Kingdom. You must now all gather in the light, for whenever and wherever two or more are gathered in My Son's name, you know that He will be among you to guide you. Call upon your Guardian Angels often, My children. You have forgotten the angels. Do you not now know of them? Do not listen to the mockery of the world; they seek to take the reality of the Guardians of Heaven from you, so that you can be sent to Lucifer. When you have great sorrow or trial, call upon your Guardian Angels. Ask My Son for help from the Father. Do not seek comfort among man, for he has none to give you. For man has become arrogant; man has become self-seeking; he loves the pleasures of the flesh.

"Man has become uncharitable, he has cast aside the truth in the Book of Light, choosing to rewrite the works of the prophets of old. You will not rewrite the book to adjust it to the ways of man. You must bring man to follow the ways of his God. How long do you think He will tolerate the abominations being committed upon your earth in the house of God? How long, My children? My child, you must always recognize Me. You must always also recognize the faces of the deceitful ones. You must be cautious in your associations. There is no deceit in Heaven.

"The spirits that come to you from the Sacred Grounds of Long Island, when they appear there to you or at your house, they are true. The spirits that appear to all Seers are true. The Rosaries that were sent to you, My child, they were sent to you at My request, though the people did not realize that it was My request. It was sent at My request. I caution you anew, beware of the evil force that surrounds the Shrine of Purity, for you now, in your area, have a little shrine. It is not a public shrine, it is your own private shrine. They will try to stop you with all cunning and deception, so call much to your Guardians. They wish to save you from all unnecessary sufferings. I tell you this My child."

Our Lady says: "This part will be private for a few moments."

Now Our Lady says: "My child, do not be depressed for Me. My children, will you not listen to My pleas?

"You will kneel, My child. You kneel before Me. My child, the Great War will soon begin and will soon take place upon your earth, [and] in your nation, Great War. The war that shall begin shall be between Russia, China, and the United States of America.

"This war shall last for a short period of time. Part of the United States shall be made communistic and part will remain democratic. Part will be controlled by the Kremlin and part will be controlled by the United States, itself. In time you may win this back, but it will be very hard, My children.

"You were warned, you did not listen. You did not listen when I cried to you at Fatima. You did not listen when I cried to you at La Salette. You did not listen to Me when I cried to you at Lourdes. You did not listen at Bayside. You have not listened at any Shrine throughout the world, My children, and now the Father is angry. The Father has been angry for many, many years, but you are now angering Him supremely. You do not listen when I speak to you any longer, My children. Therefore, Great War shall soon come now upon you, for you have not listened.

"You have not changed; you do not seek to change. My child and My children, your nation shall be the first struck. New York shall be the first, then California and then Canada shall be struck and your nation shall be crippled. During your Second World War that you had, there was a great attack upon the Harbor called Pearl Harbor. You thought this attack was great, My children, then wait until you see the next attack upon your nation, a greater attack than ever has been seen in the history of the world, greater than any of the attacks done in the past by any nation upon any nation. There shall be such destruction, bodies will be charred and be unable to be identified from man or woman. They will be black and charred, with the bodies all over your nation's streets.

"No, not the whole nation, but rather especially around the outer fringes of your nation. The center parts of your nation will be more protected and have a chance. If your war should escalate, if you should not respond soon enough, much of your nation will be destroyed, but, My children, part of your nation shall be saved, a small part of your nation.

"This is the minor chastisement that shall soon come upon your world. Then many shall listen and heed Me. Many shall then know that I have spoken and have really appeared, and shall heed the next part of My Messages when I Warn: Much of New York shall be destroyed. Most of California shall be destroyed. Part shall sink below the ocean. Japan shall sink below the waters. Hawaii shall sink below the waters. The other side of the San Andreas Fault, My child, shall sink soon enough.

"A great earthquake shall soon divide your nation at the center. My child, this shall happen very soon, very soon, My child. My child, you do not understand why this will happen, but it shall. Now, My child, I do not have any more to continue. I cannot answer any questions for you at this time. I know you have many questions, My child, but they shall be answered in the future, and tell your first worker that she is doing a good job. She must continue, but she also must take a rest, for she has been overworking herself. Tell her, My child, that it is My wish for her, she must take a short rest. This Message shall be sent out soon enough. She will have extra workers. Yes, My child, you were right in telling the person you told last about this Message and about these Messages. You must send a copy to her. She may be a help, a great help in the near future. She will be a future secretary of your group in the future. My child, good day, pray now a Hail Mary in Latin, as I leave and honor Me."

"Goodnight, Mother."

"Ave Maria, Gratia Plena, Dominus Tecum, Benedicta Tu In Mulierbus Et Benedictus Fructus Ventri Tui, Jesus. Sancta Maria, Mater Dei, Ora Pronobis, Peccatoribus Nunc Et In Hora Mortis Nostrae. Amen."

****

Today is Friday, April 29, 1983.

Our Lady now has come before me. Slowly She is coming in. Yes, the lighting now is coming very clearly on the window before me, it is a dark blue, almost purple.

I hear a voice saying "Woe to the inhabitants of the earth, Woe, Woe, Woe, O Woe to the inhabitants of the earth." I recognize the voice of St. Michael. I cannot see his presence, nor do I yet see Our Lady, only the blue that surrounds her normally when She appears. There is a pinkish presence, alike to that of the presence of Jesus, a pinkish red, a very dark pink, but not quite a red yet.

Our Lady now is slowly materializing now in front of me in a blue light. The window is still a blue where she passed through on a beam of blue light. She is now assembling herself in composure.

She has nothing upon Her feet tonight, oh, but Her Rosary is so beautiful. You should see Her Rosary, folks, you should see Her Rosary. It is wooden and yet beams of light come out from the Rosary. Her robe or outer tunic is dark blue. She has a crown upon Her Head imbedded with jewels, rubies, sapphires, I don't know if they are diamonds, but they are almost whitish yellow colored stones, and there are amethysts as well. She truly is the Queen of the Universe, Queen of all Hearts, Queen of Peace.

She is taking the Rosary out in Her hands and kissing the crucifix and She is now pointing to the window. On the window there is now a large area that has turned pink instead of purple, purplish blue. In this pinkish area Our Lady now says Jesus is coming forward. He will soon join us.

"Until He joins you, My child, O until He joins you, My child, I will speak with you.

"I must speak to you of the world's situation at this time. My child, the covens in your country have grown greatly. Mankind does not realize what dwells about him. The Christian world does not realize. Some of the priests do, some are good priests, but many have fallen and do not know. They have not followed the truth. They have lost the truth - they have lost the way.

"O priests of the world, O lay people of the world, nuns of the world, listen now for I am warning you of what will happen in the future, if you do not turn back now and realize the truth. Your nation once blessed in truth has become despoiled. I have placed My mantle of blue over your nation, but much of your nation now has fallen, My children.

"I come to you now with a broken heart. I come to you with a heart of a mother, a mother who is sad for how many children She has lost. On your human earth you see before you death in your family and you long for that one person; now how many have I lost, My children. How many of you have I lost and you wonder why I cry great tears. You wonder why, My child and My children, that these tears are on my eyes."

Our Lady is really tearful; great sobs of tears are flowing down her cheeks. It almost makes me wish to cry for Her and with Her, for I know what She is speaking of.

"My child, no longer describe how I look, but repeat only:

"My child, and my children, in your nation now dwells the greatest of evils, the greatest of sins. In your nation now dwells the covens of 666. The greatest of the covens are centralized around 2 central areas and a third central area which is minimal now, but which was in the 1950's the first of the 3 in list.

"The first central area, New York City. The second central area, Los Angeles, California. The third central area, Maine, USA. Canada: if I continue on, in the City of Quebec there is the 4th central area of Coven Worship, and then the fifth, Nova Scotia in Canada.

"In the many years that I have counseled and warned you, My children, great, great numbers of these covens have sprung up. Many covens, since the time they have been found out, separated My children. As they separate, each of them seeks out 12 more members and these 12 members are tried; these 12 members, My children, then become new members, and each of these joins his own group and becomes the leader of his own group.

"Later when these groups are educated in the satanic art, these groups then divide and recruit new members again. Thus, My children, you can see the systematic plan of Satan, for he has convinced each of these groups that he is true. He then takes over their souls; as these souls are taken over slowly, one group at a time, each of these groups slowly becomes a cancer to your nation.

"My child, this brings back memories in your mind. Do not worry, for these memories shall not be harmful to you. They shall not be harmful. They shall be beneficial to the Mission that you do remember what you remember of your experience. It shall be beneficial, My child. Remember this, do not worry.

"My child, you have felt sad this week. Do not despair; your position in life at this time is due to your own error. You must work out your own amount of time, for your time on earth is not that of worry. Your time on earth is for penance and atonement.

"Offer your suffering each day my child for Pope John Paul II. My children, I tell you now your Holy Father - very soon there shall be an attack upon him. Very soon, your Holy Father, our Vicar of Earth, your Pope of today, your Pope for the past 2 years has been trying and trying and trying again to bring peace to the world. I say 2 years, My children, for during these 2 years he has been trying the hardest to bring peace to your nation, to bring peace to all nations. My child, your Holy Father shall soon go through great suffering if not death. If he is gone the Anti-Christ shall then sit upon the Throne of Peter. It is conditional unto prayer, but it is almost certain that the Anti-Christ shall sit upon the throne.

"My child, you worry too much.

"My children, offer more prayers, more sacrifices. Your Holy Father is in need of them, and the souls in Purgatory, My children. How many truly pray for them, how many? That is where self-worry comes in, that is where selfishness comes in, but what about when you go there? What will happen? What about yourself? Do you not worry about your own souls? When these souls that you have not prayed for are in Heaven, they would have been able to pray for you. Now they would no longer pray.

"They may pray, but they will pray less because of the fact that you did not pray for them, and if they did pray, their prayers would be very little in the eyes of God, because you are not deserving of the prayer. Pray for the souls in Purgatory. Pray for them all.

"Pray for the few souls who are in Hell that would not go to Hell, rather that would go to Hell under the condition that they are in; they will not go to Hell if there were prayers said for them. They would go to the lowest recesses of Purgatory.

"I do not ask you to pray for the souls already in Hell, but those few souls that would end up in Purgatory through one prayer, instead of going to Hell.

"My child and My children, My counsel is clear and direct, clear and direct, My children; I ask you to listen and heed my Message to the world. Thank you."

****

Message given to a privileged soul on Sunday, May 15, 1983.

Our Lady has come before me now, or the presence of her is before me. I can see a blue presence, an aura, coming through the window, coming directly before me. It is a good feeling to see Her again, as for a while She was not here. It has been a while since I have last seen Her. I feel a comfort of a loving Mother alongside me. Our Lady is wearing all blue, as She is materializing now from the mist which She travels in. You see when She first comes, She is like a beam of light or mist. She is now before me. Upon Her feet She has nothing except a little blue sandal with a pink rose. Her sandals are blue, though a light blue, almost like a wicker type of sandal, but they are blue with little rosettes on them. Our Lady now is putting Her finger to Her lips:

"My son, at Fatima, I came, I spoke, I requested and I begged of the crowds and I warned the crowds through the Seers, Jacinta, Lucia and Francisco. I warned them of what was coming. They did not listen to Me and so a war broke out again. At Lourdes I warned you, I warned you, O Mankind. Did you listen? No. And at Necedah I warned you all. Have you listened to Me? No, you do not heed me, you do not heed Me. At Bayside I warned you, at the Shrine of The Lady of the Roses. Do you listen to me? No, you do not heed Me.

"O Pastors of the World, you specifically should know that I am appearing, but you deny My presence. You deny Me. To deny Me is to deny My Son. You, who are representatives of Him, are denying Him, are denying Me, and are denying your entrance into Heaven in your future. You will suffer great years in Purgatory, or many of you may also fall to Hell. O Pastors of the World, You are becoming too open to the ways of mankind.

"My child, I am the Patroness of your Country, but Satan is slowly, slowly now, very soon in his manner, taking over your country, O mankind. I am your Patroness. Pray to Me, Pray to My Son. Pray to the Saints, and most of all, pray to your Father, but Satan is slowly taking over your country. Your country will lose, will lose its pride. Your bald eagle has been plucked. He is now a charred skeleton.

"New York shall soon be as such a skeleton, a skeleton of its former glory. Its obscenities shall be killed. It shall then be a 'nation apart' which will be perfect, shall be purified by fire, both manmade and celestial. California shall have the same fate.

"O Pastors of the World, do not think that you are safe! Do not think that you can mock Me and mock My Son. Do not, O Pastors of the World, think that you are safe from Our Will. Our Will, upon you, is that you would do good or be punished for it, when you come to Us. How many of you Pastors now upon earth, are no longer doing good? How many of you no longer can see the Truth? O Pastors of the World, Heed Me. Turn back now, before it is too late. Already, within your country, is the destructive force to destroy one part of your nation, a major city. Already around your nation, is a force, a task-force, which is waiting, in lieu of destruction of your nation, to take over your nation. Satan has his plan, well within the Kremlin. Satan has been there, yet Satan is also in your nation. Satan does not sleep, My children.

"I do not call him Luciel, I call him Satan at this time. Before, I used to call him Luciel at one time when he was in the Heavens. That was his name which meant "light-bearer," but now mankind has become the light-bearer, so I am no longer at this point able to call him Luciel. At this time, as I speak of him as Satan, he is no longer with us. He is against Us and he has been against Us. He is a Fallen Angel. He was never stripped of his powers, My children. We in Heaven do not sleep, My children, and he for that same reason does not sleep. As you mortals sleep he roams your earth, still seeking to cause terror, destruction and evil. Death and torture to him are no folly.

"The Covens of your nation, My children, have grown greatly. They are now all about you. Your nation is soon to be destroyed, My children, of the glory, destroyed to the point where there shall be no glory left among your nation.

"My child, two of your workers no longer believe. Two of your workers must no longer be left among you. You will send them the Message, but you will no longer request their help for they do not give help, but rather they will hinder your Message and Mission.

"The man from Pennsylvania is true, he does believe. My child, you will tell him that he has done good in receiving the names and sending the names. His part, his only part in your Mission must be to find people. My child, your future secretary's health is at this time waning. My child, you will work with her in the near future, but I do not say the present future. I say in the future, but near can be many, many days, months, days or months. My child, Jesus is now coming, you will Heed Him."

Now there is a pink light coming before me and this light is so bright, so bright that I cannot see the image coming forth. Our Lady is still present, but Jesus now is coming forward. Yes, I can tell it must be Jesus. When the pink lights come normally, Jesus comes with them. The light is so bright, it is amazing. I have never seen a light this bright, not even from Jesus in the past. He's now before me. He is wearing a red cape and a white robe, a beige/white robe or tunic, the dress-like clothing that they wore in His days. It is made of a really different material, a heavy material. He now has his fingers to His Lips and He is saying "Repeat, My child:"

"Pastors of the World, you must go back. You must return to the old ways. The new ways are not pleasing to Us in Heaven. I did not wish that My Mass was to be changed. If I wished it to be changed, I would have come and told you so. I did not, therefore, you must bring back the old Mass.

"My hand is coming down slowly upon you, and when it reaches, there will be no escaping My Wrath. I am a just God, but you have tried My patience, My children. I have warned you many times. My Mother has warned you many times. You do not listen. You do not listen. I have shown My wounds to many, many, many throughout the nation and throughout your world. Do they listen, do the people listen when they see or hear of My wounds? Very few listen, My children, very few. My wounds are reopened by every sin committed by mankind.

"I tried to die for all, but not all could be died for. I did not pay the price for all mankind because many will not accept and if they will not accept My suffering for them, then it is their folly, their own fault that they do not be saved.

"My son, the priest who you are thinking of at this time, he is a good priest, but he is confused. He says you must go through an exorcism prayer before you are able to be saved if you have been in a Coven. In many cases this, My child, is true, but in your case it is not, for you were never a true member of that coven.

"My child, much of the rain cried this day is from the Angels of Heaven. They are washing your nation. Your nation is so paganized in sin, that the water that falls are to purify part of it. The Father sends them to purify your nation, to purify your world. That is what rains in part are for, but your nation has been polluting the sky. Acid rain is the effect which comes from tampering with what God sends. That is what acid rain is, My children.

"My son, I have given warning after warning to many Seers throughout your world. I have appeared to many. I have appeared at most shrines throughout your nation and your world, at most Catholic shrines to at least one member of the crowds. I have appeared at the Litchfield Shrine of Lourdes in your nation. I do not mean the Lourdes of France, but I mean the Lourdes Shrine in Litchfield of Connecticut. I have appeared there to one priest. I have warned him of the future. He did not heed me; he believed that I was a demon appearing to him. Such is the way with many priests nowadays. They will see and still not believe. My son, you no longer need a spiritual director, as you were at one point told to seek out. You no longer shall seek out a spiritual director, for in your area there are none who would be a good spiritual director for you.

"They do not believe, they will not believe, and they cannot believe. The Bishops will not allow it. You may speak with a, if you wish, but you must pray before speaking. You may speak with the Bishop if you wish, but you must pray before speaking, for I have given warning after warning to mankind and do they heed me? No.

"My children, accept and learn by these warnings from Heaven. Your country, the United States of America, and many countries of your earth are near to a great chastisement."

"I choose for this apparition the title "**Our Lady Of All Holy Titles**" for My Mother. She then came to you and She told you of this name.

"My son, do not despair or be depressed of your present state. You are doing good at this time. Remain with the present course you are going and do not worry. Leave your life in My hands. Should the trials become great, should the pains become great, remember My suffering. Remember the Walk of Calvary, remember the pain and the blood I shed for you, and offer your suffering to Me. For great are the number upon your earth who could use them. My child, heed the Messages of Heaven, heed the Messages of the past. Go back and reread all My Messages from the true seers throughout your world. Reread them, and pastors awaken from your slumber, for you have fallen asleep.

"You who mock me and say: "When is He coming?" I tell you, I will come to you without your knowing and shall slip in upon you. You will not realize I am here. Many of you shall die before the Chastisement, before the Miracle, and before the Warning. You do not know your hour of death, for only We in Heaven know. The Father, He alone knows along with Me and the Spirit.

"Pastors, can you say that you will guarantee yourself Heaven when you go and you mock Me, you ridicule Me and you do not listen? You do not heed.

"When you were warned and you know, can you then say that you will have Heaven? No, I tell you I shall cast many of you out. You shall be immediately turned away. Many, I will say, shall be saved through prayers and sacrifices of others, but some of you, if you do not turn back and at least heed, you shall fall. This warning is a warning that is strict and it is given in due purpose. O My children and My child, it is needed. Amen. Good day."

Jesus and Mary are now floating through the window in a wisp of smoke, blue and pink smoke. It is colorful. Jesus had on a beige/white type of robe or tunic with the cape of burgundy or maroon type of red, like a felt. I forgot to mention earlier that he had a crown upon his head bedecked with jewels. Our Lady had a blue shawl with a type of cloth upon Her head as well, covering Her hair and a crown upon Her head as well, bedecked with jewels. The King and Queen of Heaven - how beautiful - how beautiful.

****

May 21, 1983 – Saturday, Eve of Pentecost

Our Lady has been before me for a short while now. She is dressed all in blue and She is crying.

Our Lady says: "We don't wish to see any of Our children lost to Lucifer. He now gives all God's children battle. There is such turmoil in the world that we cannot come to you as often. We are needed badly in the battle of the spirits. We listen to all that call us. We will answer all who come to us in belief.

"My child, you will have no fear at speaking out for Us. For to accomplish your mission from Heaven this will be necessary. Unless you pray for the souls that are falling into Hell from My Son's house, many of you, O mankind, will be affected by the disaster that lies ahead of you. Yes, My words were given in the same vein many years ago. They too were not heeded. Did you act upon them? No, you hid them from the world. What will you do now? Yes, I warned you many years ago that Satan would enter into My Son's house. You did not listen. Now he is there. Have pity for all men of sin.

"Have pity for those who respect My Son and have fallen into the web of deceit of Satan. They will all be answerable to us, more so for they were given the grace to fight this. What is the darkness, you ask me? This darkness is a blindness of heart. Yes, you too can be conditioned to accept error. You can be conditioned to be confused and no longer recognize the truth. You have a free will to go your own way; should you fall you must fall alone. We will not let you be taken as Innocent Souls.

"If you are unknowing to these things, then we will not also let you take innocent souls along with you. You are treading on My Son's house. You are now taking it and making it a place of self-gratification for arrogant man, who follows after his own master. Your love of money has been your downfall. Yes, you are misguided. There will be much suffering for those who stand to defend My Son's house. This can never be destroyed, for there are many who honor Him as well as there are now many who dishonor Him, but the foundation is solid. The foundation is My Son's.

"O mournful heresy, whatever will we do with you? Satan is now banding his disciples with My house. We watch this and My Mother's Heart, yes, My Heart, it is torn, I am your Mother. As I am Your Mother and I see you all going about in sin, My Heart is torn. Your prayers are sorely needed for your priests, your cardinals and your bishops. The heaviest attacks are upon those with the most influence in My Son's house. My children, you are now on the edge of a great disaster. Pray as you have never prayed before. I need not relate again that I have cried throughout the world, that I came with a plan of salvation. How many have listened to my pleas? How many have understood that We bring willful disaster, not upon you. No, for the disaster is not willful. We could only allow you to have your balance, in measure of what you have sown.

"America, you have grown fat on your luxury and starved your souls, for this you will not escape the trials given in the past to your fellow man. You will not be free of Chastisement. O, Woe I say unto you, you have turned your back on Myself and My Son. You worship evil, thus you have been allowed to set demons upon your earth from the Abyss. Those who remain with Us and "do" to the end Our work, will have no fear. We will protect them as all will be turned to good for those of well spirit.

"We look upon the most despicable of sins being committed in the disguise of the name [of] humanism, modernism, and all true Satanism. You build your ladder to Hell. Yes, We promise you many, the ultimate victory. I shall carry the light with the world in spite of the plan of Satan. Atonement, prayer, and sacrifice. This we ask of you all.

"I struggle, My children, to reach you all. I have much help. Many arms are needed. I ask your help and the help of those who have love for My Son. Do not permit those evil infiltrations to desecrate the Body of My Son. 'As you Sow, so shall you Reap.'

"My Son's house is now infiltrated, My children, with many agents of Hell. Recognize the signs of your times. When a man of God has fallen from Grace, he can be blinded to the truth. His way back will be of heavy penance. Seek, and you shall find the road back. Travel on the side road and you enter the Abyss. Many in the house of God have accepted their blindness. The Seat of Peter - all trials coming from the Abyss can enter from the men of Perdition.

"A constant vigilance of prayer must now be kept throughout your earth. The time for your Vicar has been extended, but only for a short time. When he is removed from the Seat of Peter, the man of dark secrets is waiting to enter. Pray, Pray, Pray, My children, for your Vicar will soon have an attack upon him if there is not enough prayer.

"Sin has become a way of life for many of you. Come out of the darkness. Woe to an unrepentant generation! The number counted saved will be in the few. Coming soon is the Ball of Redemption - and how many will burn in its great flame? What was to happen in 'the future' shall be now. The Father now leaves this decision upon His children. The fullest measure of responsibility is planned for the condemnation upon all parents who do not safeguard the souls of their children entrusted in their care. We see a foul example in many homes. We see an uncaring and permissive attitude on the part of many parents. Woe to the parents who disregard this admonition now to prepare the souls of their children for what lies ahead.

"Men of Science, you are ever seeking, but never reaching the Truth. Man shall be set up as a point of object of worship as the human. Blindness and darkness lead many into the Abyss. I have warned you of this before.

"I am the Queen of Heaven and the Mother of all upon earth. I am a Mediatrix between God and a Mediatrix between man. I come with Graces in abundance. I will dispense all to those who join Me in rescuing their brothers and sisters. Many manifestations by means of conversion and cure shall be brought upon many."

And now Our Lady says there is a scene I must view. She says to title it:

THE PUNISHMENT OF NEW YORK

Oh, it's horrible; there is a scene now before me. It's like I'm there, but I'm not there. I'm viewing the scene but I'm not feeling the scene. There is a ball. It is swinging. It seems to be going very fast and coming throughout the sky. As it passes over, there are great particles of dust. There are people standing and coughing, and falling and it's as if they can't breathe. It's choking. It's like a dirt falling from the sky. Now there are large rocks and oh, there are some people falling now. The people are falling. Some buildings have fallen and people are running away, but there is no place to run because now there are waves that have started very, very high. The waves are now 12' high and they are pulling into the land. And I see now, I see part of

New York. Oh, now the comet is swinging over and it's not just New York, It covers the whole land, but I see now, Our Lady now, She is pointing over to the right and there is a map, and I see little dots of light, I see, one, two, hree over on the side of the map.

It looks like New York down to Florida. I see one, two, three, four; it looks like eight or nine candles now. Then, over toward the center, there are about maybe 15 or 20 candles. And over it looks like Washington down to Mexico. I see very few, only maybe 4 candles. Now Our Lady is coming over and now Our Lady says I am to listen and not repeat. I must shut the microphone for a few minutes; I'll leave the tape running.

"You will remove now from the sacred schools setup within the Districts and of the house of God the filth and abominations in print. You will restore Truth to the schools controlled by the house of God.

"All clergy who do not accept the truth, and follow their vocations with pride and Godlessness as representatives of God shall meet the fate of the fallen angels. Confusion and delusion are among the works of Satan. You have been given the truth. You have been guided in the truth, if you have remained close to My Son.

"We are permitting all, at this time, manifestations and evidence of miracles more abundant than ever in the past, in the history of your world. By this means, We shall use this to fight the armies of Satan. I promise, as the Mother of God, and Queen of Heaven, to bestow upon all who come to My Sacred Places of abundance, upon this world, powers within the Sacramentals of theirs, for Cure and Conversion."

Our Lady says again, I am to silence the microphone. Again Our Lady says to listen. In front of Our Lady is appearing numbers 19 - 1964. All publications of truth will be found prior to this date, all publications of the Bible. There is only one other Bible that is printed, to be followed at this date. The name D ... Oh, Douay Rheims. Yes, she says Douay Rheims is the name. Follow this Bible. This Bible is good, or any printed before 1964.

Our Lady says: "You will notice, My child, there are no changes in Heaven. The nuns must bring their skirts back to the floor. The greatest of punishments, from the Eternal Father, will come upon them if they do not. Eternal banishment will be given to many of those who have abandoned their vocation and been led astray, but with self-will by the plans and guiles of Satan.

"I do not have to repeat, My child, the great sorrow in Our Hearts for the abominations being committed in your world against the Sacred Heart of My Son. See, My child, My heart pierced with sorrow."

Oh, it's horrible. Upon Our Lady's chest there is a great heart. It is covered with thorns, and the pain is evident upon Her face. It makes me almost wish to cry at this point, myself. Her heart is covered with thorns and there is a sword now piercing it. Oh, the sword is now taking the figure of a cross and there are flames now erupting out from the heart.

Our Lady says: "The Flame of My Immaculate Heart's love for your nation, for your world, for all the children of God." Her Heart is bleeding.

Our Lady says: "I would give every drop of My blood, as My Son did, if it would only change the course of events of your nation and the World, the course of the events that will happen. Shut now, My son, the microphone. This is the end of this section. Turn the cassette over and again begin.

"My child, you will tell the man from Illinois that his Mission, in regard to your Mission, shall be to receive names for you and to seek new names. This only, will he be allowed. This only. You now have two people seeking names for you. The first, so far, has only sought one name and shall (unless you do seek him out, and send him a letter yourself) not send you this name.

"My son you will tell the woman who you have called once already, that she has done great work for your Mission, that We appreciate it here in Heaven. We of Heaven, have sent great peace upon nations in the past. Great wars will soon begin. When these wars begin these few people shall have protection. It shall be from Heaven as long as they continue upon the Missions of peace. They shall have Our protecting arms over them. But do not be overconfident and think that, as soon as you leave, that that would continue. You must pray the Rosary at least two decade sets, each day, if they cannot continue with the full five and fifteen that would be appreciated by US in Heaven. My child, My children, wear the Rosary around your neck, The Miraculous Medal, as well as the Medal of St. Benedict. These metals have great protection for you.

"Invoke St. Padre Pio. Yes, he is among Us in Heaven. He is a Saint. Invoke St. Benedict often, for he is a powerful saint. Invoke him. When you feel the snares and temptations of Luciel, invoke St. Michael, for he is always among you.

"You cannot see him nor any of the other saints, for they are on the Spiritual Plane, My children. You, My child, can see them when they are near you when We will it in Heaven, from Heaven. You will be willed to see them in the future at some point. You have in the past seen St. Michael, My child, so you know the reason why you cannot see St. Michael at this time, as you have longed, at this moment to see him. The other saints, We do not wish you to see at this time, My child, but in the future you will.

"My child, your Mission is going well at this time. Tell your assistant, and present secretary that she is doing a very good job. We in Heaven, bless her at this time. She has a great sorrow at this time, though she does not realize it. A great sorrow is about her. A great sorrow is about you, My child as well, though you do not know it or realize it, but be not afraid. If worse comes to worse, you still have Us with you.

"Be Not Afraid; Bless you, My child. Goodbye."

****

Message given to a privileged soul on Sunday, May 22, 1983 – Pentecost Sunday

Our Lady has come before me again this day and She says to me that the Message has not been completed from last night. She says that I must tell, now, everything that She tells to me, word for word.

She says: "My child and My children, a great war and strife are soon to be upon your country. My sons, do not join the armies of your nations willingly, for many of you will not return. Mothers and Fathers, do not send your sons to the battlefield, for they shall not return. Many sons have been lost. How many sons have been lost through the battles of your nation? How many mothers and fathers have wept because of their children's deaths in the battlefields of your nation in the past and on the foreign battlefields? How much American blood, young blood, has been shed because of war? War is a punishment for your sins. Do you not realize, O mankind, that every sin you commit brings you closer to war, every sin, for war is the punishment brought upon you by your own sins?

"War shall soon happen, and when it happens, there shall be no turning back until it has ceased. The duration of this war is in your hands. The time-span shall be taken by the amount of prayer. Prayer is what it is in conditional. With prayer, this war would not have happened. But how many times have I pleaded and asked of you to pray, and how many have listened? Very few, My children, very few. This Message is strict, but, My children, what do you expect? We have tried and tried. You have not heeded. You have not listened. We have begged for many years. We begged at many shrines throughout your nation, throughout the world. How many have heeded? Very few, when you look at the nucleus of people upon your world. Your nation has slowly fallen. It was once under My mantle, but many are under the wing of Satan as well. There are now more under the wing of Satan than there are under the wing of the Angels, under My mantle. There are more under Satan than there are under God. You must pray to bring them back, My children, for Prayer Only can bring them back – prayer, and atonement, and sacrifice.

"When you feel sorrowful, when you feel that there is nothing left for you, pray, My children, pray. Many among you are suicidal, many among you wish to die. DO NOT DIE, do not kill yourselves, for this is listening to Satan. Satan has a strong hand in the lives of many. They do not believe in him. This is his greatest weapon upon mankind, his greatest armor. For he can attack without being known, without being expected. Many deaths have occurred because of him; many deaths.

"When you are feeling sorrowful, pray, My children, pray. When you are feeling happy, pray. Pray at all times, My children, at all times that are free. Pray - make your life a daily prayer. Every transaction that you do, pray. Every transaction that you do, pray, for God is among you. He is about you and He can be with you and in you at all times, if you will pray.

"When you go to your Churches, do not go to Communion before going to Confession, if you have committed a sin, for if you do this, you have committed a greater sin and must again go to Confession and confess that as well. But do go and receive Communion. Do go to your Confessionals. And you who are not Catholic, go to your daily prayers, your daily meetings, if you have them. Go to your religious affiliation of your Churches, and Pray - Pray at all times. Go to your Masses at least once a week, but if you can daily, go daily.

"Dear children of God, heed Me now, for this is the last effort [of] Myself, My Son and Heaven. We come to many Seers now throughout the world. But this is one of Our last efforts when We plead through our Seers. We plead for peace, We plead for humanity, We plead for you, My children. O children of God, may God bless you.

"Goodbye now, My child."

****

Message given to a privileged soul by the Blessed Virgin Mary on May 28, 1983 – Eve of Trinity Sunday

"Walk honestly in the day, not in rioting and drunkenness, not in chambering and impurities, not in contention and envy. I say to you, O mankind, love thy neighbor as thyself, for love of neighbor worketh no evil. Love is fulfilling the law then. Now is the time for you all to awaken from sleep, for now your salvation is soon to come or your darkness shall continue. Therefore, cast off the works of darkness and come and put on thine armor of light. Put ye the Lord, My Son before thee and stay from the ardor of the flesh and its concupiscence. Not in disputing - take who is weak in faith unto you and aid their faith.

"He who sits with you to eat, judge him or her not by how he or she eats, but how much God must love this person He created and if this person has ill manners, do not judge him or her for this lest you be then judged by thy God. Instead teach this person manners for who made~ above another man? Only Satan can do that, for God the Father creates all as equal in His image. Man could never transcend higher than his God, but this is the idea of the Satanist of your lands. Do not heed them. So judge not another man, for only the Lord sayeth when he stands or falls.

"In the name of the Lord Jesus Christ you are now gathered together. As you are gathered, My Son, the Good Shepherd will separate you as sheep on the right of Him and goats on the left of Him. Those on the left, under them He shall open a chasm, and they shall forever fall into the bottomless pit of fire and brimstone. They shall be burning forever as the devils do. Those on the right shall have been bathed in their own blood as martyrs and shall be handed the white robes and shall enter My Son's Kingdom.

"Men and women should not run about as Jezebels, harlots and pimps, because then they are as dung in the streets before My Son. A man or woman must choose only one mate, for anything more is sinful. If a man goes to a woman when she is in her monthly time, he commits a double sin and he must go to his priest for this immediately. He or she who commits any act of fornication commits therefore a sin of his or her own body. You are not your own, you are a temple of the Holy Ghost. Remember this, for He is within you, and without, about you. I speak this to you all by indulgence and by command of the Eternal Father.

"O men of earth, I look about you and I see you worshipping money and statues of demons and demi-gods of the underworld. Do you not realize that only My Son in the Trinity within the Father and the Spirit is God? I am Queen of Heaven, but even I am given very little reverence or notice. But I do not seek any reverence for Myself, only for My Son and thy God. If you do not turn back now and pray, then can you expect Us to allow the continued struggle of our Vicar for your sakes? If he dies it is because you all have killed him through your sins and your lack of prayer, your lack of atonement for your own sins, let alone anyone else, and your lack of sacrifice.

"My son, you have been discovered by your associates of high degrees about you. They seek to have you hospitalized for a long time because they do not believe in your Messages from Me. Worry not of what they say, think or do, because no matter what happens, you are under My mantle and are destined to one day join Us in the Kingdom of My Son.

(Our Lady to me in private - but included here)

"My little one, I tell you now that the advice of your associates was good when he advised you to obtain a postal-box at the Post Office, for Satan, Lucifer will soon send many against you. This will cause great trouble if you let them find out the address of your own, or your assistants.

"My sons among the clergy, be proud of being Servants of God. Have more faith in My Divine Son's Providence. Love My Son, Love Him. You seek a great Chastisement upon your Nation. Bring back the statues, and St. Michael - bring him back.

(In private to me - but included)

"My son, I seek that you heed My Directives to you, the Directives of the past and of today, I will not see you as often when your court appearance is gone by. Alone you will not be when before the judge. I place a High Angel with you.

"Goodbye now, My son."

****

Message given to a privileged soul by the Blessed Virgin Mary on Corpus Christi Sunday and Monday, Feast of St. Norbert, 11:00 PM to 12:15 AM, June 5, 1983

Our Lady is coming. I can see a blue call color at this moment all about my room. She has sent this blue luminescence of which only I can see at most of the occasions in which she appears.

I have now put a question before Our Lady. Now the color of the light is fading into deep, deep purple which means now She is answering my question, which was "Are you going to give a Message which brings much sorrow to your Heart? The color purple, as you will note, is for sorrow, suffering, or the Passion of Jesus. Now the color brown is present and the scent of cigar smoke. I think I should be surprised, but no, I know what it is. It is a saint from Heaven. A priest of the Capuchin Order from San Giovani Rotundo of Foggia, Italy - Padre Pio. Now he and Our Lady are both present and Our Lady says: "Hear out this saint and what he tells you to write."

Padre Pio: "My spiritual son, you must repeat now in print what I say:

"Russia, the Kremlin, is planning a great war upon your nation in a major attack. The Kremlin has the egg of war already set, and it is in New York in an abandoned subway. Listen to the High Queen's warning, for she has already warned you of this in Flushing Park, Long Island. O my son, you wonder how my words come to you in English. This is through She, the Queen."

Our Lady is wearing a purple mantle and a blue sash with a yellow robe or tunic.

"I, My child, worry about the stubbornness of your Holy Padre. He will not listen. He was warned by Veronica. He has not heeded her warnings. He must have faith and believe, or it will be too late for him. He will die. Soon he will leave Rome. Be prepared now. Store your blankets and water and sufficient foods ready at hand. The Warning is soon.

"During the Warning do not step outside your doors. If you do, sadly you will not return. Do not wish for the Warning, for much destruction will happen in the time of the Warning. During the Warning make adoration on your knees and pray for a quick end to the Warning. It, the Warning, will be of a short plan of time, duration, but the amount of time will be conditional to prayer. Explain, My son" (me) ... Our Lady means that the amount of time of the Warning will take is going to be conditional on prayers, and the acts of man.

Our Lady: "My son, the thing you are not yet capable of doing is explaining the Warning. Therefore, I find it necessary to tell you that during the Warning, the sky, it shall roll back as a scroll and will turn white as snow. There will be a great set of upheavals of nature all about your earth, and lastly the souls of all mankind will have revealed before their eyes all the offenses that they gave the Father of Creation. Many shall die of sheer shock and fright when they see what that they have done."

****

Message given to a privileged soul by the Blessed Virgin Mary on Wednesday, June 19, 1983 (in Honor of God the Father on Father's Day).

"My dear children of America, I come to the Seers in your land because I wish to guide you on the Road to Heaven. Your land is rich in material wealth and could be rich in spiritual wealth as well.

In your nation you all, on the general part, feed yourselves well. Not much of your nation knows of what it is to starve to death. You grow fat on material wealth and you slowly lose the Soul of Prayer.

"In your land you have too little an amount of poverty. Soon this will change. You cannot offend your God in the manner of, which, that you do because soon if you continue on the same path there will be a great famine set upon your nation.

Why do you not help the refugees of the wars in the foreign nations? I speak of the children -- children who are now homeless, father and motherless. I speak of the children in Africa, Israel and other such war- torn countries. The parents are killed by shelling and by other means and the children escape but to where do they escape? I ·tell you: They escape to hunger, starvation, famine and more war. Can you now stand before My torn, bleeding Mother's heart and say to Me now, that you, O mothers, fathers, sons, and daughters of America, that you cannot share but a small portion of your major wealth?

"If your nation would but try the Wish of the Father, instead of rebelling and living in luxury while your brothers and sisters starve, you would find peace in the world. Remember, I told you all in the past, war is a punishment for man's sins.

"Mr. 666 and his agents of war lie just off your shores, lying in wait, for the proper night or morn to open a full scale attack upon your land and Canada. Should there not be a full scale change among the people of your nation, then what happens will be allowed in the Will of the Father.

"We have allowed Satan to take over the elements, and as such, he can use the weather to destroy much of your nation's food supplies. Already he has caused the floods and the rains, which flooded the East this spring. He is now flooding the North and Southwest. The North and Southeast shall soon feel great heat.

"The heat will be sent by Satan to wither and burn the crops. The crops shall not be as easy as in the past for the farmers to grow. Check with your farmers, you people who doubt My words, you doubting people of today, and pray for your Pope of today.

"Goodbye now, My son."

(Today Our Lady wore blue only and nothing on Her feet. She looked very sad and sounded very sad.)

****

Message given to a privileged soul by the Blessed Virgin Mary on June 27, 1983, Feast of St. Cyril of Alexandria.

The sky all about me now, outside here where I am right now abiding, is filled with clouds and thunderstorms, around and about. It is coming in now; it hasn't quite yet began to rain. It's just the wind at this point and right now there is a presence of a light blue mist hovering quite near, remaining where it is.

Earlier this morning a voice spoke to me, Our Lady, which said: "Tonight you shall receive a Message.

Prepare yourself and be ready." and told me to await Her here at this time. At this moment, a green light is coming and a pink light as well, a mist-like light, and Jesus is coming forward from the pink light.

He says: "My son, you question of what to tell the woman, the woman who wrote to you. You will tell her only this: that is she is welcome to join in the Mission if She wishes. There will be, as I told you in the past, no major miracles and no names given. There shall be no signs given.

"If any workers question this, or wish to know the reason why, tell them this only. As I've told you in the past, My child, tell them this: "He or she who has faith, let the faith stand alone. Let it stand forth. Let the faith be as a light, a guidance. By faith and works of [a] moral nature you can test the truth. As you test the truth, you shall find it and when you find the truth, you will know your answer, for Satan cannot hide long his way. The Works of God and the works of Satan are akin only in one way. They both work only in their own way. Satan's will be evil and God's will be good. Our Working will be good, the Father, The Spirit and Myself, and My Mother."

Jesus is now beginning to fade. Before he fades I'll describe him. He is wearing a sort of leather type of sandal upon His feet which crosses about the arch and sort of like the Roman type crossing in "X" shapes up the leg, as far as you can see, which is not much above the ankle, and he is wearing the same toga that he always wears. I say toga, but it's like a gown, cream colored and He is gone.

St. Michael is coming forward from the green light and he says: "Woe, Woe, Woe to the inhabitants of the earth. Woe, Woe, Woe." He is immense, he covers the whole yard before me and just about, in the space between the trees and he is now vanishing too.

I sit and wait on Our Lady. She is still there, a blue presence. Our Lady has come before me at this point as I knew She would because of today's Feast Day.

Our Lady says: "Do not fear the lightning for I am protecting you. Describe Me, My child."

Our Lady is wearing blue, a blue mantle, and a blue robe. She has nothing upon her feet. She has a golden colored tassel or belt about Her waist and Her hair is pulled back into [the] mantle or shawl. She is putting her finger to her lips.

"My children, your nation and all nations must no longer allow the mass slaughter of the young, the innocent. Abortion, My children, is a foul crime to thy God, far more foul than any other crime you could commit aside from murder. For my children, it is murder and do not the Ten Commandments of thy God (in the past) command "Thou shall not kill?"

"Then Why, My children, why have you committed murder after murder in your lands? My child, this Message may be hard to understand, for some, but it must be sent out. Your nation, of all generations and nations; this generation of your nation, it has committed mass murder.

"The women of your nation do not realize what they do when they kill, by abortion, their child. Daughters of the land, listen to Me now, for I come to warn you that many of you are in lieu of losing your soul. I come to warn you that, though you are in lieu of losing your soul, you can turn back now and pray and make reparation to your God. I come to warn you, daughters of your nation, to turn back before it is too late.

"Fathers, Mothers, do not allow your children to wander freely about your nation, for now Satan seeks many victims. He plans his attacks well by taking the children. He takes them, forces them into sex slavery, and then he takes their souls. As he takes these children, he causes anguish to you, parents, and tempts you, and many of you he claims.

"Do not allow Satan to control you. My children. Honor My Son, Love Him, Go to Church more often, Go to your Churches. My Son is among you. He has not left. He is among you, O mankind. You must learn to love My Son. Love Him. Do not cause Him more pain and suffering, for He is thy salvation. He died for your sins. He tried to 'die for all' but He could not die for all - many of you would not let him die for you!

"My child, this is your Message for this day. There will be no more to this Message than this. It is short, strict, and to the point.

"This short rain is enough to revive the crops, but Satan will soon send along many great heats and your nation shall become as a desert."

****

1983, Third Quarter Messages

Message given by the Blessed Virgin Mary on July 2, the Feast of the Visitation.

A presence has come before me which as yet has not identified itself or himself, I could say, but has said that I will receive a Message today from the Virgin and from himself.

He is a very puzzling character. He's just standing before me. He wears a red form of almost like a dress type clothing. That which Jesus' disciples might have worn, so I know he must be one of the saints. He already has answered a question of mine by just reading my mind, which a demon cannot do. So, therefore, I know he must be a saint. He has not yet identified himself as yet.

Oh, now he says: "I am St. Christopher, my little son. I tell you now the Church has dishonored me. No longer do they go forth and say that the children should wear my medal for protection when they travel. The people should put my plaque in their car, their vehicle of transportation. Long have I been the protection of travelers. The Church has taken this right from me, though, by making many people no longer aware of my presence.

"Soon, in your country a great strife will come forth if there is not prayer. You, my son, should warn your president that there are some who seek an assassination upon him. He shall be removed if he does not watch his step. Your President may have many flaws, but then no man is perfect, aside from the Son, the Son of God. You will pray to me for your President, as he will not pray to me, for I am not of his faith. Goodbye now, my son. Be prudent and wait."

The presence has now vanished and before me another presence is started. From the bluish color emerging, Our Lady must be coming. Now through the blue comes forth a brightness, a very bright brightness and almost blinding light and it is taking on the characteristic figure of Our Lady, but she is not dressed the same today. She says: "Describe."

Well, I don't really know where to start, but I guess I might as well start with the fact that her robe is covered with golden star shapes from her neck to her feet. There is no belt about this sort of robe. The sleeves, they come to Her wrists; she has a Rosary in Her hands. She is wearing slippers which are as blue as the dress, where it surrounds the stars and in the center of each of these is a golden ribbon with rosettes on it forming almost like a knot. Her hair and Her ears are completely covered by a black veil which has covered the third of Her forehead. The veil though does not hide Her face. On Her head she has a golden crown with no other ornament other than a little red line through the middle. She is smiling.

Our Lady says: "The description is correct." But I am puzzled, and She says: "Do not be puzzled. This is the attire I wore when I appeared at Pont Maine of Pont Maine, France. Yes, I appeared to the children, the Seers. All the children there saw me in that town, throughout that date. The parents did not see me. It was January 17, 1871. How I wish that other visions I have given would go as far as this had gone. For I was known of, at one point, under this apparition title. The Church has almost all but forgotten about it though. This is not good - they must remember. They must remember.

"My children, you must pray for your president. There is a vile attack from Satan coming forth soon in an attempt to remove him from among you. You will pray for your senators, especially the good ones, for Satan seeks to remove them too.

"You will pray for peace, World Peace. You will pray for time, time before the ending of all, as you know it, which is soon to come. The Warning will be first, then the Miracle, and then the Chastisement.

"Within your nation lies the greatest of evils, My children: Abortion, Pornography, All sexual acts of carnal nature, Rapings, Bestiality, Homosexuality, Lesbianism, All sins which were condemned from the beginning of time in the Days of Old.

"What is becoming of your country that they allow the communist parties to grow? Are you, O American population, blind to what is happening about you? Do you not realize what is happening? What I have warned of? What I have given Message upon Message of in the past?

"The communist party seeks to take over your United Nations, your United States, [and] the World. For remember it was said by the communist rulers at that time: "Better for ¾ of the world to die and for the remaining ¼ to remain communistic than for there to be two different governing forces in the world. One must remain and the other must be destroyed." This was said long ago. Do you not realize that when you allow these communist parties to grow that soon they will revolt and try to take over? Are you blind to the amount that they are of, in people, the communistic parties within your nation?

"And the covens, they have grown greatly, My children. Guard your little children, for they shall soon disappear if they are not guarded. Do not allow them to go freely about without proper guard. Keep the Sacramentals upon them, for Satan seeks many sacrifices. He knows his time is short. He will try to claim any soul that he can. Protect your children – protect them.

"My children, if you pray, if you pray hard, you can turn about the clock of the forces which Satan has put against your nation. By this I mean you can have your rains correctly and the suns correctly without having pure sunlight without rain, and the crops to wither without having pure rain and no sunlight to dry the rain and the crops to drown, without flooding.

"Your nation could be lavished again with lower prices, with crops, if you would but pray and make the intention to feed the world, not to starve the world. For remember, I told you, your nation is among the wealthiest of all nations and could easily feed all of the starving people of the world.

"Remember to pray the Rosary daily, to wear the scapular. Remember to Honor My Son, to Love My Son. Do not disobey him. Do not dishonor Him. If you have sinned do not go to Communion without going to Confession first. For then you create a greater sin, a sin upon your soul.

"Pray for your pastors, pray for all priests, [the] clergy; pray for all of them for they are under attack by Satan constantly. Pray for them that they may all see the light soon.

"Knee l when you receive Communion if you can. If you must stand, then stand, but tell Jesus that you would like to kneel. Tell Him for if you at least tell Him, you bring much relief to His heart. Do not receive Communion in the hand. It is better not to receive than to receive it in the hand, for this is sacrilegious.

"My children, tell your priests that you wish to have many Holy Hours, many Holy Hours, and go to them and pray. Pray always a constant vigilance of prayer.

"Goodbye for now, My child."

****

Feast day of St. Anthony of Zacaria – Eve of St. Maria Goretti, July 5, 1983.

There is a blue presence coming through the wall before me. This presence is a presence I know to be Our Lady. It is taking form and Our Lady is now beginning to take form before me. She is wearing a golden belt about Her waist. She is wearing a white robe or tunic and She wears a blue robe around this white inner robe, or clothing. She has on a blue mantle, flowing down half-way around her back, covered by a white mantle. Upon Her feet She has only two little rosettes. Her hair is completely covered by Her mantle.

Our Lady says: "My child, in answer to the question you have in mind, you will tell our assistant by the name of the initials "P.R." that he will send to you the addresses of those who wish to have the Message. All except for those in the City of New York.

"I say all but the City of New York for this reason. In the City of New York there are a few who might cause trouble. It is better that they not know of this apparition. Already many in New York know or suspect who you are, My child. Therefore, We request that you only tell P.R. that he must mail to you all the addresses he has, except for those in New York. If he wishes, he may mail along to you those in New York, but you must not mail to them yet, My child. I will instruct you as to who to mail to in the future, in private as you go through the list in the future. At this time you must only concentrate on all except those in New York.

"My child there are many in the Canadian Territory who would be willing to receive the Message fully and openly. Two, about this letter. Soon you will receive a letter. You have been mentioned to about this letter. You will respond to this letter, My child, personally. It is from S.G. in Pennsylvania.

"My child, listen to me now as I warn you of the future, the future of your nation. My children and My child, great tribulations will soon come upon your nation. Already there have been great heats and great floods. Soon there will be great plagues upon your land, minor plagues. There have been plagues which have been incurable. There is a plague that was God-sent recently within the past few years:

Before me now, on the side of Our Lady there are appearing letters in gold: A. I. D. S. AIDS, underneath it American Immunity Deficiency Syndrome.

Our Lady: "My child, know full well, that this plague was sent by the Father. This plague goes among the homosexual crowds within your nation. There are others who catch it when their systems are weakened, but it goes mainly among the homosexual crowds of your nation. It was sent as a punishment and a warning. But has mankind heeded this punishment and warning, and turned back? I tell you no he has not.

"My children, Farmers of the Nation, Farmers of America, Farmers of Canada, it is God who sends to you the rains. It is God who sends to you the sunshine. It is God who sends to you your bountiful harvest, but it is also God who takes away your harvest. You must pray, you must pray well, and you must pray hard and devoutly. At times God will take away that which you would wish to have, but in those times He is testing you. In these dire days, these ending days of your world, as you know it, your world will become a testing spot for all. You will be tested as the metals which are hammered in the fires. You will be blasted clean of all the evils and you will be purified.

"In this manner you will be ready when My Son returns to take up many in the rapture, before the great war, during the great war, but after the Warning and during the Miracle, and before the Final Destruction, the Chastisement. My child, you will turn off the cassette at this moment and you will wait and listen, but not repeat on [the] cassette until I tell you to, for I have much to tell you in private.

(Pause on the Cassette)

"My child, you will repeat: The Churches must become again places of prayer. The Churches of My Son, the houses of My Son, they must no longer be meeting halls for people to talk and gamble and socialize in.

"No! That is not the purpose of them. My Son's house is for sacrifice of [the] Mass. My Son's house is for prayer. My Son's house is a Tabernacle of Heaven on Earth. My Son's house is a place where man can go before his God, in the physical presence and talk to Him and feel that he is in front of his God.

"Jesus is present in the Sacrament. I tell you the Churches, they must not be any longer, I repeat again, they must not be any longer places of meeting halls. They must be returned to places of prayer. For We see many Churches which now are as meeting halls in the Church part itself.

"In the lower basements of the Churches it is permitted, but when it goes before My Son, before the Tabernacle, the meeting itself, this is not permitted. This is sacrilegious, for remember when My Son was on earth, He went into the Temple, the Synagogue, the Synagogue of His Father, the Father of all Creation, and He threw out from the Temple the money exchangers and those selling things within the Temple. If it was sacrilegious then, and He threw them out then, do you not think that it is sacrilegious now? And that he would wish you not to be there in the same manner. O you who run these sacrilegious meetings within the halls of the house of My Son, to gamble within the house of My Son is sacrilegious.

"The Nuns, the sisters, they must return their habits to full length. They must wear the habit. We see many sisters now who no longer wear the habit. We see many sisters now who cannot even be identified as sisters, for they no longer wear the garb of the Nun, but rather they wear the street clothes of the modern woman of today. This is not good. If We in Heaven had wanted this change, We would have told you. We did not request it, so why did you change? Nuns, sisters, listen to Me now, your Mother, turn back, wear the full habit. If your Mother Superiors will not allow you, at least wear the short habit.

"And women within the Churches, you must wear head coverings. For you offend the angels and more than that you offend My Son. You offend Him when you do not wear a head covering. You have angered My Heart against you, for you have not listened, My children.

"Many times in your nation, in other nations and throughout the world, I have warned continuously and continuously, never ceasing, that the women must wear head coverings within the Churches. It is a sign of subservience to the husband, who is head of the family and even single women must still wear the covering upon their heads, a prayer shawl or a bonnet, or some form of covering. For it is as if you were shaven in front of God, in His presence, when you come before Him not wearing a covering upon your head. The Churches of today, they say that they have changed. They will tell you that this is not needed, that it is not mandatory, that a woman wear a head covering, but it is necessary. And the men must never wear a head covering within the Church, for if they do, they then offend the angels and their God.

"My child you wonder why this Message is being given in such a slow pattern on this date. Why I am taking so much time? It is because I have grown tired of pleading throughout the nations, throughout the world. For many years now I have pleaded at Fatima, I have pleaded at Lipa, I have pleaded at Bayside, I have pleaded at Garabandal. I have appeared at Knock. I have pleaded at many shrines throughout your world. Yes, I have pleaded at Lourdes and many other sites in France, Italy, Belgium, Yugoslavia and many countries. Many have tried to lighten the burden upon My heart and blessed are they in Our Presence, but many, far too many, still weight the balance to the left. There must be many prayers to weigh the balance back to the right. My child, you wonder why I wear two mantles upon this day. I wear the white mantle for purity and the blue mantle for Myself.

"Should there not be much prayer in the future, your nation and many other nations throughout the world will face a great war, far greater than any war known. This war will happen no matter how much prayer eventually, but it can be held back. My children, if you would only learn to accept what We say to you and pray, pray a constant vigilance of prayer, you would find that much of what We warn would be held back, to happen at a later date. The Father is merciful and His Heart is moved easily, but there must be great public assemblies of prayer throughout your nation. There must be many people within their homes praying constant vigilances of prayer. There must be prayers ascending to the Heavens as little bullets, missiles to Heaven.

"The Rosary: this is the greatest weapon you have, [and] the Way of the Cross, the Stations of the Cross. This too will bring peace if it is said devoutly - the prayers of St. Brigit of Sweden, written for Our Saviour, for your Saviour, My Son, Our God Jesus.

"My children, My Heart is torn as We see the great obscenities in your world – Pornography, Rapings, Murder. Much of the rapings and murders in your nation are being committed by those who read pornography. Pornography is printed by those involved with Satan seeking to seduce the soul, and cause the person who would otherwise not do this kind of sin to commit great sin. This is all for now, My child."

****

Message given to a privileged soul on July 11, 1983, by the Blessed Virgin Mary

"Before me now is a presence of which I have been awaiting since last this presence came to me. The presence is that of Our Lady. Our Mother and Queen has on a deep purple mantle. I have already found out the response, but I will list the question for you all first. I asked Our Lady in my thoughts if She would tell me if the purple is because of the Mission and myself.

She responded to me that "Satan sought to stop the mission before it begins to take roots, take hold, and then spread to the corners of the earth. Mr. 666 will use his many powers against you, My child, as you can already see him doing. Continue describing, My child."

Our Lady is wearing, as I said before, a purple mantle upon Her head. Under Her mantle, She has on Her blue robe and white dress or garment. Upon Her feet She has nothing at all. Our Lady has a very pretty face, which is shadowed by Her heavy mantle. Her hair is not to be seen. By this I mean She has it completely covered. Her Rosary is also beautiful. Her Rosary is connected to Her waist by being drooped through Her thin golden belt. The Rosary is of all colors and when I look at it, it is actually clear white. Although it is clear white, it does reflect out in clearly visible rays, colored light. She is so beautiful that you could not imagine Her beauty. Here on earth Her statues are only that of clay, carved in an image of a woman, in comparison to Our Lady's queenly beauty. Our Lady says that I have more than sufficiently described Her. Now I must await Her Message. She has now put Her Rosary in Her hands and is beginning to recite it. As She recites it each single bead is beginning to give off enormous color. The colors are like little rivulets of light which quite resemble the graces given by Our Lady upon the crowds at Her public shrine manifestations.

Now Our Lady is at the first decade and is reciting the Our Father. As She is doing so, She says: "Watch, My child." Oh, now the Our Father beads are all beginning to emanate a line of colorful solid beams of light. This Our Lady says is: "My child, this is the blessings and graces We give from Heaven to those who are about you now. My child, I will continue now to pray and you will join Me in this procedure of blessing those about you, for without My Grace many of them would be unable to get the strength to continue the struggle of which daily life is for many of them. Now We will recite together the rest of the Rosary on My Rosary beads, My child."

I reached out before me and held each huge bead with Mary till the end.

****

Message given to a privileged soul on July 12, 1983 (1:00 AM), by the Blessed Virgin Mary

"My child, about you now you can see the worst of the evils and the worst of the human terrors which come from the State of Connecticut. These are the ones, who if left without My Grace, would all have remained under Lucifer's wings. Our prayers have given them a chance to find My Son's Kingdom, My child.

"My Son, if you wonder why Mr. 666 was allowed to cause this trouble, you must only do one thing to make clear to you what I mean. Just because there is against you a total injustice, sent along by Lucifer, you will not worry, for I tell you We in Heaven are all using this attack for the use of your presence in prayer, during an appearance to cause My Graces to fall on those around you who otherwise would be unworthy of them.

"My child, tomorrow, you will move to another, better place near Rhode Island, so do not worry about what may happen tomorrow. You, My child, will be going to where We will pray each night on My Rosary, when I come to you. There will be more graces spread, as you will pray for them at this place I mention, for two weeks, until July 26, 1983. Today, you must not worry about any longer, My child. I say this because [if] you allow yourself to continue to worry and be nervous, not believing My words to you, you will end up not sleeping tonight. My child, this is all in regard of this matter that I will tell you at this time, right now.

"My children of earth, I tell you now the world is as a pit of vipers, about you all. Many of you are vipers, but how few of you are truthful with Us? How many of you who think that you are in the army that will fight for Heaven are really vipers at heart? Because of your evilness, your cruelty and your hatred, of your brothers and sisters upon earth, I am forced to say that many of you upon earth are vipers at heart. You must all atone for your evilness of heart. How, many of you would ask, so I will tell you how. You will go to your religious leader and confess your sins, then go forth and do that sin no more. (By this Our Lady means never to do that same sin again).

"My children, some of you are denying My Message, saying that some of its content is perverse or untrue. I showed to this Seer the disgusting process of abortion for reason. This reason being that mankind heeds not the Directive to tell all that abortion is forced murder of the unwanted sons and daughters of the Father of Creation. I gave you thus in graphic words, by My Seer, the way to warn mankind of what happens during this evil procedure.

"This is all for now, My child. I will be back tonight, My child."

****

Message given to a privileged soul on July 12, 1983 (11:30 PM), by the Blessed Virgin Mary

Our Lady has appeared without the usual wait for Her to materialize. By this I mean, She has come to me while I was asleep and awakened me.

Our Lady says: "See, My child, I told you that the place you were going would be a whole different scene. Was I not telling you the truth? I cannot lie. Here you will live for the next two weeks of your earthly life. Here you will pray every night on My Rosary, My child. Now We will pray."

Here we prayed one whole Rosary on Mary's Rosary beads.

"My child, now that we have completed the Rosary, you will now see before you written in gold letters on your wall, a poem. This you will now write out, My son, for it must be eventually given to the world."

>The world is now a great cauldron of sin,
>and as such a Ball of Redemption is all you will win.
>
>Your money is what you all love, and is all you see in your realm.
>We have love only for the Father, the Son, and the Dove, up within My Son's Heavenly realm.
>
>You must pray now for your Most Holy Father,
>Otherwise Satan will remove him with little bother.
>
>Pray now for Holy Mother Therese,
>That her Heavenly help may continue to increase.

****

Message given to a privileged soul on July 13, 1983 by the Blessed Virgin Mary

It appears that again Our Lady may be seen only by myself, and no one else.

She says: "My child today at 4:00 Satan will begin his form of mental sexual torture upon you. You will, from all around you, begin to hear the voice of those under his wing. He seeks to drive you insane. Therefore, you must pray constantly as never before, My child, for guidance, health and peace of heart and mind, even while you are surrounded in an unholy war, a maelstrom. My child, We shall pray, then I shall leave. Now we pray"

We prayed and then She left before me.

****

Message given to a privileged soul on July 14, 1983 (3:00 AM), by the Blessed Virgin Mary

Our Lady has awakened me.

She says: "Tonight We will pray, not now." Now She only wishes to talk to me and through me to the world. "Pray for your President, O American Citizens. Soon without prayer, he will be removed. If he dies your country shall go on to worse times. The next President may not be a good one; he may end up under the wing of the Antichrist. I say he may, because this is not definite yet; yes, time and prayer will tell the answer to this.

"Even in Rome, Italy, your Holy Father, Pope John Paul I, is not safe in his securities at this time. Should he again leave Rome, Italy, it will, without a full turnabout of the world to prayer, mean his demise. Your world now in its present state of being does not deserve the holy continued struggle of your Pope, Our Church Leader of My Son's Holy Church upon earth."

(Myself) I smell roses now and Our Lady is saying now: "My little son, I shall give you a grace now that you did not expect from Me to bring you in this situation. Theresa wishes to come before you now, as she has a Message for you and the world."

Our Lady is becoming now four times brighter than the brightest light that I have ever seen before. She is dazzling and bright, with a deep blue light which also now is beginning to get tones of deep rose red within it, in streaks of moving light. She is brighter by far than the sun at midday or noon. I'm sure that if it was not Her, the Queen of Heaven and Earth, that I was viewing, that I would already have been blinded by the light. As it is, I must keep my eyes squinted to view Her because She is so bright. Now, as I'm viewing Our Lady before me, behind Her, I see now a large, large white nothingness.

Our Lady says: "The portal into Heaven and from Heaven. Keep describing now, My child"

Now, in the white circle that Our Lady calls the portal, I see a figure is coming forward. The figure is very much like that of Theresa. Yes, it is St. Theresa, The little Flower of Jesus. Theresa says now, that I must repeat what she has to say.

> "You must pray, if you know what it is to love.
> Shed your love in prayer on the Pope through the Dove.
>
> Pray to the Mediatrix of all true Holy Grace.
> Beg Her to put Her heart in your heart's place.
>
> Guide yourself in Jesus, the Savior's Holy face,
> Not in, or by the sun and planets in space.
>
> Be humble in all the prayers in prayers you do,
> With this alone Jesus and Mary will get you through.
>
> If you lead a life that's prayerful and even sound,
> Then you will one day be led – as the saints, Heaven bound."

"My Spiritual little one, I tell you now, you will call My poem **"Loving And Praying Your Way To Heaven**."

"Goodbye now." At this point both vanished from before me.

****

July 14, 1983, Midnight 12:00 Thursday, till 1:30 AM Friday, July 15, 1983

I am now seeing before me, a bright flash of light, it is a flickering blue, green and now bright white circle of light. Oh, I now know what it is, it is Our Lady's portal. I am now seeing inside the circle. Now, I hear a voice; it is Our Lady.

She says: "I wish I could, My child, take you elsewhere, but it is the Father's wish that you stay till such time as you get out by your earthly standards."

I can see now within the portal. There are many, many angels present within the portal and there are different kinds of angels. They are all mixed together in a crowd, but I will attempt to describe them. There is one set which has glowing bodies of circular light. These have wings which are long, but they are like downy goose feathers. Also, I must say that there is one thing that none of this type of angels has in common. This is their faces. There is one that's like an eagle, one like a lion and the others are hidden behind thousands of other angels. There is a type of angel that looks like a blob of bright light with wings of downy, soft looking feathers. These appear to have no heads, as we would know it.

There is a type of angel which looks like little children that have wings. They all resemble little boys and girls, but it is not easy to view these as they are so brilliant with blinding lights that it hurts my eyes to cast my eyes upon any of these type of angels.

There are some large angels. They must be archangels because I can see Michael, St. Michael and St. Gabriel. Gabriel sys to me: "Honor God and Pray to me when you travel." St. Michael says: "Mankind must place me back in to the house of God's Son. Mankind is soon going to wish that they were praying to me because Satan is now weaving his way among all of mankind. Soon it will be too late to pray. It is almost too late now. Should your nation not begin to again pray to me, soon even I will not be able to help your world."

Now I can see our Queen and Mother Mary. She has come among the crowd of angels now. Now, all but the childlike angels have moved to the sides. All of the children are opening up Our Lady's robe tail behind Her. Now, She looks like a real regal Queen. "Should I describe you, Mother?"

"Yes, My little son, the people will wish to know what I look like."

Our Lady wishes me to describe Her, so I will. She has a long flowing white robe on and the angels are holding the bottom of it up. She has on a long flowing white mantle and a beautiful white gown. There is a belt of which I believe is made of miniature links of spun and weaved gold about Her waist. Hanging from it is a Rosary which has wooden beads and is made with solid gold colored links. The Rosary, She is grabbing it from about Her waist now and She says "My child, We will pray soon, but for now you will sit and watch. I feel it is the least I can do for you since you have not a thing to look forward to where you are now. No joy, except when I come to you. Since I have asked you to undergo these tortures by being at the spot that Satan had set a trap for you, and you accepted My request, that we may bring prayer into the prisons, I feel l owe you this time of joy."

"Alike to Veronica, My child, you too are suffering for all mankind. Continue to pray to St. Jude, My child. We may send you to a psychiatric facility for a time, then release you, but then maybe We will not. Remember, you mast pray to St. Jude for your release. Should you fail to pray one day, your fate will be sealed to where you are now residing. I single handedly chose you for this mission, because I felt that this was the best way that you could suffer for Us. I wish that I could do what you are wishing now, My child, but it would still your heart. You see now only that which is My portal between Heaven - never could We allow you to see further, for that type of joy would still your heart.

"My child, We could not, therefore, allow you this. You are always in Our hearts, so persevere, My child, until the end of your lifetime. We had said you were being attacked by Satan. This is true, for you were attacked by Satan, but We led you to his attack for reasons already mentioned to you. Is it that hard for you, My child, to understand? Persevere in prayers."

The Seer: "I love you Mother, please help me, please allow my suffering to cease. Theresa in Locution, told me the value of suffering, but I cannot handle this. I love Your Son, will He not help me?" (here I was crying in self-pity). "Please Mother ask your Son to have me released from prison to a psychiatric facility and then home."

Our Lady: "My son, stop pleading; when you go before the Judge on July 26, 1983, I will make an attempt to help your case, but only if you continue to pray to St. Jude and My Son and Myself. Relax and watch, now My son." (I relaxed for 15 minutes and I still felt sorry for myself.).

"My son and My children, love is giving of one's self for another. The second greatest love one can give another is to suffer for his brothers and his sisters in My Son. The first great love a man can give is to give his life for another person to live."

"Mother, I love you; let us please pray now on your Rosary." Our Lady conceded and we prayed.

"Now that we have prayed, I must leave, My son."

She vanished by going farther back into Her portal and then I only saw white; next, this too vanished.

****

July 15, 1983, Midnight Friday to 1:45 AM Saturday, July 16, 1983

Our Lady: "My child, I am soon coming."

Now before me there is a pinpoint of light on the wall. This is now growing to a wide circle of light before me. The complete circle is white and clearly present against the green wall before me. Now I, as of yet, cannot see within the circle. It is a giant blob of white solid glowing light. Now within the portal circle I can see a shadow only as of yet. Only I am able to see this light, and also write by it. I know this because a prison guard has passed by my cell and he has not seen the light from the portal. Now from the shadow within the portal is coming a feminine hand.

Our Lady: "Come, My child, into the portal. You will now sit at this desk I have placed in the portal, My child, and write the words you still have as yet to hear. I love you, My child, that is why I grant you this request, which you mentally gave me. I can take you into the portal, but not into Heaven. My child, do not even think of an attempt to get up and follow My portal to Heaven. For the angels would stop you and if I were not there you would be hurled back through the portal into your cell. Then, I would be forced to abandon today's part of the Mission. I say I love you and I love you as only a Mother could love her children."

"Mother, how long will I be caused this suffering that I am now undergoing? When will it end?"

"My little one, I have already told you that you must undergo this suffering until July 26, 1983, and maybe even longer, so do not question this issue any longer, only pray on it. Describe now in your words what you see about you now. My child."

I see all things now in white, except for our Holy Mother and the angels. There is here within the portal no floor. The desk is floating with me sitting at it, and Our Lady is standing or floating in front of me while the angels move about us by flying of their own ability. It is very calm and serene within here. The sky all about is white and bright, while about Our Lady it is blue. Around each angel, flowing from within them, is an aurora of solid yellow light which is very bright. Our Lady is wearing a green billowing cape and there is the customary blue mantle above this, with the blue robe under the cape. Our Lady is wearing a white dress or tunic, that is. Around Her waist is a belt made of solid gold immature links.

Upon Her feet She has slippers which are quite different from any I have ever seen Her wear, or heard of Her wearing. Her slippers are made of a glass which is inlaid with pure gold and appears to have some kind of cushion inside them for Her feet. Upon the middle of the top of the toes are roses made of golden colored glass. About Our Lady is a distinct odor or smell now. The smell is that of roses in midsummer in a garden of roses, all in full blossom. The only thing is that the odor is hundreds of times stronger than an earthly garden of roses. I am sensing an air of sorrow about Our Holy Mother tonight and now She says: "Describe My face."

Our Lady is very sorrowful and tears are streaming down Her face, Yes, Our Holy Mother is crying very profusely now. She is weeping. Oh, now I can see why. Yes, now I can see why and I too, am being caused to cry also.

Jesus has entered the tunnel or corridor, portal also. But He is on a heavy wooden cross now and He is moving on the cross, moving in pain, Jesus has upon His head the crown of thick thorns. Jesus' body I so covered with the scars from the scourging that He underwent while before the scourer. The blood is pouring from His body and I will use a quote which St. Bridget coined long ago in her 15 prayers. "The blood is flowing from the body of Jesus as the grapes which are pressed in a wine press."

I had to stop writing for a few minutes, a few minutes ago and this was because I too felt the passion and death in the portal here for a short time. I here now will enclose the dialogue which went between Jesus, Mary and I.

"My Son is going through the Passion again and you too, My little child, will now experience parts of the Passion and death which My Son is now undergoing for the sins of all mankind."

"Mother, please no, I do not wish to die yet."

Our Lady; "My silly little son - do not worry. The death you will undergo will only be a temporary one."

At this point, I was carrying the cross looking out at Jesus in a crowd of people. Then I was in the crowd looking in at Jesus. Then I was Jesus again, walking and I fell 3 times On the first fall my shoulder opened wide in a wound, and the muscle was then bare and Oh, the pain it was unbearable. I was wearing the crown of sharp and long and thick thorns which were cutting and digging into my scalp with each time that my forehead moved by action of my blinking my eyes.

I got up and continued on the walk to Calvary and fell the second time and my knee was scraped bare and open and at this point I was switched back to myself and again Jesus went to continue the walk to Calvary, and then He was thrown down to the ground and we again switched places and now I was upon the cross and Jesus was in the distant crowd watching me. I again switched back with Jesus and watched as the King of all Creation was dying slowly by bleeding to death.

Next, I was the one upon the cross and I felt myself slowly die and my head went to the right and then I was floating free of my body, and it was all white and then I found myself sitting back at the desk, in front of Our Lady and Jesus was no longer there to be seen.

Our Lady then said to me: "My child, I wanted you to experience death, because some day you will be before a crowd of people and I will ask that you explain what death is like. So that then they may be able to know what death is truly like. Should you also wish to know another reason why that you were chosen for the death sequence, I will tell you why now.

"We wished for you to know that in death, at the moment known to you as death, all pain ends, and you see your body separate from your soul. As your body remains below and you [will] float slowly in an endless void until it is deduced which way your soul will go - to Purgatory, to Heaven or maybe very sadly, to Hell, the abode of the damned in Lucifer's own very dark burning pit.

"Woe to those who die to the unending death, for even their soul is dead, and as such there is no way that they will ever see Us. They will be lost to Us forever to float forever in a sea of endless fire that will never die and will endlessly burn in Hell as the demons which already are there. For during their lives, they were just like the demons incarnate and living and they died without asking the Father to forgive them for their evils of heart and soul.

"My child you must all pray for the Poor Souls of Purgatory, who with even but one Rosary may find Purgatory instead of Hell. Pray your Rosary for earth's sinners, which means for all mankind, each and every man, woman and child. No man is free of sin, so thus you must pray for all men of sin. My child, you and I will pray now on My wooden Rosary. In the name of the Father, and of the Son, and of the Holy Ghost, Amen."

Our Lady kissed my Scapular and said: "Tell all My children of earth who wear the brown scapular that if they kiss it often, they will receive signal blessings from Me and will at the end of their time on earth be aware that they will soon die."

"Goodbye now, My child."

****

Saturday, July 16, 1983, 12:00PM and Saturday, July 17, 1:00 AM

Now, before me the portal has opened wide and Our Lady Queen of All Heaven and All Earth is stepping out before me.

She says: "Please describe Me, My poor little one. I wish to tell you so you may tell all you meet at a later time that each and every sin puts a dagger in My aching, loving Mother's heart."

Our Lady now is coming the rest of the way out of the portal and She - oh, oh, I can see Her face now and She's very sad looking, in fact I have never seen Our Holy Mother look so sorrowful ever before. Our Mother,

Queen Mary, has on a regal crown covered with stones all over its base. This is lightly placed over Her mantle which is a deep, deep blue. The stones in the golden crown, some are red and resemble garnet. Some are white and resemble and almost definitely are diamonds. Some look light purplish color. These I would say are amethyst. Some are also green, and about the green, I have noticed two different things: one is that some of them are jade stones and some are almost 'see-through' and yet are light green. A rare and very precious stone - I don't know this stone's name, and would not even chance to put forth a guess on that matter.

There are also what appears to be star-shaped purple and black rocks on Her crown. When I say star-shaped, I mean round with the shape of a star imbedded within the stones or gems. Our Lady is now saying, oh, oh, "Star sapphires, My child, that is the name, they are star sapphires." Now Our Lady's robe is, a deep, deep blue; Her dress is white and She has her customary gold belt, made of miniature links of gold which are all interwoven. I have never seen such metallurgy craftsmanship upon all of earth, upon earth.

Her robe is trimmed in a border of what appears to be gold foil. The foil is [a] ¾ inch border around Her robe. Also, around the bottom and top of Her dress hems She has a golden foil trim, but this trim has a design shaped into it. It looks like a bottom of a wavy awning like you would see on the streets.

Oh, now upon Our Sorrowful Holy Mother's chest, I now can see a complete human heart beating. It's beating and it's filled with so many miniature daggers. Oh, it's horrible, the suffering that She must have to undergo, because with each beat of Her heart, there is now blood dripping and leaking out from Her heart. Oh, Mother, must I view this?"

"My child, others must know of this scene you are viewing - that is why you are viewing it. Now, My child, I will no longer make you view My pained heart, but you will remember what you have seen. My little child, be light of heart, am I not here, am I not all joy and happiness to view? I will be your happiness only when you leave yourself open to Me. My child. Let us recite the Rosary now, because it now grows quite late and you will be awakened at 6:00 AM tomorrow morning.

"I will pray, Mother, yes, on your 15 decade wooden Rosary, but Mother, where is it?"

"Do not despair, My child, I have it looped through the back of My belt. Thus it is behind Me - that is why you cannot see it. I know that you were thinking I had forgotten it, My child, but I never am without one of My Rosaries. You must realize that I hear every thought that you think and as such I can answer any questions you think, even if you did not mean the question for Me. Take heed in your thoughts, My child, as I said, I can read your thoughts."

Now Our Mother Mary is taking out Her Rosary and She has made the sign of the cross both on Herself and then upon me. "I believe in God.. ."

After the Rosary Our Mother Most Holy, Most Beloved and Most Blessed said: "Goodbye for now, My child." Then She walked or stepped backwards into the portal and I could see Her slowly begin to move backwards within the portal. Then the portal itself began growing slowly smaller and smaller. This kept happening until the portal itself began to vanish and finally did vanish.

****

July 17, 1983, Sunday 12:00 Midnight, till July 18, 1983, Monday 1:00 AM

Before me now on the wall is a small pinprick of bright light and it has all the power of love of Our Lady. I know It is Her portal, because the moment the light appeared I felt like I feel only when Our Lady, Jesus or the saints are present. Now the light shape is widening into a circular or oval-shaped portal doorway. Now I can see a solid hole in the fabric of the space of the cell wall. The hole steps to a warp in the very fabric of Time and Space, the portal of Heavenly-making used by Our Heavenly Queen, Mother Mary. Mother Mary, Our beloved Queen is floating slowly to where I am from within the portal. Slowly, She is coming forward and now I can hear Her voice echoing through the tunnel.

She is saying: "My child come now and step within the portal. Yes, that's it now await Me at the gate or doorway of My portal, only just inside of it. I will guide you to the desk. Come now, My child, hold My hand and We will leave the door, but do not let go until we are at the desk."

I am now at the desk to write this, and am writing what has happened since Our Lady and I have left the portal doorway. "My child, I know you are happy to see Me, and it is partly to make you happy to see Me, and it is partly to make you happy that I have chosen to bring you into the portal. The other of the reasons that we are in the portal is because I am now going to take you on a trip. You will not like where We are going, My child, but I must ask you not to worry; after all I am with you, am I not? The place We are going to view is called Hades, My child, or if you prefer, Hell. It is the domain of the King of Evil and Demons, Lucifer, also called Luciel, Abaddon, Apollyon, Shutan and Satan, among his other titles. Now you will sit and write just what I have said, while the portal slowly brings Us to the opening of the Abyss and then into it."

Now, I am back to the present and We are traveling into a tube of solid white. I will describe now Our Lady, how She looks. I now see our Lady is wearing a solid golden crown upon Her head and Her mantle is a deep blue. Our Holy Mother's dress is a clear and beautiful deep white. The white is like fine pure sugar, it is that white. Today She, Our Queen, is wearing the usual belt made of solid golden miniature links. Going back to Her crown, now I notice that it resembles the Fatima crown, except for it has no jewels upon it. Our Holy Mother's robe is a beautiful sugar white also and She looks familiar to the way She had looked somewhere else in some other apparition. Our Lady is now getting ready to speak because She has told me now to hush.

"My child, you must tell which apparition. It's as I came at Lourdes that I now come here, but with one added difference: I am now also wearing a crown. My little one, you will now describe what is appearing below Us and as We descend, you will describe all of it to the best of your ability to do so."

Now below me there is still a white vastness as of yet, but if our Holy Mother says to watch and describe what happens down below, I will. Oh, now below us there is a change beginning to happen. The flooring below Us is now the color of charred earth. Now as We come closer there is a deep hole - Oh, it is very wide and all around it are hideous creatures. They all look slightly different, but they all have horrible monstrous faces. Some have horn and some don't. All of them have hooves for feet. Mostly, they have the color of red, brown or black for skin, that is, if you can call the scaly stuff skin. Every one of them has eyes which are almost, in fact, they are horribly hypnotic, the eyes are. Some eyes are black, and most are red, but all are hypnotic. They all have wings.

Our Lady wishes to speak: "My children, the eyes of a human only need but be looked into by the eyes of a demon, and though the human mind does not perceive their presence, the demons do hypnotize in [the] process of temptation of a human being."

Now I see the hole itself. Our Lady says: "Abyss, My child." There is a coating of burned charred soil within the hole; Now I can see near the top only darkness as we move down into the hole, that is [the] Abyss. There are some souls who are chained on the wall here.

Our Lady says now: "There are many walls and levels of, and in, the realm of Hell. These are covered by those who did not merit the flame of farther down. These are the ones whose greatest fear, thus greatest punishment, is Eternal darkness. Many of these could have been saved had they but said they were sorry to their God before death. Sadly, We had to condemn them to Hell. They suffer here as great as those who are in the flames below them. They will suffer until the end of time, which is never, for all the endless time of eternity. Describe more, My child."

Now on the walls as We are moving downward, I can see many demons crawling and slithering about. Many resemble snakes with wings and these are more repulsive than the other demons I have had to view so far. Now, ohh - it's getting horrendously hot down here, and there is much light as well. Now We are standing in a globe of energy, Our Lady and I, and the flame, flames, oh, the flames of the far lowest recesses of Hell are burning about the globe which is surrounding Our Lady and myself. Now, ohh, it's horrible. "I cannot look at it, Blessed Mother!"

"My child, do not test My wishes. Mankind must hear of what exists in the bottomless recesses of Hell and you must view and describe it in order that they may know of what you are now viewing."

"Yes, Mother, I'm, I'm sorry; I'll do as you say."

There are people with distorted features of face floating about, rolling in and burning in the flames. Their spiritual skin is on fire, but the fire does not seem to consume their flesh. It just keeps trying to continue to burn without any consummation at all. There are demons above the fires and they are hovering and stacking people on top of each other in the fires. The new arrivals, as they would be called, are falling constantly, from the opening of this seemingly endless chasm, into the arms of the demons who hover above the fires waiting to stack people in these fires which will burn for all eternity. Part of me feels sorrow for these souls down here, while another part of me understands God's position to punish forever souls who would be like Lucifer, the Devil, forever evil in intention.

"My child, feel no sorrow for those here in this place. They came here of free will. Many of them never wanted to see Heaven or God, or the Angels or Myself. Listen to them, My child, and repeat what you hear."

Demons: "Be gone. Why do you torture us so? We could not and did not want to see you. Yes, we can see the Queen here with you, but if we could get to you, you would be dead now."

Our Lady: "You see, My child, they did not wish to be among Us ever and there was, therefore, no way We could accept them among Us. Now, My child, We shall go down deeper in the flames and view one more spot, that you as of yet have not viewed - the place where Michael will cast Luciel, back to, soon, when My Son returns.

"Notice, My child, the chains are not filled; they are empty. Luciel now lurks and wanders your earth in a chain of destruction which is ever widening. Lucifer has a major legion of demons who obey and assist him in his battle against human mankind, and the forces from the Realm of Heaven. Satan walks the earth seeking to steal away souls from earth for then he can add them to those in his kingdom, now burning for all eternity. Now, My child, you have viewed Hell. You have viewed the Realm of the Prince of Evil, and you have viewed the realm of which souls are falling into as fast as the rain droplets of your month of April upon earth, combined with the snowflakes which fall during the months of your winter season.

"Now, My child, since you have viewed these things, you will notice We are no longer descending; We are now ascending toward the top of the Abyss. We are going to pray a Rosary before I send you back into your cell until 12:00 midnight when I again will come to you."

We prayed a Rosary and I stepped out of the portal and slept for the night.

****

Monday, July 18, 1983 – 12:00 Midnight till Tuesday, July 19, 1983 1:30 AM

Our Lady: "Wake up, My child, I am here."

These are Our Lady's first new words to me on this night. Now Our Lady must have come the usual way and entered into my cell through Her portal. This is the only way She could have come inside my cell, which is locked from the outside now at this time.

Our Lady is saying now that the Pope must be prayed for. The cardinals must be prayed for. "It is not wrong to pray for yourself, but you must pray for other people as well as yourself, for this is in itself true love of thy brothers and sisters. If you in any way of truth feel that you wish to pay a person who has died a favor back, then pray for them. Pray for all the Poor Souls in Purgatory. Pray for all these souls who would go to Hell if not prayed for as they die. Pray for the conversion of sinners.

"Go to your Churches more often, My children. Pray to My Son in the Eucharist Most Holy, My children, and receive Him at least once a week on your tongue. If you can do so, do so daily. Kneel before My Son when you are about to receive Him in Communion. Pray the Rosary daily and kneel if you can.

"My children, you must do something about the abortions in your country, for they are leading many down the road to Hell and damnation. In your country, the mothers are murdering their children and many of them, the mothers, are now sterile because of abortion. Why, do you, O mothers, think that you will be allowed to continue with the evilness and butchering?

"Do you think that the Father will allow this evil to continue much longer? No, I tell you now He is going to soon send upon you what you have earned justly, a great ball of fire, the Chastisement. I tell you, My children, the Warning is soon. If you knew how soon you would be on your knees during each and every moment of your spare time praying, begging and beseeching the Father for more time before the Warning."

****

Monday, July 18, 1983, 12:00 Midnight till Tuesday, July 19, 1983 1:30 AM

Our Lady: "Do not pray for the Warning, but rather for more time before the Warning. No man, woman, or child is safe when they step from within their homes, to the outside world. You are not all safe and secure now, especially in the continental United States of America.

"Upon this nation, Lucifer, the Prince of Darkness plans two major attacks – an attack from within and an attack from without. The attack from within comes on many major fronts:

1. The American Communist Party is seeking many new members and they are finding them.

2. The Masonic Lodges are sending out many members to find new recruits among all the major business places in your nation.

3. The American Witches International of Wicca and the covens, they are seeking new recruits.

"These three major groups are a major part of the wealth within your nation. Just before your nation is attacked in the second major attack, which will be from without, or outside your nation, most of the money within your nation will be removed from the banks. Thus, your nation, except for all its gold, will be poor. Then the American Military will not have the money for expenditures.

"The second attack will then happen, and off the shores of your nation the massive Russian submarines will then attack by first sending Russian armed troops and then more weapons in a full scale attack upon the shore-lying military installations of your nation. Once these are knocked out, it will not matter if all the other military installations in your nation try their hardest. The shores of your nation will be under the Kremlin's major control from Russia. This will also follow suit in Canada and then in Mexico. Only prayer can hold this major attack back, but I fear you are too late, My children. My children, prayer can hold it back, but it will eventually happen. It is an eventuality.

"Describe now, My child, what you see, what I look like."

Our Holy Mother Mary has on upon Her feet a form of slippers with roses at the toes. The slippers are made of some type of animal skin. The skin appears to be dyed a light sky blue. The rosettes upon Her slippers are deep red, like blood, but they are flecked with gold splotches. Along the dress She is wearing, is a ¾ inch trim of solid gold foil at the ankleline and at the neckline. Her dress is a sugar white. She has a belt made of miniature gold links all interwoven, and upon Our Lady's head is a deep blue mantle and it is trimmed with a ¼ inch border of fine gold foil. Her robe is a solid deep, deep blue and She has a trim of ¾ inch border upon the edges of Her robe. Upon the head of Our Lady is a great golden crown bedecked with many jewels, under Her crown the mantle almost totally covers Her head.

Today Her hair and most of Her face as well, does not show through Her mantle. Her mantle, well it resembles the material thickness of burlap, but it is made of a material as soft looking as silk and as shiny as that of deep, deep blue satin. Our Lady's Rosary is a - oh, she has two Rosaries, one Rosary is made of wooden beads and has a wooden crucifix.

The links are made of pure gold that glistens as Our Lady is holding out Her Rosaries. Oh, oh, oh my, the

Body or Corpus on the cross, it looks exactly as Jesus looked upon the cross when he died upon... it is flesh and blood colored and all the wounds are exactly in place on the cross. It is amazing to behold this cross. The Rosary has 15 decades of wooden beads each 3 inches long by about 1.5 inches wide. Our Lady's other Rosary is made with golden links and the beads are made of clear crystal which is see through only when no light hits it. When the light beams which exude from Our Lady hit the Rosary, the beads are multi-faceted [and] send out aurora borealis type lights. This light is like that of light broken into [the] spectrum of the colors that compose it, by a prism.

Our Lady: "Now My child, We will pray, then I will leave."

****

Tuesday, July 19, 1983 till Wednesday, July 20, 1983 – 1:00 AM

Now before me, I can see the portal has opened and Our Holy Mother is here now to speak to me and through me to the world. Now Our Lady has Her finger upon Her lips and now is instructing for me to listen to Her.

"My child, I only wish today to say that:

(1) All must say the Rosary.
(2) All must go back as before Vatican II in My Son's Church.
(3) Abortion must be stopped in your Nation.

"Now it is almost too late for your nation. The Warning, Miracle, and War, and then the Great Chastisement are very soon to be upon you now. Now, My child, I have already joined you and We will pray the Rosary."

After the Rosary Our Holy Mother left.

****

Wednesday, July 20, 1983, 12:00 Midnight till Thursday, July 21, 1983 1:00 AM, Feast of St. Lawrence of Brindisi – Priest and Doctor

Our Lady has come and is before me now. I am beginning to experience the joys common only to when She is present before me. Now She is ready to speak to me and all of us through me. Her finger was just upon Her lips, but now She is speaking to me.

Our Lady says: "My child, tomorrow you will ask (priest's name kept silent) to get a Rosary. He will get you a pair but they will be missing a bead in the third decade. This you will not worry about for the wooden Rosary is still good as long as you recite the missing bead. My child, all must pray the Rosary and you will now pray a Rosary with Me. I have at this time nothing to say that would be different from what I have already said."

****

Thursday, July 21, 1983, 12:00 Midnight till 1:00 AM July 22, 1983, Friday

We prayed a Rosary only today.

****

Friday, July 22, 1983 - 12:00 -1:00 AM - We prayed a Rosary only today.

****

Saturday, July 23, 1983 12:00 - 1:00 AM - We prayed a Rosary only today. (Feast of St. Bridget - Nun)

****

Sunday, July 24, 1983 12:00 - 1:00 AM - We prayed a Rosary only today.

****

Monday, July 25, 1933 12:00 - 1:00 AM - We prayed a Rosary only today. (Feast of St. James - Apostle)

****

Tuesday, July 26, 1983 - 12:00 - 1:00 AM - Feast of St. Anne and St. Joachim (Parents of the Blessed Virgin Mary)

We prayed and She said: "It will be hot for a long while, My son. The fires are upon the earth." (Hell is open and the devils are among us.) This is what she meant.

****

Friday, July 29, 1983, Feast of St. Martha the Virgin 11:05 – 12:05 AM

Before me now is a pretty woman named Mary. She is truly the Queen of the Universe. Truthfully the gospel writers were correct in saying that She is brighter than the Sun, because She so bright that when I checked a single moment ago, I could read a book by the light being emitted from Her Most Heavenly countenance. I used to be amazed at first that only I could see the Virgin, but now I have grown quite used to this phenomenon.

Our Lady is wearing the usual blue mantle and robe, both trimmed with a quarter inch border of solid gold foil. Her dress or tunic is white, in color. It's as white as sugar or pure salt. Our Lady has upon Her feet a pair of usual leather type of sandals, only this time there is no rosette on the toes of the sandals. Our Lady's Rosary is made of golden links that are connecting the wooden beads together. The cross is wooden with a human flesh-toned color mixture to the golden effigy or corpus on the cross.

Our Lady is saying: "My child, if only all mankind could recognize My Son, the way that day's saint did, if they but realized the presence of God among them, mankind would not have so much strife. My children, the great heats of your summer will continue. I have warned you of the approach of the beast - Antichrist. He came. He is here. He is among you all now, born in Palestine. I have this warning and a bit of knowledge for you now.

"Many demons are among and about you now. Many temptations are given to you all each day, by the agents of 666, about you now. No man is ever free from temptation and no woman is free from temptation either. In your nation especially, the demons are seeking for possession of little children. They seek to cause the little children to murder - Murder Parents - Murder Brothers - and Sisters and any others who might be present at the time.

"Remember, long ago the Apostles of My Son wrote in the Book of Life that in the end days of our generation. it would be father against son, mother against daughter, and all because of mankind's sins. I cannot tell you how much My heart is hurt looking down upon your nation now. The sins of mankind are very heavily weighing the scales to the left."

"Oh, Blessed Mother, I know that this statement is a sign that things are not good in this nation any longer."

"Yes, My child, that is true, the Death Angel is in your world, My children, and he plans to bring such terrible, terrible destruction to your nation. He plans on eventually taking with him back down to Hell, ¾'s of Mankind, in the final destruction of your world during the Chastisements.

"The only true weapons that you have against this evil being of destruction are the Sacramentals and prayer. You have been given My Brown Scapular and My Rosaries. They are to be used as such. He or She who dies enclothed with My Scapular will not suffer the eternal fires of Hell. All should wear this Sacramental. One need not be a Catholic necessarily to wear a scapular, for I gave it to all mankind, not just the Catholics.

"In a like way also was given to all mankind the Grace of the Rosary. These beads of prayer should be prayed daily, even many times a day, if you can fit it in your schedule. There is not one person on this earth who has no free time with which to pray the Rosary. If you feel you cannot fit one Rosary in your day's schedule, then try to say as much as is possible.

"My child, you still do not seem to comprehend the full power for joy and miracle-bringing which can be said to be enclosed within a single Hail Mary. Yes, My child and My children, one Hail Mary can save a soul from Hell and bring it to Heaven. In some cases one Hail Mary can save the life of someone who is dying and in many hospitals miracles have been obtained for people on the verge of death by one Hail Mary.

"One Hail Mary can save a soul in Purgatory from sufferings which would have otherwise been continued upon them. One Hail Mary in every case, causes all of Hell to tremble, and puts fear into every demon's mind, including Lucifer's. Now if one Hail Mary can do all of this, is it then not a smart decision to pray My Rosary, which has 53 Hail Mary's in the five decade-Rosary, and 153 Hail Mary's in the 15 decade-Rosary? My children, I love you all, but I leave the decision of World War or World Peace in your hands. Should the world not pray more, major war and destruction will come upon all mankind.

"Goodbye now, My child."

Our Holy Mother has just now stepped back into Her Portal and both have vanished.

****

July 30, 1983 Saturday, Feast of St. Peter Chrysologus, Bishop and Doctor, 11:00 PM – 12:00 PM

"My child, more funds are needed for the foreign missions. Every day between the number of 10 and the number of 200 children die in just the country of Ethiopia alone, not to forget Africa and Malaysia's poor sections.

"Your world is in such great famine, and yet as We look about now, We see you set your tables with huge gatherings of food, and set to feast while they suffer of famine. You do not even remember to pray for these poor little ones I speak of. Yes, some of you do, but those who do are in the few. Political issues are no reason for your world to hold food from any neighboring nation which is in need. I assure you that he who gives monies or food goods along with medicine to even but one of these will eventually find a route of peace in their life. I say a route of peace and mean by this a road which will be guided by God until you climb the final road to receive reward at the other side of the gate in Heaven.

"Your nation supplies, and Russia supplies, many smaller countries with nuclear supplies for reactors, but I tell you now, not all of these supplies go into these nuclear reactors and many of these supplies are converted into hidden nuclear weaponry. Many nuclear supplies within the past 20 years have been listed as missing within your country and within Russia. I tell you now these have been brought to many of the smaller countries, which are preparing for future defense should war arise, as We in Heaven have warned you all, that it will arise quite soon.

"Your question, My son, about why Jesus will not come, or has not come to visit you: I must inform you that you are wrong because He has been with you many a times secretly since you came to this place. My Son would not leave you in these times of trial. He is with you when you call to Him, and He hears your prayers. Before God your prayers are quite strong.

"You will now begin making a list of people who have died recently so that you may pray for them, for a time period of at least 3 weeks. You will find the names in almost any newspaper of your land. My child, you will also pray for any person whose name is sent to you. I must inform you that many will find relief much quicker by your praying for them.

"I, in the past, have given you warning of a plague and of another and another; and now there are many plagues among you all. Some plagues lie dormant for long amounts of time, making the doctors of your land think that a cure has killed all traces of a disease or plague. My children, the plague of the Middle Ages of England is on the rise now in your country. Rats, My children, are the carriers of this disease. The Black Plague, also called Bubonic Plague, has killed and will kill many. I gave a very simple way of cure for this disease or plague before it reached the shores or inner confines of France, to a Miss Marie Jahenney in olden days.

"This cure grows in your country as well, but not as commonly. The cure that I speak of is called the Hawthorne Tree. The part of which is used is the leaves of the tree. The leaves may be picked when they are newly formed. When they are older, they are just as fresh then. When the leaves fall off of the Hawthorne in the fall season, they are just as powerful.

> "The leaves should be cut from their stalks and placed upon a pan, which is covered with a metal foil, which upon your earth is known as tin foil.
>
> Next they should be baked, but only until they are brittle enough to break into miniature pieces when touched with a finger.
>
> Then an emptied tea bag should be filled with one teaspoon of crushed leaves from the Hawthorne, and this should be steeped for a few minutes to a half hour.
>
> After this the tea should be slowly drank. In this manner a cure is given forth, but this tea must be used until all traces of the plague are gone."

"My children, unless you all pray much more, the situations of other plagues shall arise within your country. Already now in your country the rat population is growing very fast. These rats carry a plague which is yet unknown to your scientists. Their plague will be unable to be stopped by modern science. It will be God-sent upon you.

"Goodbye, My son. Pray your Rosary."

****

July 31, 1983 8:00 PM Locution

"You will soon have trouble. You may end up serving time, My child, for the devil is lining evidence against you. I will be with you to bring you through - just call on Me. Pray your Rosary tonight; you forgot it last night.

"Goodbye now, My son."

****

August 4, 1983, Feast of St. John Vianney, Cure de Ars, Priest – 12;00 – 1:00 AM

"My child evil has escalated threefold in your world. We must now pray Our Rosary. (We prayed 5 Sorrowful

Mysteries.) My children, Satan again is lurking your streets as he lurked in Sodom and Gomorrah and Atlantis. and they fell under the fires and wars. So shall it be among you all now. Man repeats his same stupid mistakes over and over again. He listens to Satan and this precedes his fall. Many in your land need exorcisms.

"The priests who perform this ritual should before doing so, invoke the intercession of St. John Vianney and St. Benedict and St. Michael the Archangel, also St. Francis and St. Theresa. Just these names before Satan, cause pain to those who are in truth possessed. Also My Name and My Son's, will cause these demons to speak if We will them to do so, which we usually do.

"My children, an exorcism should not be performed within a block radius of anyone who has no Sacramental or especially no Scapular or Rosary, because Satan will then, instead of leaving for Hell, go before mankind in a new body very quickly and attempt to destroy the priest who is performing the exorcism. No man should attempt to do spiritual battle with Satan alone. This usually will result in instant death for this man, and he may lose his soul.

"My child, there is hope for Our race, but much time is being wasted. The Father is angered by the witless stupidity of the human race in ignoring My warnings and My Son's warnings. There must be much more prayers or sadly all of the world will be caused to suffer much, much trial and much strife. I will be with you again tomorrow, My Son, on My Feast Day of August 5th. Goodbye."

****

August 5, 1983, Friday, Feast Day of St. Mary Major, Mother of God, 10:00 – 11:00 PM

"My children, We in Heaven are all crying for all the souls now that We are losing. The Gates of Heaven are open, if you'll but come to Us in prayer. The Gates of Hell will not envelop you if you pray. If you pray you will enter instead into the Gates of Heaven.

"My Son is suffering still, even in His Spiritual Body... suffering for the sins of mankind. Each year that passes Jesus is caused (by man's sins).to suffer more. Jesus is there also when Satan tempts you, so why must you fall, in rejection of Him…into sin? God has in the moment of creation, created mankind with an inborn knowledge. Later man gained the Knowledge of Good and Evil. But what has he done with this? Man has begun to live in total evil and is now at the point where without a change, the end of all as you know it is at hand. It is very hard for man to enter Heaven, but it is even harder for a man to enter Heaven who is very rich. The only road which is truly easy is the Road to Hell.

"Your burdens and your sorrows, My children, I do not think you realize... these are but added graces of your life, for the joys of the Kingdom are easier to obtain when you accept your sufferings you may have while upon the earth. If you live as St. Francis of Assisi, a very lowly life upon earth, you will gain an even greater life in the Kingdom.

"When you have suffering, you have a Key to Heaven, providing you do not curse the suffering or He who allows it upon you, for I tell you, if you pray it will be lessened and you will feel better. If you curse your suffering and then God, you will lose your easy Key to Heaven. Heaven is won by suffering and if one does not suffer in any way upon earth, that one and same will not enter the Kingdom.

"All suffering, one day, will pass and if you are not with God at that moment then you can only be with the adversary Satan at that moment. What will it gain a man to lose all his sufferings upon earth? Then he would, if he had no suffering on earth, have to suffer long in Purgatory if he was ever to reach the Kingdom. Some people suffer this Purgatory upon earth in great pains every living day, and as such, may offer these pains up to the Father for other souls who have died and are suffering in Purgatory.

"Yes, My child, you are correct. If you pray for the people listed in the obituary pages in your newspapers, you will find that they are thankful as they pray back for you. You will now begin this process, My child. For two weeks you will pray for each soul you see listed in your newspaper today and on each day to follow.

"Goodbye now My child." She has now vanished in Her portal.

Our Lady wore a blue habit and mantle with a blue robe and She had nothing on Her feet this evening. She had Her hair completely covered by Her mantle, no hair showed. Her Rosary was made of large brown beads.

****

August 6, 1983, Saturday, Feast of the Transfiguration of Jesus Christ 10:00 – 11:00 PM

Jesus: "My child, you will hear My voice now and write My words. Yes, the answer to your question is yes. We in Heaven have been very happy to hear the prayers for you. Many are the number of they who are now praying for you. You, My child, must not despair. You must accept the present situation. Have you not read the Message My Mother gave you yesterday and understood it? Be of good cheer. Remember for each suffering you undergo, if you offer it to Me for the poor souls in Purgatory and the Holy Father John Paul II, you will have great stocks stored in the Realm of Heaven for when it is your time to join Us. Continue to pray, My son. My Mother and yours will soon be here. I say 'and yours' because She is the Mother of All. Goodbye now, My son."

I had been in the middle of a Rosary when Jesus came, and after He left, I finished the Rosary and Mary Our Mother and Queen appeared through the portal and came forward. She is very beautiful, stunning and very regal, queenly.

"My child you may describe me, but there you just repeated yourself twice in the same statement. This can be confusing to those who will read the Message. My child, describe Me, how I look."

The Queen and Mother is wearing a blue mantle with a blue habit and a blue robe. Her tunic is a whitish color and the belt about Her waist is golden in a fine weave of linked golden woven links. The belt is made with a skill such as I've never seen upon earth. Upon Her feet She is wearing nothing this evening. She has very tiny feet with skin as white as a lily. Our Lady is blushing; she is embarrassed by my description.

"I'm sorry, Mother, but I will continue with my description now." Our Lady is holding in Her hands a wooden Rosary. It is made with golden links and a golden corpus which is on a wooden cross.

"My children of the world, I am your Mother and Queen. **I am The Lady Of All Holy Titles.**

"I came at Fatima, at Lourdes, and many other places. I am the Queen of the Universe and Mother of thy Lord Jesus Christ, and as such, I command you all to pray. Pray the Rosary; it is the Key to Heaven. The Rosary will save your world, if you will but pray upon it in large groups throughout your land. There is a group of people throughout your land which is an army for Me. The Radio Rosary Stations are this army. Pray with these stations and pray together. Make one solid Rosary across the land, link to link, chain to chain. If you all again begin to pray now, a short time of peace may come to you. If you do not, then the time of complete world peace of which I promised you at Fatima will not come about, and you will all go onto worse things then. Pray. Pray Hard. Pray Much.

Goodbye, My child."

****

August 8, 1983, Monday, Feast Day of St. Dominic, Priest, 12:00 – 1:00 AM

"My children, on this day I bring you a most urgent Message from Heaven. I have many times now warned you all of the submarines surrounding your nation, the United States, and Canada. Now because of so little prayer they are also about the shores of Iceland, and Hawaii, and soon without prayer they will also surround the Philippines. All free world nations shall be surrounded while the communist parties work within the countries. Are you all so asleep that you do not heed this, or see this all happening about you?

"Again, I tell you: Following the laws of Stalin, the communist countries will preach peace, but be preparing for war. When they think that all trust them and all are not prepared for their attack, they will attack then.

"In Leningrad of the Soviet Union, the leader of the evilness has devised a cunning plan to make all believe in his false plan for peace. He has already used this plan and many [are] trusting him now to never be the cause of war; but I tell you all and warn you all now with fair warning, there will be major war led by this Soviet leader.

"A child, write to this leader, pleading for him not to start war with the United States. When he received this letter, he then thought to invite her to the Country of Russia and show her every spot in which there was no war preparations. As he planned, many news reporters from your nation followed her to Russia. He showed total peace during her stay, so she and the reporters would only see peace and calm. Thus many fears were cancelled out, and he set in motion his major plan for the beginning of a world war such as has never been since the beginning of time, nor will ever be seen again, for so little will be left after the destruction.

"Now this 11 year old female from Manchester, Maine is home again and the communist Soviet leader, who invited her for a time, is now planning a full scale major war. Planning is almost complete and almost every tactic of the setting up for this war is now in place. When every free island or country is surrounded, and your nation is caused to go broke by the Masons --the covens and many of the communistic regimes in your nation taking all their money out of the banks all at once -- then war will come to your whole world and the Ball of Redemption will soon strike you all. Your nation will be especially hard struck in this Time of Destruction. I tell you that this cannot be stopped, but it can be held back from coming upon you for an amount of time, if you all pray.

"Go down upon your knees, send each bead up to encircle your world with a shield of prayer. Eventually, as man continues to sin and commit all manner of evilness, We will send this Ball of Fire upon you to cleanse the earth of the evilness. Remember the cities of sin, Sodom and Gomorrah, and what happened to them in their evilness. So, in part will it be upon your world. Read and learn by My past Messages to you all and also remember what the Father allowed to happen to Pagan Atlantis. The continent warred between itself, North and South - both sides were super advanced in weapons, and all this did was [to] destroy all record of them. They destroyed their continent and caused it to disintegrate into the waves, leaving no trace of themselves left. I told you all this in the past, but to no avail; the few prayers gained are too few.

"There must be many more said, or your world will destroy itself as Atlantis did, for you will disintegrate much land with your bombs. You will heat and poison your atmosphere and you will cause the ice to melt and the waves to cover you all. That which is not covered will be struck by the Ball, nothing will be left upon the face of the earth. Only then will My Son bring the 144,000 who will be saved back to your world, which shall be wiped clean and shall be as a desert.

"By prayer, water and food will be provided. In like manner will all other necessities be sent to the 144,000 chosen beloved children. I am not trying to scare you, My children, but this will all happen and this Warning will be heard by all before this will happen. So I tell you now again, pray, pray, pray. Pray hard with all your heart's love, for not only yourself, but for thy brothers as well. Go back and reread all Warnings given throughout your world.

"Pastors: Do not stop your flock from reading these Warnings, for they were given for them. Why, O Pastors do you not allow My Messages to My children to be given to them? I will tell you the answer: It is because of Fear and because of Pride. You are afraid of anything you cannot see or comprehend. Your pride is hurt because many of you are not central figures in your Church. You are afraid to see a Seer lead crowds twice as large as you can obtain yourself in prayer.

"Your Pride has caused you to sin, My Pastors. Turn back now before it is too late. Many of My shrines have not been truthfully investigated. Many of the Messages from those shrines which were truthfully investigated and found true, have never been read by many Catholics in your world.

"The children - what do you teach them in their catechism classes throughout the world? You teach them only of loving their brother and their God, but what of the teachings of the Bible? What of My Messages and My Son's? We in Heaven hear very little talk of Lourdes or Fatima, or La Salette, or Pontmain, and all the other places We appeared.

"If you want a good nation, if you want a peaceful world, and you wish to hold back war, then teach the children of these things, and more than that, how to pray. My child, see that this Message is gotten out to My children very soon, in print, for each one who reads this will have heard My urgent Warning and will be able to make their own choice. We will save many through this Message. You will pray, My little son, pray and Pray Hard!

"Goodbye."

Our Lady has now vanished. Our Lady wore a green cape tonight and tonight Her Rosary was all golden except for the corpus on the cross. Everything else was the same as the "Statue of Our Lady of Grace" looks.

****

August 10, 1983, Feast Day of St. Lawrence, Deacon and Martyr, 12:00 – 1:00 AM

"It is good to see [you] - you look so well this evening, My son. My children, We in Heaven have heard your prayers and a brief relief is on the way to you in the Northeast. I warned that the heats would be great and the rainfall little or none. Was I not correct? I cannot lie and tell you that everything is going well when it isn't. Since 1904 your Northeast has never been this hot for so long a time. It had been hotter for brief periods, but never for so long. The time which has been hot affected all areas South and East of the Dakotas: Nebraska, Kansas, Missouri, Tennessee, Virginia. Your corn and soybean crops have been spared this year, but without prayer, your citrus crops will soon begin to fail. Your country is sending large amounts of cattle to the market, thus prices will he low now, but then prices will rise next year because there will be a lack of food-animals. Also there will be famine which shall kill off many of the cattle which are left now.

There is one truth to the studies of Darwin and others like him. They say that the Father created dinosaurs as well as the creatures about the world in this modern day. This is true; man did not, however, evolve from the ape. Those few cases of bone which are part human and part ape were caused by mutants between ape and man. There were many mutant strains which soon died out and left their bones. Man did not evolve from the Ape.

"In Drumnadrochit Province in the country of Scotland there exists an unidentified creature family. This creature family of living dinosaurs of the water which survived as eggs during the last freeze-over of your world. This freezing I speak of is that which you call the Ice Age. You surprise Me, My children, by not recognizing a creature that you have many times before seen the bones of in the past. This creature is known to your men of science as the Ellanasaurus.

"Another creature exists unknown to many - it exists in Africa, but unlike the Reptilian dinosaur Ellanasaurus, this creature does not lay eggs. This second creature I speak of lives in the misty swamps of Africa and is called Brontosaurus. The Africans call it the Mekele-Mbembe. These two wonders of their times were thought extinct by your scientists, but they are not. Soon, however, if man does not take measures to protect these two families of their kind, they will be extinct forever and this is why I am taking so much time upon this issue tonight. In the schools many are taught the evils of evolutionists' lies. Thus, We in Heaven deem it necessary to explain the mysteries of your world which evolutionists can only guess at. My child, now you will continue to pray your Rosary after I leave.

"Goodbye now, My child."

"Goodbye, Mother."

Our Lady tonight explained the mysteries of that which have been puzzling many of us for years. Now the scientists have been blown away in the wind, with their theories about saying the creatures were probably instances of evolution which have not died yet. Yes, tonight Our Lady disproved this theory.

****

August 11, 1983, Thursday, Feast Day of St. Clare, Virgin, 2:00 – 3:00 AM

"My children, your Churches today, what has become of them? You are taught of what the truth is, in the most part, but you do not believe what you are taught. You have not taught My children right, My Pastors. You have not taught any longer of the Fires which exist within the afterlife plane of Purgatory. This is wrong! You must teach of this, for many will fall into there which might otherwise have been saved. Many no longer believe in these places of afterlife. Sadly, because many of these who are among you all, do not believe, they are sinning in many ways, thinking that they will not be punished for their sins. Many, or most of these, will end it all in Hell, for their non-repentance for their sins.

"California is coming closer to the time when it will lose all of the area west of the fault line. It will sink in the waves. The proof of what I say can be shown in the San Joaquin Valley, where there at the present time is an area of the fault lines tremor which carries a 6.7 on your scientific devices called the Richter Scale. $31,000,000.00 damage was caused on May 2, 1983. I warned once before that without prayers, there will be a massive earthquake of which will cause California to fall, Japan to fall and which will divide the USA and Canada in the Middle. Already in San Antonio, Texas on July 23, 1983, there was a large earthquake of 3.4 Richter Scale. This quake was the first quake in the area since 1973. The quake struck in a manner which seems like nothing, so far, but this will eventually cause the Fault Line that exists to move apart in this spot all the way up to Canada. The quake that occurred happened at 10:25 and shook the countryside.

"My child, you will now pray your Rosary and do not forget the Holy Father in your Rosary.

"My child, goodbye."

****

August 13, Saturday, Feast of St. Pontian, Pope, and St. Hippolytus, Priest-Martyr, 12:00 – 1:00 AM

"I am upset, My child, yes I am upset."

I was not going to describe what Our Mother is wearing, but I feel I should, and Our Lady is nodding "Yes." I know she is going to speak of the Papacy tonight. I hope he is okay still. She says he is. Our Lady is dressed in a yellow dress with a purple mantle.

Her belt is golden and is the same as Her usual belt. Her robe is bluish, pretty sky colored. Our Lady has a wooden Rosary which is a deep dark, mahogany color. The cross is wooden with a human colored corpus or body. Our Lady is crying... her tears are flowing from Her eyes. She is putting Her finger to Her mouth and She now is saying, "Repeat, My child."

"My child, there is a plan afloat against John Paul II, Our present Vicar. Today, My child, at Lourdes 20 people were arrested as three people among them tried to bomb My Shrine. The group called by the title "Stop The Priests" is trying to get a chance at the Pope. Pray hard, My child, pray that they do not succeed in their attempts. Your knowledge of what is happening at this time is very little; let it be opened."

Oh, Oh my, that is truly happening. The Pope is going to Lourdes and he is to be attacked if there is not enough prayer.

"Yes, My child, it is so. Now you must go and pray to the Holy Ghost for the Holy Father also, I will give you the Litany of Jesus' Life that you will pray with Me and write as you pray later, but for now I will leave you.

"Goodbye, My child."

****

August 14, 1983, Sunday, Eve of the Feast of the Assumption of Mary Immaculate, 12:00 – 12:30 AM

"My child, recently your scientists discovered the star Vega has planetary matter floating about it, but this does not change anything. There is no life in the Universe other than on earth, in Heaven, and in Purgatory and sadly in Hell. The fact of their discovery is true. The one fact that they forget to mention in your news media is what they are viewing happened five million light years ago. So, as they say, what they see is a planetary system forming around a one billion year old star, they are seeing something that went on over five million light years ago. The planetary system is completely formed and there still is no life upon it, nor shall there ever be life upon these planets, as any of the other in outer space, only upon earth will there ever be life.

"Your men of science are ever learning, but they will never accept the truth, or any other truth that I have always spoken of. They will continuously try to explain away miracle after miracle that the Father has sent upon you. I have told you that Abortion is Murder, but still the scientists deny that from the moment of conception a life is a life. I have said that the test tube baby is a lifeless creature of the Abyss. Yes, still they create the test tube baby very often now.

"I have said that there is no life on other planets, but mankind still believes that there is a life on other planets. I have warned of many things which would happen, so man would pray for his brothers and for more time before the Final Chastisement, but did he do so? No; sadly, he did not. I have grown weary, My children, and this is one of My last times of warning you. If you do not pray, the end as you know it, will be hastened upon you.

"All religions must be as one before God. Worship in your own ways, but do not argue over who is correct in his belief. This only breeds discord and division. "To Divide Is To Conquer" and this is the Plan of Satan! You must all stand up and fight for your country with your God. Stand as one with God. All religions must stand together, all Christians

"I tell you now, My Son is soon to take souls up in the Rapture. So be prepared for this time; you do not know when it will happen. It could be at any time of the day or night. If you have followed and obeyed all of My requests, you will have nothing to worry about, My children, for then you will be among those saved. If you have not, then change your life before it is too late. Pray the Rosary daily. Catholics and all other Christians attend your Churches and heed what your Pastors teach you and your Reverends teach you, for they are My Son's representatives. When they speak heed them. My child, I am now going to leave you. Be sure and send out these Messages as soon as possible or tomorrow.

"Goodbye now."

Our Lady cried through Her Message tonight and She needn't be asked by me what She was crying for, because I already know. She is weeping because of all of us, Her children, are ignoring Her pleas and Her requests which She gave long ago, and is still giving now

I ask you all: Isn't it about time we all stop hurting Our Blessed Mother's torn heart? Is it so much for all to sacrifice 30 minutes of our 24 hour day to Mary and Jesus in prayer? If you saw how She was weeping, you would be praying at every moment possible.

Please won't you pray so we can save our nation and bring a smile back to Our Queen and Mother Mary? She loves you; don't you love Her enough to pray and make Her smile? She has given so much for us all. She has not rested since being brought up to Heaven as Queen of All the Universe. She is our very best friend in the whole world. The Queen of the Universe has on many, many occasions had the chance to warn us and has done so. Now why don't we heed Her requests and put a smile back upon Her face, Okay? Good day.

****

August 15, 1983, Feast of the Assumption of Mary, 12:00 – 12:30 AM

The portal has just opened and Our Lady has come forward and is now stepping out of it. Our Mother is wearing a blue mantle today with a blue cape flowing behind Her. Under the cape She has on a blue robe with a golden trim upon the edges of it. She has on a very fine golden link belt about her waist, and Oh, Her Slippers are very dainty and pretty. They are golden and they have miniature pink rosettes upon them. Her mantle almost totally covers Her face and what there is that is visible of Her face is hard to see, because of the light being emitted from Her body. Our Lady is so bright, that She looks five times brighter than when I've looked at the sun in the past or a car headlights. five times brighter than them. Now Our Lady is putting Her Rosary in Her hands and is holding the cross at Her lips. She is nodding now for me to listen and repeat. Yes, she says to repeat.

"My child and My children, I came to counsel you all again on many things tonight. There are many plagues upon your land now. Diseases and other forms of plague will abound now. Many will not be able to be cured by any means of Modern Medicine known of today, but only by our concentrated prayers. One Plague is incurable and is carried among many of the sexual deviates of your land and in other countries. This plague I speak of is the "American Immunity Deficiency Syndrome."

"A second set of plagues will be able to be cured or stopped if the disease is found out about in time. This second set of plagues is carried by the mosquitoes of your land. This plague will be especially heavy in the Massachusetts and Connecticut areas. It is the disease known by the doctors as Elephantitus of which that this second set of plagues consists of. Spraying for mosquitoes will stop some of them, but only prayer can sufficiently cause this plague to end it once it begins. The plague will stop during the winter, but will begin in worse proportion in the spring, without prayers.

"A third plague is coming upon you in the Eastern Coastal Area. This plague will be carried among the rats. The rat population shall greatly increase. The Black Plague or Bubonic Plague of which infected much of Middle Age Europe is now on the rise in your nation. Prayers, My children, Prayers - The only answer is found in Prayer. You must pray and pray hard; it is almost too late.

"My child, due to a problem soon to be announced to you, you will have at this time, a period of withholding the Messages. This Message and the other Message before it will be sent out, but you will wait for two weeks, before sending out the Messages from August 16, 1983, a period of two weeks. I will announce to you the time of when you will send these out to the general public. You will, however, have your assistants to type and prepare enough copies for all areas but New York and Connecticut. However, in New York and Connecticut there are three exceptions to this rule I have just given you. You will listen, but not repeat the names in print.

"Repeat, My child: On the topic of the Bible, I have not recently told you this because of more important issues, but now the time is ripe for telling you all. You must not read any Bibles in print after the years 1965-1966. The new Bibles have been changed and are no longer correct.

"Revelation 6:6 is often misunderstood, therefore, I shall now explain the mystery of this quote. This speaks of the time when the crops shall be as they are now in your country. (Many in utter destruction because of the weather.) The quote of the Oil and Wine refers to the Holy Oils and Holy Wine used by the Priesthood. 6:12 is exactly as it is written in literal form. This will soon happen upon earth, the sun and the moon.

"Revelation 7:1 refers to those areas in the Midwest at this time where there are great heats and no winds. This will eventually happen to the whole earth, but is beginning in the Midwest of the United States.

"The pages of Revelation are turning fast, My children. Prayer can only slow them, but it can give you precious time for saving souls before the Final Destruction. The Babylon of Revelation, 17:15, is the once proud, but now debased state of New York in your country, the United States of America. The reasons are many. Need I list them all? Among them are the major evils:

1) Prostitution; 2) Pornography; 3) Witchcraft; and 4) Homosexuality.

"From this once proud state, the worst of these evils is sent to all states of your country and also many and most foreign shores. Also, it is the major city for the import of evils from other nations and countries of your world. (17:15) confirms this quote.

"The bomb which I spoke of a short time back in My Messages is described in 17:16 of Revelations. When it explodes it will eat the flesh of many around it in the New York Area. The state shall be made desolate of life and the land shall be charred. Soon when Satan gains control of the United Nations and then of Rome, three days later, the bomb will explode.

"Revelation 18:21 refers to the flood which will come and cover the then desolate State of New York and many of the surrounding East Coastal Cities. In Revelation 18:23, Words 44-51 refer to the witchcraft covens now existing in New York. Verse 18:24 refers to the victims of the covens - those who were murdered by them, in the New York Area.

"My child, you now will pray and pray hard for all those who are sinning tonight upon earth. I am leaving you now, My child, but you will be having another Message tomorrow.

"Goodbye now, My child."

Our Lady is now backing up into the portal and now the portal is already beginning to vanish. It is almost gone, and now it is gone. My friends, I too am requesting for you all to pray to God that the Bible pages turn slowly, and that our demise will be held back from coming upon us.

****

August 16, 1983, Feast of St. Stephen of Hungary, King, 12:00 – 12:30 AM

"My child, you had fallen asleep while praying. You will write all what I tell you now. Your country, the once proud United States of America, the plucked bald eagle, whatever shall become of it? Because of mankind's sins, a new tactical and more potentially destructive weapon is being developed. A new form of intercontinental ballistic missile is being developed now in the United States and has already been developed in Russia, The Union of Soviet Socialist Republics. The weapon at impact will send out microwaves at a radius five to ten miles from central impact zone. It will kill all plant and animal life within its ten mile radius, including all bacteria and other disease organisms. It will create a sterile atmosphere and also make that area unsafe for human occupation for at least a two month period, while it keeps emitting microwaves.

"My child, you are correct in being frightened, for the next war will be a Fierce War. It will not end as quickly as many of your politicians and American Military believe. No, it will last for many months and three-quarters of mankind will die in the war and from the Hand of the Father with the Ball of Redemption.

"There are many Russian Satellites about the skies of your planet now, with the capacity of destroying whole and complete major United States cities and also destroying other satellites or blocking transmission between earth to satellite and back to earth communication systems. Major war is soon to befall you all. Will you not listen to Me and pray for peace?

"I do not ask for prayers out of vanity, but out of necessity. Mankind must go upon his knees now and pray, before the Father causes you all to be forced to your knees in fear, but then it will be too late for many.

"Look at all who have died in the past wars, outside of your country, in the foreign nations' battlefield. See now in your hearts that I cannot lie, and then I tell you the Third World War is soon, and will take three-quarters of your world's population to their death. I am telling you only how many will die, but in your nation, there are so few who actually realize what real war is like, how it is to see their relations in the streets and sidewalks of your land, bloodied or burned, [and] charred bones with no flesh.

"You do not realize what is coming upon you. You are almost beyond the point of no return. You must pray the Rosary and pray it well. If you do not pray, the end of all as you know it will be hastened upon you all. There is hope in prayer and all religions must be together as one before the Father. You must all see yourselves upon a battlefield now.

"You are in the War of the Spirit - each prayer knocks the enemy (Satan and his army of evil) back a fewsteps on the battlefield. You can pray at any time and any place. You do not have to pray aloud. You can pray to your God in silence which is just as good.

"My child, you will now pray on your Rosary and you will not despair of your present situation. There are many things in store for you yet in your future. I cannot reveal them to you now, but I can only say that this situation will be over soon, and you will move on to other better things and times. The Messages will never cease until the war begins or until the Warning and Miracle. But I beg of you, My child, no matter what situations may befall you, you do not deny My coming to you.

"You may choose now to continue to repeat or listen in silence of your pen to what I have to say now.

"I will repeat it."

"Very well, My child, then so it will be. I know of your persistence and your strength of will. I know of your strength, and your weaknesses, of your desires. I chose you to work with because of many reasons, many you already know by now. You are among the degenerate teen generation of your 'fastly coming to an end era' of time. You would have been lost without Our Guidance. You will one day lead many to us.

"You are a suitable link in saving souls, as are the other true Seers. My child, there are many who do not believe in you. Many of them are trying now to stop your assistants from sending out My Messages to the world, but they are not evil just because of this. No, they are only confused as to the truth. Pray now, My child, upon your Rosary.

"Goodbye now until Friday, when I will return to counsel you again."

Our Lady is now backing up and as She is going into the portal She is blessing me. Our Lady is now in the portal and it (the portal) is beginning to vanish.

****

August 19, 1983, Feast of St. John Eudes, Priest, 12:00 – 12:30 AM

I was sleeping as Our Lady has just awakened me for this Message She is giving tonight. I will not, therefore, be able to give a description as She is now ready to speak. I will only say that She is wearing Her usual blue and white and Her gold belt. She has nothing upon Her feet.

"My child and My children, there are many blasphemies upon your earth now, and now your scientists seek to play God in yet another way. Once they only tried one of the worst things, Abortion. They tried Vitro Fertilization. Now your scientists are attempting splicing of genes in the act of altering the height of a person. This will not be from God; they will be from man and of Satan. Do your scientists have no fear of their genetic engineering?

"Your scientists also seek and have now already begun to develop a Genetic Bomb. This bomb is dangerous, and in the process of its development they shall destroy not only many of themselves, but also many others around them. This plan is being developed in a government facility in a highly populated part of your country, to bring this bomb forth. The bomb will consist of a plague-like set of different types of radiation-altered germs containing death-producing cancerous genes which will kill people quickly because the genes will be radioactive. Genetic Radioactive Warfare - is this what you want? Pray. Pray without ceasing. Pray constantly, for if you do not pray, it will be too late.

"My child, pray on your Rosary now. I am leaving. Theresa will soon join you now for a short poem Message."

I prayed a Rosary, just until the last word of the Hail Holy Queen Prayers before I noticed a movement in the portal before me. I finished and St. Theresa said "Salutations" she stepped in from within her transportation, Our Lady's Portal.

Theresa: "Repeat, little one:

I speak to you now of the Genetic Bomb which they now seek to develop.
Without prayers I tell you it's your nation that it will envelop.

Russia the Bear is guided now by an Angel who is slyly wise.
Upon this bomb this serpentine Angel does have his eyes.

I do not seek now to spread to you all a fear,
But rather to speak to you of its effect on your atmosphere.

I know that this much you already do know:
It will be spread by the winds that always do blow

You were warned in the past in Biblical form of term,
Of the bomb which would come with the genetic germ.

If this bomb is allowed to be created,
Then soon your country will be ill-fated.

"My child, you will call this Message **The Genetic Bomb**.

"Goodbye now."

St. Theresa is gone now; I have been staring at the portal as she left, and she was praying on her big wooden Rosary beads as she disappeared and then the portal itself was gone.

I will attempt to simplify what Theresa's words mean. She is initially telling us to pray, because if we don't the bomb will be successfully created or the Gene Germ will escape its creator's laboratory in our atmosphere, thus killing many Americans. When she says in line nine about the Warnings being in Biblical form, she does not refer to the Bible, but actually means the Messages of the Virgin during the years at various places, [Who] has spoken of the event in some minor detail alike to the Bible's reference in the Apocalypse for the modern times.

****

August 20, 1983, Feast of St. Bernard, Abbot and Doctor, 12:00 – 12:30 AM

"My child, tonight I must again give counsel to you all on Abortion. The number of abortions in your nation has steadily increased. There must be more prayers said for the poor little ones. Go to the doctors of the world; I say to you now: you who commit these acts of abortion are accused of murder before the Eternal Father. If you do not repent before death, you will find your place in the Legion of the Fallen Angels and Satan, when you leave your earthly shells. I ask you: How dare you take the life of these little ones? You call yourselves doctors, in your world, but I tell you, you have defamed your profession. You are worse in your dealings than the butchering murders of the Third Reich in World War II, who murdered almost three quarters of the world's Jewish population.

"Hitler found his place as a major demon among the Legions of Satan - shall you too gain Satan? You seek to speed the hand of punishment upon you. I cannot hold My Son's hand back from descending much longer. There must be much prayer; the Rosary holds back the Warning, but it will soon come upon you, and the Great War, the Miracle, and then sadly the ending of all as you now know it, The Chastisement. The Ball shall descend from your atmosphere and shall destroy all that is left at that time upon your earth.

"My child, this is today's Message."

****

August 22, Monday, Feast of the Queenship of Mary Immaculate, 1:00 – 2:00 AM

Our Lady is all aglow in a blue radiance [of] white and gold colors. Her feet are bare.

"My child, today's Message will be short. Women and men of the world, how many times must I counsel you on the evils of Pornography? When a man reads and views this impure immoral trash, he begins to form motor images of the same thing happening in real life. Much the same is the action of the thoughts of a female who views the books. This is one of the major evils which will bring the Chastisement upon you. You wallow in sin. Come out of the darkness now, while you still can. You are under the dark hand of Satan. You must pray and, as such, move into the Light of My Son, Your Lord and God, Jesus Christ.

"Goodbye now, My son. Pray your Rosary" She is wearing Her usual clothing of blue.

****

August 27, 1983, Saturday, Feast of St. Monica, Widow, 3:00 -3:30 AM

The Angel of Death is among you, My children. He walks not only in your country, the United States, but also among all of the other nations in your world. Should you not all pray much now, he will seek to obtain more control on your world than he already has. He seeks to gain the complete control of the City of the Papal Throne, Rome. He seeks to spread his evil errors until everyone in the world will be of the Religion of the Beast.

"Full power of the Abyss is behind Exterminatus now, just as behind Lucifer himself. Do not question the power of these two major demons of Hell, Exterminatus and Lucifer himself, but pray instead that you will not fall prey to their evil intentions.

"If mankind would stop the mass murder of the miniature ones, then a time of peace would be granted through the Father to the world. Your country seeks to be the Peace Keeper in your world. You are told very little of the actual thinking of your government in your nation towards the wars on the foreign battlefields. Pray constantly a vigil of prayer. Pray that the effect of these foreign wars does not increase and make need for more of your country's children to be sent to the foreign fields of war. Mothers and Fathers, do not allow your children to go to these battlefields. If they go they will not return to you the same. Many will die and those who do not will not be able to lead a normal life anymore, due to the rigors of war.

"You must not allow your children to indulge in Rock music, for Rock, Acid Rock, and Light Rock are all music from the Abyss. I have counseled you all many times before on what to do when you have these types of recorded music in your home. You must unreel or erase all tapes that you own containing this type of noise that you call music. The plastic recording known as records must be cracked or otherwise destroyed as well.

"My child, pray now. Goodbye."

****

1983, Fourth Quarter Messages

Upon the hour of 3:00 I am awaiting a vision from Our Lady and Her Son, Tuesday, November 15, 1983. The feast of St. Albert the Great, Bishop and Doctor of the Church.

Now the sky blue color of the wall is beginning to dissipate into a variation on the usual appearance of the portal of Mary Our Queen and Mother. The portal is encompassing the complete and whole wall. Now, I see white and can very faintly hear the angels singing within the portal. There is now a figure that is coming forward. As yet I cannot make out who the figure is, but he is dressed in a flowing robe of solid Kelly green, trimmed on the edge with gold foiling or gold leaf of some type. He is carrying a shepherds staff made of solid wood.

Now, I can see he is about to speak: "You have not mentioned that I am brown haired with a beard and that I am bare footed. I am St. Joseph. Did you not recognize me?

"Yes, my little one, you will bring children forth in a tight situation in your future. You are wise to test me by a question that you think, but do not speak. You will have to test more often the spirits who come in this way to you. You must no longer leave the staff down on the ground. You must pick it up and fight off the wolves who surround daily the sheep whom you were sent to help shepherd, My Son's sheep.

"You have not been heeding your dreams in the past few weeks. Had you heeded your dreams when you saw the people of the battlefield, you should have prayed, and thus have saved many lives. Many of the young men you saw begging for prayers could have been saved had you but prayed for them. Many died and were claimed only through the prayers of others, but your prayers could have put them back into health and life as well as our having been able to claim them for My Son's Kingdom.

"Some of your dreams had requests for these prayers and the others were for prayers for the release of certain souls from Purgatory. You have been lax in your prayers. Yes, the list of those that you must pray for is long, but you must pray it anyway.

"I will not be here often on visits for the guidance in the Mission, but you may request for my aid in your prayers.

"Goodbye son, heed your Queen now. Goodbye."

Now St. Joseph has stepped back into the portal and has begun the backward floating process. Our Mother, Most Holy, Queen of All, is now coming out of the portal. She is dressed in a dazzling dress like garment, more like a queenly gown. The color is like the bluish sparkle of a diamond; a very light blue, like the dawn sky in spring on a cloudless day. The gown is inlaid with a border of golden foil trim about the edges. The mantle is pure white. She is wearing a sash of which seems to be made of golden links. This She has about Her waist. She is speaking now in a very soft, sweet and queenly voice.

"My little one, you must pray more often. My children, the world shall soon undergo great turmoil and the sins of abomination shall be a major leading cause (the first leading cause which is abortion) for the outbreak of the Third World War.

"My children, pray that the Syrians do not set themselves alongside the Red Bear of communism for if such an alliance occurs it will be devastation for most of the world. I do not mean to say that there is no alliance already existing, yet the War Treaty Alliance that the Bear seeks with Syria must be prayed out of existence before it is completed, for if the two join forces the Key of War will be turned. If the two do not find equal ground together in a War Treaty Alliance, then the Key of Peace may be found in Syria.

"You have been given many signs of this ending soon to come - ending of your era as you know it. You will hear rumors of war, but you must not go to war physically. Go in spirit through prayer and sacrifice. You must pray that the wars end and that the major world-destroying war does not happen, for three quarters of your nation then will be destroyed. Those who do go to fight on the foreign soils, many shall not return. Your President can send forces under the Title of Peace Keeping Forces (Marines, Army, Navy, Air Force) but what will bring actual peace, We hear many of you ask? Peace is Love of God, Nation, Fellow Man, and

Prayers, Most of all Prayers.

"You must not continue to sin without repentance. You ask what sins We in Heaven refer to? The sins of Impurity, Carnality, Abortion, Murders, Homosexuality, leaving all manner of Virtue behind.

"My children, your nation will soon be in grieving, for a representative of it shall soon be killed. Prayers must be said for all government leaders.

"My little son, Jesus is coming now, so heed well His Message both His public and His private one.

"Goodbye, My little son."

Now She slipped into the portal and vanished into a pink type luminescence from which Jesus now is coming forward. He is in a tan colored or possibly ecru or off white colored garment, through the brightness of the light I cannot tell accurately which color that the tunic He is wearing is. He has long hair which is brownish in color, but the light emanating from within Him is causing His hair to look like it has streaks of flaming red within it. Now He is beginning the Message.

"My children, you must heed the Messages of My Mother in the past. Heed them and obey the requests She has made. For if you do not, My Hand will come down.

"Goodbye, My son."

****

(This Message is given out of sequence. We thought it was important and, therefore, it is given ahead of the other Messages, at Mary's request.)

December 7, 1983, Feast of St. Ambrose, Bishop and Doctor, 3:00 PM, Eve of the Immaculate Conception of Mary (Message with description placed afterwards)

Our Blessed Mother: "The iniquities of the nations are exceedingly great. Soon the nations shall be filled with the blood of those who create the abominations of iniquities and perversions.

"Many among you believe that the Lord is not God, and that He does not see the errors of today's modern ways of sin. His eyes do see the evils and He shall not spare thee and have pity on thee much longer! His hand is coming slowly down upon you, and when it strikes, the destruction shall be great.

"Mankind, in his evil ways, has provoked the Wrath of The Father in the past, and not only the Father do you provoke, but also the Holy Spirit of Life, and My Son Jesus. You now provoke the Wrath of the Triune Godhead, and I cannot hold back this Wrath of God the Trinity back from coming upon you much longer.

"Prayers, My children, prayers, I beg of you now as your Mother and Queen, pray unceasingly, offering your entire day as a prayer. Catholics, pray the beads of prayer I gave to you all so long ago. There is very little time left for this prayer, for you have waited far too long. I grow weary in My travels between the nations. So few listen to Me. O Woe! What great numbers of souls shall be lost now? And Why? Because mankind refused to listen to Me. I warned you all with ample time for change from the mountains of La Salette. Did you heed Me? No. Again I warned in Marienfried and at Lourdes, again at Fatima and many other places. Did you heed Me? No. I have come to many other places as well, but have I been heeded? No.

"I now will tell you, My child and children, of the latter days, the Secret Mystery of the Five Special Blessings given upon the Rosaries I Blessed to be sent out. These are the blessings mentioned to you on February 14th.

(1) The first Grace is that I personally will come to the bedside of the people who die that have prayed but one complete Rosary on these beads... with true devotion in their hearts. I will assist them in the trials of death and I will claim their soul before My Son saying: "I Love It." Thus that soul will not, even with mortal sin, end earthly life in Hell (Note: This does not mean that one would not spend many years in Purgatory for unforgiven sin.).

(2) The second Grace is that if one continues to pray and meditate each day on the Mysteries, they will attain close to perfect faith.

(3) They whom are prayed for will have a better chance of finding cures and conversions that will last.

(4) The fourth Grace is for the souls in Purgatory. Every time a complete Rosary is said in their name, on these specially blessed beads, a soul from the lower recesses of Purgatory will be raised to the stage of Purgatory that lies just before entrance into Heaven. Here they will await the First Friday after they have been raised, and will then enter Heaven.

(5) Those who pray on the beads, 15 decades every day and wear (along with praying the beads) the brown and green scapulars will find that they will almost always have close to perfect health, and if they are already sick, they will find a gradual cure of their illness, if it is not a God-sent type of illness meant as a cross.

These, My children, are the Five Graces.

"My child, I am going to answer the questions that you are now requesting of Me. You will not place the questions in writing. Only the answers will you place upon this Message's written form.

Answer #1- Yes, within your own judgement you may do so.

Answer #2 - She may do so, but she will remain nonsexual in the new relationship until the death of her previous husband. She can marry, but should she have sexual contact to this man prior to the death of her previous husband, for this reason: She was faithful to him, he left her and now she is alone with a child. A man may be found who is willing to accept her as a nonsexual woman and then only may she marry. Should she have sexual contact to this man, prior to the death of her first husband, then she will be guilty of adultery in the eyes of Heaven. Only after the death of the last husband is she not guilty of adultery if she has sexual contact. Her life will be hard, but this is the cross We have placed upon her. Tell her to offer the sufferings of her loneliness up as a sacrifice for the Holy Father and the souls in Purgatory.

"There are many other questions you have, My child.

"You will, my child, continue to pray for those who request your prayers.

"Yes, My Son Jesus will bless those who pray daily the Rosary.

"Yes, The Warning shall be soon.

"Yes, the answer you gave the man who requested to know about the New Age Movement was correct. They are anti-religious and are supported majorly by the American Communist Party.

"No, My child, the Messages shall not cease in the near future.

"One more question only shall be answered. Yes, you may do as your assistant requested; have the major mailing in Illinois, provided that you are mailed the letters of those who request prayers from you. And you may give guidance to some people who request it. However, you must not forget to pray to the Holy Ghost.

"My beloved little son, you shall now hold up your Rosary, for I wish to place an additional small blessing upon it. Now, My son, you will pray as I am leaving, the "Ave Maria" very slowly.

"Farewell for now."

Our Mother came to me at 3:00 PM on December 7th and She was dressed in a white gown with a blue sash and [a] gold, very thin, belt just below the sash. Her mantle was sky blue and was trimmed all about the edges in gold, about ¾ inches, as a border. Her wooden Rosary was beautiful. It had large wooden beads. Her hair was hidden beneath Her mantle and it did not show. This is how she looked today on December 7. 1983.

****

This is the Message given to a privileged soul on the Eve of Christmas, 1983, by the Blessed Virgin Mary and the Lord Jesus, and Prayers of St. Michael.

Our Mother has come now and is coming towards me.

She is saying: "Be silent, My little one. Write of how I look and do not speak. Write the Message and do not speak, as this will clue those about you to know that you are seeing a vision of some kind. They would question you, and you would be unable to tell them, in order to keep your identity closed secret, as a Seer of Heaven for mankind. Describe now, My son."

Our Queen is dressed in blue completely except for Her feet; upon Her feet She has on a pair of, I would say, slippers. They are made of an animal-flesh type material, and they are an off-white or ecru color. Mary, Our Queen and Mother, is wearing upon Her waist a golden colored girdle or belt, made of miniature golden links. Upon Her head She is wearing a mantle, which is a light blue, or sky-blue color. Her dress, or tunic, is a sky-blue also, tonight. Her robe is a deep blue, a navy blue, like in brand new blue jeans, Our Mother's hair does just barely show through the mantle She is wearing tonight. Her hair is a light brownish color, and ohh, Her face, because it is shadowed, was hiding from me the fact that Oh, She has been crying. Mary looks to be about thirteen or fourteen years of age tonight, and She is the most beautiful that 1 have ever seen Her, this evening. Her robe is blowing in the wind tonight and Her cheeks are quite a rosy color.

You see, even with my being inside the building, on the physical plane of existence, She is in the spiritual plane of existence where there are no walls to surround Her and keep the cold wind from blowing about Her. Now She is aglow with a bright luminescence which is very warm. Oh, the wind is no longer striking at Her robes so fiercely. She is aglow with light, like a miniature sun. The equivalent of a summer breeze is all She now has reaching to Her through this ball of light which is emanating from within Her.

Now Our Holy Mother is lifting from upon Her side Her Rosary. The Rosary is a clear crystal that is sparkling with dazzling colors, and it has a golden linking between the beads. This set of links between each bead is so shiny that it shows no traces of any other metals; it is pure gold. The crucifix is of wood, a light colored wood, which now Our Lady has in Her small hands. She is lifting it up to kiss it, and now She is making the Sign of the Cross in a manner as if She was blessing someone or something. The blessing, I have a feeling, it will be explained later in the Message. She is nodding, 'Yes.' The Crucifix is now raised and glowing.

"In the Name of the Father, and of the Son, and of the Holy Ghost, Amen."

Now She is ready to speak, for She has said: "Repeat in print now."

"My child, I cry for the state of the world. The wars and the destructions shall not cease, but rather they shall continue to grow. And "Why must this be?" you ask of Me, My little one. It is because man refuses to hear Me. Because man does not listen, and because of mankind's sins, Wars are punishment for mankind's sins. Mankind must pray and pray continuously, and not in the future, but now, not tomorrow. When the wars come to your shores, you will not be able to resist them in your present state of worldly affairs.

"At this time in your country, very few possess the ability to resist a full-scale attack upon your shores. At the time when this comes, there shall be few with weapons of protection upon your land. Without your prayers, My children, they will come upon you, and the destruction to your once-proud nation, the Eagle, or United States, shall be great! How many great destructions must there be before you will realize what is now happening about you? There have been many in your lands, and you now have still to come upon you, the destructions I have, in the past, spoken of. Never has the Father allowed mankind to be so sinful for so long of a time without sending upon you a major destruction. Remember Sodom, the city of sin. Its eventual sudden destruction had been warned of, but man did not heed. Fire rained from the sky, and so it shall be in your day, as the Father, and My Son, send down this Wrath, and the destruction is great upon you.

"My blessing, My little one, was given upon the Message. My blessing will be given to all, as they read the Messages that I give to you now.

"War approaches and it is closing now, to [the] time when there will be no peace upon your earth! Prayers, My children, prayers; this is all I ask of you – Prayers and Sacrifices. Remember to pray your Rosary, and don't just 'lip-service' the prayers, but concentrate upon the Mysteries. Also at this time, there must be many Litanies and Prayers of Petition said for My Son's Church and the souls in Purgatory.

"Now, My child, the blessings will be given to yourself and your assistants in the Mission to find the Litanies I will request you send out with the Messages, because these Litanies have been forgotten by most upon earth now.

"You will also print the simple Prayer of St. Michael, and you will receive a prayer to two other Saints tonight, as well. My child, await My Son now; I will be leaving now."

Now the light about Our Queen and Mother is growing a deep blue and She is now beginning to rise directly through the roof, and Ohh, as She is going, a deep pink light is now coming through the ceiling; it is a very bright light. Now Jesus is coming out of the light's brightness, or I should say, He is dimming the brightness down a bit about Himself, so I can see Him clearly.

Now Jesus's robe is a burgundy color of red. It's like a velveteen type of a felt. His hair is a reddish-brown in color and is flowing down on His back. It is also being wafted gently in the wind blowing about Him in the Spiritual World. Now His tunic is an ecru or whitish color, and it looks also to be of a shade close to beige. He is wearing nothing upon His feet and He is a very stern looking (but loving still) God tonight. I feel so peaceful every time I have Jesus's presence near to me. He is so peaceful, yes peaceful! How I wish everyone could see and feel what I am seeing and feeling now.

Now His lips are not moving but, as I watch Him now, I can hear His words:

"'My children, you have now in your world many sickly minds. Mankind uses the word 'insanity' for those who are committing acts against society, but he [mankind] does not realize that sin, in any form, is pure insanity. I am a Just God, but I warn you now My Hand is coming down and the destruction shall be great. Mankind has been warned and warned, but he refuses to listen. Soon, in his arrogance, it will be too late for you to even hold back the time of this punishment.

"I will say this: in some small, areas it is getting better, yes, but then on the over-all the balance is too far tipped towards Luciel's reign on your world. When this happens, that he takes the throne, know that My Coming again is near. You, upon the earthly plane of existence, have allowed the United Nations to be used against you by letting the serpent into the United Nations. The United Nations are now at each other's on every issue they discuss.

"My children, you all were once told Syria was the leader or 'stopper' for the beginning of the Third World War. Now I tell you again, be watchful of the actions in the area of Egypt, Palestine, Syria, and need I continue the list? Palestine shall flow with blood. Lebanon shall flow in young blood! You must pray now, for your sons are dying, not for your own country, but for a war which shall break out, with them there, or not, if you do not all pray now.

"My child, heed My Mother's instructions on Prayers. Await now, St. Michael.

"Goodbye, My son, and all My children of earth."

Now as Jesus is going up into the roof and vanishing, He says: "In the Name of the Father, and of the Son, and of the Holy Ghost."

He is gone now, and I hear a voice, and only see a brightness before me, which has wings like St Michael's, protruding from it. Oh, it is St. Michael in the form of light surrounding him. I was unable to view him.

He says: "Do not bother with a description now, my little one. I must speak to you now of a prayer. You will invoke St. George in this way."

A New Litany of St. George

Lord, have Mercy on us. *Christ, have Mercy on us.* Lord, have Mercy on us. Christ, hear us. *Christ, graciously hear us.* God, the Father of Heaven, *have Mercy on us.* God, the Son, Redeemer of the world, *have Mercy on us.* God, the Holy Ghost, *have Mercy on us.* Holy Trinity, One God, *have Mercy on us.*

Holy Mary, *pray for us.* St. Joseph, *pray for us.* St. Michael, *pray for us.* St. Benedict, *pray for us.*

St. George, Thou who drove out the serpent-dragon, *pray for us.*
St. George, Full of Patience, *pray for us.*
St. George, Most Just, *pray for us.*
St. George, Most Prudent, *pray for us.*
St. George, Most Courageous, *pray for us.*
St. George, Protection against the dragon, *pray for us.*
St. George, My Protector, *pray for us.*
St. George, Guardian of Cities, *pray for us.*
St. George, Guardian of virgins, *pray for us.*
St. George, Guardian of the sickly, who were caused so by Satan, *pray for us.*
St. George, Terror to the demons, *pray for us.*
St. George, Protection for Holy Church, *pray for us.*
St. George, Illuminated from On High, *pray for us.*
St. George, Silent and eloquent, *pray for us.*
St. George, Shining, as a Star, into Eternity, *pray for us.*
St. George, Learned Expounder- of Mysteries of God, *pray for us.*
St. George, Fragrant blossom of Heaven's Garden, *pray for us.*
St. George, Powerful in word and work, *pray for us.*
St. George, Refuter of Luciel's Errors, *pray for us.*
St. George, Model of Holy Death, *pray for us.*
St. George, Solid rock of Hope and Help, *pray for us.*
St. George, Mighty Defender of the Faith, *pray for us.*
St. George, Bright Mirror of Temperance, *pray for us.*
St. George, Protector of the Persecuted, *pray for us.*
St. George, Unshakable Pillar of Fortitude, *pray for us.*
St. George, Defender of Justice, *pray for us.*
St. George, Trumpet of Eternal Salvation, *pray for us.*
St. George, Conqueror of Devils, *pray for us.*
St. George, Companion of Angels, *pray for us.*
St. George, Protector of those who invoke thine aid, *pray for us.*
St. George, Cherished by Jesus, *pray for us.*

Lamb of God, who takest away the sins of the world, *spare us, O Lord.*
Lamb of God, who takest away the sins of the world, *graciously hear us, O Lord.*
Lamb of God, who takest away the sins of the world, *have mercy on us, O Lord.*

Pray for us, St. George, *that we may be made Worthy of the Promises of Christ.*

Let us pray: O God, who has sent St. George to remove the devil-dragon from breathing out his pestilence upon the city, send him again upon earth to cast out Lucifer from our cities, as in the days of old. Answer, for us, the petitions we send up to You through St. George, our Intercessor. Amen'

(End of Litany of St. George).

St. Michael, (still speaking): "Now, my child, we - will you please recite with me my Prayer for the benefit of those who do not know it."

> "St. Michael, the Archangel, defend us in battle;
> be our defense against the Wickedness and snares of the devil.
> May God rebuke him we humbly pray;
> and do Thou, O Prince of the Heavenly Hosts,
> by the Divine Power of God, thrust into Hell Satan,
> and all the evil spirits who wander throughout the world,
> seeking the ruin of souls. Amen."

"Now, my child, the Prayer to St. Gabriel:"

> "O Blessed Archangel, St. Gabriel, we beseech Thee,
> do Thou intercede for us at the Throne of Divine Mercy in our present necessities;
> that, as Thou didst announce to Mary the Mysteries of the Incarnation,
> so through Thy prayers and patronage in Heaven, we may obtain the benefits
> of the same, and sing the Praises of God,
> forever in the Land of the Living. Amen."

"My child, you will now gather as many Litanies as it is possible to find, and print them out, in with the future Messages.

"Goodbye, My child."

Now St. Michael has vanished.

****

Messages given to a privileged soul by Our Lady and an angelic Messenger, Feast of the Holy Innocents, Eve of the Holy Family, December 28, 1983, 11:00 PM

I had been sleeping, and it is about 11:00. An Angel has come to me and has shaken my bed until I have awakened.

He has now said unto me: "Awaken, little one, it is nearly time to see the Queen of Creation. The Mother of All is coming now from Heaven to give you a Message."

At these words I sprang from my bed and opened the door of my closet to look for my pad of paper and my pen. Thus I now have [a] written account of what has happened tonight so far. Now I am awaiting Our Mother Mary. Now the Angel is saying: "Behold, the Queen of All Creation is here."

Now the space in the room on the side of my bed is becoming luminescent with bright sparkles of white light. Our Lady is radiating light from within Herself and, truthfully, She is the "Lady Clothed With The Sun," as mentioned in the Apocalypse of St. John the Apostle. Now Our Mother is pointing downward to Her feet. She is standing upon the Serpent and its head is beneath Her feet.

She says: "One day, with enough prayer, I will crush this Serpent's proud head. You will be instructed, in the future, to have a medal cast. The details of this medal will be given to you in the future. You also may be given instructions as to where to have the medal cast at.

"Describe Me now, My child."

Now the serpent (beneath Our Lady's feet) has disappeared from beneath Her feet and Her bare feet are hovering just above the cold floor. She has on a blue robe, white tunic, blue mantle, and a golden-link belt about Her waist. The edges of the mantle and Robe are trimmed in an outline of what looks like a 1/4 inch solid yellow gold trim of foil. She is very beautiful.

Now She is beginning to speak: "I have come tonight, My children of the World, for this reason: to warn of five deaths if there is not enough prayer. Senator Kennedy of Massachusetts must have much prayer said for him now, and in the near future. He has been instructed by many Seers in the United States, that if [he] does not change his opinion on a certain issue, that he would follow in the steps of his brother John, who is now here, over the veil with us. Very soon he will encounter a brief illness which will come upon him suddenly. This shall pass before the public reads this December 28, 1983, Message in print. After this time, there must be much prayer said for him, or else he shall be removed from among you. All of you must pray that this does not happen.

"Your President - there must be many prayers said for him because there is a plan for his removal.

"In England there is a plan for the assassination of Elizabeth, the Queen, and Her Son, Charles. You must pray, as well for Your Holy Vicar in Rome, along with all the Cardinals, Bishops, and Priests. Your Vicar is in danger even in the city of Rome.

"My children, you must pray your Rosary every day. Prayers only will save you all now. There is nothing else that can. When the ones under the wing of the Adversary come forward and assassinate these I have mentioned, you will have a World War. These attempts, with enough prayer, will never happen, but without prayer, the deaths are immanent, by assassination. The forces of Antichrist are gathering now.

Now Our Lady is vanishing, and as She is vanishing in the puff of white light, She is saying: "Pray the Rosary. In the Name of the Father, and of the Son, and of the Holy Ghost. Amen." Now She is gone.

The Angel is still beside me and he is saying: "You will be receiving another Message on the 31st of December; be ready, for it will be your Lord and God coming to you."

Now the Angel has vanished, and all is as it was before.

****

New Year's Eve, Eve of the Feast of the Solemnity of Mary, December 31, 1983, 10:55 PM

I have skipped the description so as to go on to the actual Message itself.

Jesus: "My child, you will obey the Directives that have been given to you in the past. You have recruited a new worker. You do have permission granted to give your first name, for this person's personal knowledge. You will not give your last name at this time. My Mother, the Queen of All Holy Titles and Apparitions, will not be here tonight.

"Little son, you have a large Mission ahead of you, one in which I will ask you to follow all the instructions I give you without excuses or forgetfulness.

"I, your God, have found there are many flaws in your society. There are many who should never have been born, for the crimes they commit against the small ones of the world. The ones who force the kidnapped toddlers into sexual activities that are done painfully.

"Those who force these activities by starvation of the children until they submit, so they may eat! When they are fed, the food is treated with hormones and these hormones make the children's bodies have a natural desire for promiscuity. Through special hormones and drugs known as 'Pixie Drugs' in your world, these children develop adult-like, sexually deviant, child-sized bodies that will never grow to their full height or weight, due to the treatments they have undergone. They will be dwarfs with fully developed bodies. Those who do these foul crimes are guilty of one of the foulest crimes in the eyes of all Heaven, since pornography was first developed. These children are dwarfed purely for pornography. It would be better for these, that they were never born.

"I say unto you now, O perverse mankind, repent now before My Hand is forced to come down quicker than any expect. When My hand comes down upon you, the Chastisement will be great upon your earth. My children, there is only one thing to save your earth now: Prayer, Atonement, [and] Sacrifice. I am a Just God. I do not like to see fights and quarrels between My Creations. My children, quarreling over what Religion is the correct Religion is going to get you nowhere. All Christians must align themselves together for the battle against the Antichrist.

"My child, I will again be with you on January 4, 1984. You will describe My feet and tunic only, on January 4, 1984"

Jesus now has vanished.

****

1984 Messages

Eve of St. John Neumann, Bishop, Feast of St. Elizabeth Seton, In Honor of Blessed Andre Bessette, January 4, 1984, 11:00 PM

Jesus has now come into my room. He is wearing an ecru or tan colored tunic tonight. He is barefooted and the tunic He is wearing, almost covers His feet.

Now He is talking, but not through His mouth: "My child and My children, I have come to give a Message to the world about slavery. I, your God, created mankind: man and woman, both. I did not intend for man to subject women into slavery into foreign countries. The slavery I speak of, is prostitution slavery, where a woman is taken from her country and brought to another, to act, or dance, or sing, while in all actuality, they are brought to prostitution brothels where they are forced into prostitution. Every country in your world is guilty of this foul crime. In My eyes your world now is covered with this crime, and many others. It is in a state of sin worse than in the time of Noe, Sodom, and Gomorrah. You all know the fate of those times and those cities, so what then will you now expect for your cities of today? Do you expect anything less? I say unto you now, the destruction upon your world will be three times worse than most could imagine.

"Without sufficient prayer now in your world, sea shores will crumble, and earthquakes shall rock your lands. Waves will submerge many coastal cities. Many other cities shall have either extreme heat or flash-floodings. I ask you now: Is this what you want? Repent now, for soon I shall return, and when I do, it will be too late to go upon your knees. Now is the time for Prayer, Atonement, and Sacrifice.

"My child, you will retire into prayer the rest of this night until 1:30 AM. You must pray the Rosary, and the Prayers of St. Bridget, in honor of My wounds.

"All who read this will be blessed specially."

Now Jesus has vanished and I must pray.

****

Message given to a privileged soul (Michael) by Our Lady of All Holy Titles, Feast of St. Hilary, Bishop and Doctor, January 13, 1984

Our Lady: "My children, now in your world there must be extreme Prayer, Atonement, and Sacrifice. Now is when the final chance is present for this 'Time of Peace' to come about. Pray that your present Vicar in Rome does not have another attempt upon his life, for he is the key, along with Russia, Syria, and the United States, for World Peace. In your world now, there is a great evil force that has built itself up. You can, and must all overcome this evilness at this time, for it is the 'time' when, with prayer, will come the time I spoke of at Fatima. Peace eludes you, My children, only because not enough pray. I have personally asked your Vicar in Rome to begin now, a Mission of 'Peacekeeper' between the nations. Prayer is your weapon now, My children. Do not mock Us in disbelief, for then surely your days shall be shortened. Sadly many, not under Antichrist, still mock Us. Many do not realize that the truths that We reveal are for their benefit; instead, they mock Us in disbelief of Our appearances. Prayers, My children, Prayers must be said, and devoutly, not just be lip-service. Is this too much to ask of you, My children, when you consider what I have to offer to you?

"My child, you shall now add, among the Litanies and Prayers being typed, the Prayer for the Removal of the evil ones from among you whom have been returned to 'life' through the Witchcraft magic of Belial and those below him.

"Goodnight, My son."

(Belial is a major demon in Hell.)

Prayer for Removal of Those Returned to Life through Witchery

If the walking 'dead' (zombies) are encountered, and the prayer is read, be not surprised if the zombie-spirit vanishes and takes the body with it back to Hell. Prayer is more powerful than an exorcism against undead souls (those who died, yet still walk due to Voodoo).

"I tell you, in the Name of Jesus Christ, Be Gone. If thou are a Disciple of Satan, I am to tell you, in God's name to Be Gone, for there is only One God, the Lord, High God in Heaven. You will return to Hell and tell him these exact words that I have told you."

"In the Name of the Father, and of the Son, and of the Holy Ghost. Amen."

(You must say 'Holy Ghost' not 'Holy Spirit' for the prayer to work.)

Miraculous St. Joseph Prayer

(Protects from death by fire, by poison, by war, or suddenly.)

"O St. Joseph, whose protection is so great, so strong, so prompt, before the Throne of God, I place in you all my interests and desires.

O St. Joseph, do assist me by your Powerful Intercession and obtain for me, from your Divine Son all Spiritual Blessings, through Jesus Christ Our Lord, so that having engaged here below your Heavenly Power, I may offer my thanksgiving and homage to the Most Loving of Fathers.

O St. Joseph, I never weary of contemplating you, and Jesus asleep in your arms. I dare not approach while He reposes near your heart. Press him, in my name, and kiss His fine head for me. Ask Him to return the kiss when I draw my dying breath.

St. Joseph, Patron of departing souls, Pray for us."

Imprimatur: Bishop Geo. W. Ahr of Trenton, N.J.

****

Message given on Tuesday, January 31, 1984, 5:00 AM, Feast Day of John Bosco, Priest and Adorer of the Virgin Mother

I am awaiting Our Mother Mary. I was dreaming, and an Angel in my dream commanded me: "Awaken! The Virgin Queen has need of you. She will be here soon. You must prepare thyself. Be ready at 5: 00 AM."

Now I am awaiting Her. My Guardian Angel is so beautiful. He is dressed in a flowing bluish white Gown. He is barefooted, I think - No, I'm wrong; he has sandals on his feet. They are of a thin leather-like substance. Now, oh, he is pointing over to the right of the bedroom, and there is Our Lady. She is truthfully the Lady of the Light. I feel almost blinded to look at [the] Heavenly figure of light and beauty. She is dressed differently tonight. She is dressed all in white with a blue sash and mantle. Her Robe is trimmed in ¼ inch of gold foil about the edges of it. She is wearing the same sandals as was my Guardian Angel tonight, or I should say this morning. Upon Her head is the most beautiful crown, the Fatima crown. She is ready to speak now, because Her finger is at Her lips.

She is saying: "Hush, My little one, hush. Repeat (in print) what I say now to you.

"My child, and My children of the world, I have much to tell, of fact, at this time. There shall be a very predictable war in the near future. The Bear seeks to invade California. They also shall try to claim Alaska. However, with a Peace Plan, the Bear's leaders of Government (at this time) shall be lost in bloodshed. There shall be a Russian Revolution and Russia shall become a Monarchy again. The Czarina, Anastasia Romanov, must be returned to rule! If, and when, this occurs, along with the present Pope John Paul II, you will have peace in Russia, and it shall be converted. Then will come the Reign of My Immaculate Heart for a short time.

"The evil ones gather now to attempt to thwart the 'Return Plans' of the last remaining Monarch of the Bear's confines. The once proud nation that has become despoiled under communism must return to its former glory under My Son, and the Father, with the Holy Ghost. I do not say 'Spirit' for there are many Holy Spirits, but only One Holy Ghost.

"Yes, My son, it is possible that, one day, you may meet the Empress or Queen of Russia, (the Bear), when she is again in rule. Nicholas the II is in Heaven with Us. It is true that you may be 'looked to' as a source of guidance for the Elderly Queen in the future. You will beware now, My child, for many about you seek to stop you. One even believes you to be a Warlock who 'sees' the devil instead of Us.

"You, My child, must obey your dreams. Yes, the Angel did come to you and tell you that St. Monica wished for you to pray to her. The interpretation that you sought out was correct. She does wish to guide you, as she guided her son, St. Augustine. She shall be with you, My little son, at all times. Be sure to pray to her.

"You, My child, will seek back in the letters sent to you, for the one sent that called you by name. This was not sent by a Seer, but by a Spiritualist whom the Father did, in Truth, ask to write to you. The name used is, in truth, one of your spiritual names in Heaven. Our Seers upon earth have many names. They all, including thyself, shall learn them one day when it is their time to join Us over the Veil.

"My little son and My children, you will all have this instruction now:

"When you leave your homes you will say: "St. Michael, the Archangel, defend us in the battle; be our defense against the wickedness and snares of the devil. May God rebuke him, we humbly pray; and do thou, O Prince of the Heavenly Hosts, by the Divine Power of God, thrust into Hell Satan, and all the evil spirits who wander throughout the World, seeking the ruin of Souls. Amen."

"Then you will say: "St. Raphael and St. Gabriel, Pray for us."

"Good morning, and goodbye now, My son."

****

Message given to a privileged soul on Friday, March 2, 1984, Eve of First Saturday

Seer: Our Lady came before me today at about 12:00 Noon. She wore a white, gown-like, dress as tunic. Her belt was of a golden chain link weave. Her mantle was blue, along with Her sash. Upon Her head was a golden crown - the Fatima crown. Her Rosary was of wooden beads. Now the Message, itself is as follows:

Our Lady: "My child, you shall now add all the New York names you have, from the list given to you, onto your list. Those who respond positively to their first mailing, you will continue to mail to. Those who do not, you will drop from your list.

"Your suspicion is well founded, for Anastasia is not dead. No, I tell you, she is truly alive still. The true Anastasia has changed her name with the United States Government's help. The one who recently died was not Anastasia, who called herself Anna Manahan. No, she was only a double, who, with surgery years ago, was made to look like Anastasia Romanov. No, My child, I shall not give you her present name, as it might slip out at the wrong time. You, My child, have to talk. We cannot take this chance.

"My child, what I am next about to tell you, is for yourself, and the Centers of Scattered Light that help you at this time. It must not go to the public. (Pause.)

"My child and My children, there shall be another Message on Sunday, the Feast of the Transfiguration. Please be ready, My child, at 1:00 PM.

"My children, pray much for John Paul II; there is a foul plan in the works now for his removal. Russia, the Soviet Bear, is now led by one who, without prayer, will lead your world to worse times. Pray much, My children, for Anastasia, and her son, who are now in hiding with government protection. The Soviet K.G.B. and the United Communist Party of America were not to be fooled by the death of the 'decoy double'. Pray for the souls in Purgatory. Pray your Rosaries often, not just occasionally, at least once a day.

"Goodbye now, My child, and remember, be ready on March 4th, 1984 at 1:00 PM."

Our Lady then vanished, as a puff of white and blue light.

****

Sunday, March 4, Feast of Transfiguration Sunday, 1:00 PM

Seer: (at 12:55 PM) This day is not the day celebrated in the Catholic Church as the Transfiguration, however, at Our Mother's request we have titled this day's Message as the Feast of Transfiguration Sunday. The Catholic Church, however, celebrates this day in August.

At 12:59 3/4 PM there is a light now coming through the roof, and taking form.

At 1:00 PM Our Lady is before me, prompt and on time. She is wearing nothing upon Her feet tonight. I can see Her feet clearly. She has on a blue robe and a dazzling white gown. Her gown is embedded with glittering specks of some shiny material that are radiating out the light coming from Our Lady this afternoon. Her mantle is a blue with golden trim, as Her robe also has gold trim. Her face is shadowed, but She seems upset by something. Her Rosary is red tonight, completely red, but still of wood with crystal 'Our Father Beads'.

Now She is speaking. Our Lady: "My child, and My children, I have been greatly saddened today, as I must give a Message of great sorrow to Heaven and to My heart. My children, I have warned you to watch where your children go, and to not allow them anywhere alone, or unaccompanied, for Satan, Lucifer, seeks fresh victims, now for his altars.

"If you have sinned, go nowhere after dark, until you have had Confession and Penance. Those adults who are in the State of Grace have nothing to fear, for they are protected by the Angels, until they fall again to sin. Yet, as soon as they again seek My Son's Grace in Confession, they are again graced with the Angel's protection.

"In your country and Canada, now, the demons of Hell have gathered. They seek to cause many covens to do multiple human sacrifices on Ash Wednesday and Easter Sunday. Wear your Sacramentals that We have given to you, My child and My children.

"In your world we see a widespread murder of the infants. This must stop now before it is too late! Abortion is murder, My children, sons and daughters. If you do not wish to have children, then do not be so promiscuous. Sexuality was made for reproduction among yourselves, but it was not made for outside of wedlock. Yet, still you fornicate like animals in the wilderness. My children, there have been many councils on this in the past, and there shall be many more in the future.

"My child, you must beware of the one who seeks to stop you. This person, along with a false priest, and a power-hungry third person, seek to end the sending out of My Messages to you, in any way that they can. I will be with you again, My child, on March 7th, 1984, for the Feast of Ash Wednesday.

"Goodbye now, My child."

****

Message given to a privileged soul on Wednesday, March 7, 1984, Feast of Ash Wednesday, Eve of the Feast of St. John

Our Lady: "My child, you will not describe Me now, for I must speak quickly.

"My sons, among the Priesthood, the Hierarchy, Why are you not remaining Chaste? Have you not all taken the Vow of Chastity? Why do so many of you defect from your orders and the Priesthood in general? I tell you now: Once you are a Priest of My Son, you are a priest for life.

"You who leave your Parish, and your Orders: You have dropped the Staff to condemn Our children to the wolves about you all now. Pick up your Staff, My priests. Do not leave them behind; for, remember you are My Son's representatives, His Shepherds upon Earth.

"Pastors: Why do you not pray your Rosaries more often? Have you forgotten the Graces enclosed in these Beads of Prayer? They are numerous in number! Yet, still there are some, blessed and dear to Our Hearts, who do pray these beads I have given to you all. Promote the Rosary in your Churches, the Churches of My Son.

Ministers, Priests, Sisters and Brothers, All religions: You must all fight a common enemy in your world, this 'enemy' being abortion. Abortion is Murder, My children.

"My children of the world, those who hear My word, listen to Me now. I have begged for Prayer so many times, and how many heed My call? Too few, too few! Pray always, My children, in never-ceasing prayer. When you can't pray, or have not enough concentration, or think you are too busy, say: "My Jesus, I Love You; Help Me in My Life." He will hear your prayer, and He will bless you for it.

"My children, seek out your Holy Sacramentals now, for soon there will be none left in your stores. Beware of the satanic mark now being placed upon My Medal of Miracles, the Miraculous Medal. Do not accept ones with a bar beneath the Hearts on the Back of the Medal. The word 'Italy' is okay to have upon the Medal, My children, but the bar is not.

"My child, you will take one good look upon Me and then describe what I look like today. I must leave quickly, for I must appear in Spain soon. Yes, My child, I do grow weary of travel, for too few listen to Me.

"Describe, then say a Rosary."

Seer: Our Lady is wearing a dark blue mantle, dark blue robe, green cape, white tunic, or dress, and a golden belt upon Her waist. She has nothing upon Her feet now. She is barefoot. She was quite angry in the beginning of this vision, but now She is weeping and is very sad. How I wish we all could dry Her poor eyes.

She is saying: "Yes, My child, many of My statues do, truthfully cry tears of blood. Pray your Rosary now."

She is lifting Her Rosary's wooden crucifix and blessing me; now She is gone in a trail of whitish, blue light.

Now I must pray, as we all should pray.

****

Message given to a privileged soul on Sunday, March 18, 1984, Eve of the Feast of St. Joseph.

Our Lady: "My child and My children of the world, you must stop this continuous quarreling amongst yourselves. You all find flaws with your neighbors instead of working with your own flaws first. Racial slurs hurt My Son, as well as those they are spoken against. You all fight over who can lay [a] claim down that their race is more deserving of the lands than anyone else's race.

Our Lady: "My child, behold: There is an Indian Maiden before me, standing next to Mary. She looks familiar, however I cannot place her, as to where I would know of her from. Our Lady said: "Auriesville, New York." Now I know who she is - she is a Mohawk Princess named Kateri Tekawitha.

"Blessed Mother: Is she going to speak to me?" Our Lady: "Yes." "How will I understand her?"

Our Lady: "I will grant, at this brief time, the gift to understand tongues of other languages in your native English. This will be limited to, when in a vision to you, one of Us speaks, but not in English. Listen and repeat."

Kateri: "My life was as an American Indian. We were the original people to live on the North American Continent. We had no problem in most of our tribes with the English and French settlers moving in with us. However, soon they began laying claims on our lands. Next, they forced us off of our lands. The Western tribes had greater suffering, as the Buffalo were killed off by the pioneers. With them went the food and sheltering skins. The lands were soon poisoned with hatred between the tribes and the settlers and pioneers. Listen to me as I say that you must pray for yourselves and for your fellow mankind. The Father of Heaven and Creator of All has placed the sins of those days upon your generation to atone for, because your fathers and father's fathers were warned, but they did not obey the Bible. The Bible warned not to sin greatly without repentance. Did they listen? Do you listen?

"Please pray for all the American Indian Braves lost in those days due to the wars we were forced into fighting against the English and French. Pray for their souls as you pray for your own ancestors' souls. May God be lenient upon you all for a little longer. Goodbye."

Now Kateri has stepped behind Mary and has vanished. She is being replaced by a male figure dressed in light green. Oh, I know who that is. That is Saint Joseph's shape. Yes, it is him. He is now holding Jesus, the Divine Infant, in his arms. Now he is going to stand directly beside Mary. They look so regal together. Oh, now there are words appearing below them. T..H..E.. = The. H..O..L..Y.. = Holy. F..A..M..I..L..Y..= Family. The Holy Family.

Our Lady: "My child, do not be depressed in heart, for it is not your fault that your family is soon to be broken apart forever. Your earthly Mother and Father were not compatible for each other."

St. Joseph: "Do not place the blame for this upon either of them, without placing equal blame upon the other one. Both parties are equally at fault for leaving each other. I will look after and guard your Father from the snares of Lucifer; however, this does not mean that you should stop praying for him. My child, your answers to the questions in the letters sent you from the believers have been done very well."

Our Lady: "You, My child, will now begin using your complete name on letters that you answer. However, you will not put your name on the Message itself. Tell My children to pray the Rosary. It is not only a weapon, but also a solace for the sorrowing hearts of mankind when trials beset them.

"My children, too few of you know the true value of suffering. You can save many with your sufferings. Offer them for the souls in Purgatory. Only if you pray for them in this life, will you gain merit of others' prayers when you are in Purgatory.

"Goodbye, My child."

Now. Mary and Joseph, who is carrying Jesus, are vanishing in a puff of bright light.

****

Message given to a privileged soul on April 19, 1984, Holy Thursday, 11:45 PM, Eve of Good Friday and continued into AM on Good Friday, 12:55 AM

Jesus and Our Lady are both before me. The garments of Our Lady, except for Her veil, are all purple, which we know is the color that denotes suffering. The veil of Mary is like a dark blue, almost a navy blue. She has on slippers of a padded glass-like substance. They are also of a purple tint. Her Rosary is of large wooden Beads. Jesus is wearing a tunic which is off-white in color. His feet are bare. Jesus now is vanishing upward, leaving Our Lady behind, with me. As He is slowly rising He is speaking:

Jesus: "My child, you will repeat all you see and hear in the following scenes of My earthly life before I was put to death."

I see Jesus now sitting at a table. His disciples are with Him. "Mother, why do they not see Us?"

Our Lady: "It is because we are not truly in the past, My child. We are only viewing it, nothing more."

"How will I understand their speech?"

Our Lady: "Do you not remember about that? My child that already has been taken care of. Don't you remember when you spoke with Kateri?"

"Yes I do, Mother, and I apologize for questioning You in so rude of a way."

Our Lady: "Behold." Now a woman with brown hair is coming towards the Lord. She has a box made out of what looks like marbled gypsum of alabaster. Now this woman is opening it. The disciples of Jesus are now questioning her why she placed this fine perfumed ointment upon Our Lord. One in particular is saying now,

"To what purpose bring you upon us this waste? This might have fed many poor, had it but been sold." (Our Lady said this was Judas Iscariot.)

Jesus is saying something: "Why do you trouble this woman so? She hath wrought good works upon Me. Remember this, Judas - the poor there shall always be plenty of to be with you all. But I, you shall not have always. She, in anointing Me with this ointment upon My Body, hath done it to prepare Me for My burial. Amen. I say to you all now, wheresoever this Gospel be preached in the whole world, that which she hath just now done shall be told in memory of her name."

Judas, after listening to Jesus speak, is now looking very troubled. Now Judas is leaving the rest. This scene is fading away now. Now a new scene is forming. It is the night time. Jesus and the twelve are at a table. They are all eating around Jesus. He is now lifting His head to watch Judas dip with Him.

He is saying: "Amen, I say to you, one of you is about to betray Me."

In shock Judas has frozen for a few seconds. All the others are troubled now. They are saying: "Is it I?"

Jesus is saying: "He that in the dish dippeth his hand with Me, he shall betray Me. The Son of Man goeth indeed, for so it is written of Him. Woe to the man by whom the Son of Man shall be betrayed. It were better for him, had he not been born."

Judas: "Is it I, Rabbi?"

Jesus: "Thou hast said it."

Now the scene is fading away like the scene before it. Now I see Jesus descending into Hell. There is like a spot of land which has no fire on it, and here He is standing. There are many Holy Angels descending into the pit to guard Jesus now, as Satan and his evil angels are trying to pass them to throw themselves at Jesus. Now this scene is fading.

Our Lady: "My children, you must pray the Rosary and attend your Churches. You must pray for your schools and for your government leaders. Be aware of what is now going on in your government and in your schools. See what happened in Poland in the schools. Do you want your child to be sent home, expelled from school, for having a crucifix on his or her neck? Pray hard, for many things in your land shall soon change."

"Beware on the Sea Shores this May."

Now Our Lady is saying Goodbye as She is placing Her hands in the prayer stance.

Our Lady: "You will forget this Message until Saturday."

****

Saturday, April 21, Holy Saturday into Easter Sunday, 11:50 till 1:25 AM

Now I have not included how Our Lady looks today because it is the same as She looked on Thursday. She is speaking now.

Our Lady: "Behold, and describe."

Now I'm viewing again the vision of Jesus in Hell; but now He is in pure white and a gleaming golden belt is about His waist. He has begun to rise now, and the scene has vanished.

Now Our Lady is speaking again. "My child, you have just viewed the Resurrection, a scene that not many have ever seen. You will now keep the rest of the Message a secret at this time, My child. You will not even relay it to the workers. Take heed to My words because We do not wish to place more burdens on your shoulders than already We have allowed you to have."

(Our Lady was crying all during the Message of Saturday, April 21, 1984)

****

Message given to a privileged soul by Our Lord, Our Lady, and other Heavenly Messengers, June 17, Sunday, Feast of Trinity Sunday, 10:50 PM till Monday, 1:00 AM

Seer describes the beginning scene of the Heavenly Visions: Descending down, through the sky outside, and all around, even into the room I am in is a deep blue colored set of light, intermixed with a shade of light sky blue. The lights are now coming to settle into one spot, directly before me now. Now I can see Our Lady. She is beautiful. She is in the garb of Our Lady of Graces of the Immaculate Conception.

She says: "My child, tonight you will have two new friends from our Heavenly Choir. The First is Mary Ann Van Hoof Hirt. She has come to bring to you a great request to bring her words of guidance to both 'Ray's' at My Shrine in Necedah, Wisconsin. The Second is Mama Rosa Quatrini. They will now speak to you, My child."

Seer: Before me now, joining Our Lady, are four figures, and one I recognize. He's really large and handsome! That is, of course, if an angel can be called handsome. In Heaven the Saints call him, 'Golden Boy' as a nickname. His glow is as that of the Sun, only brighter. With him is St. Francis of Assisi, the companion of Mary Ann at Necedah. He too is enveloped in a glow, only his is transparent, like white light.

Mary Ann and Rosa are veiled in a bright pink light, and their vestments are so beautiful! Both of them are dressed in white robes which have golden trim on the border of the neck, ankle line, and sleeves. Mary Ann now is coming forward. I should note one thing other - she looks years younger than any recent pictures show her as looking.

She is speaking: "I know you are thinking: "Here is one whose Mission was greater than mine", but you are wrong. Your mission is equally important as is the Mission of every Seer that the Father, or the Queen of Heaven, have started. You must listen closely now as I wish you now to write to Ray P. and Ray H. at Necedah. You will tell them that I have requested of you that you direct them to reprint, and send out, the 1981, May 28, June 14, July 16, and October 7, 1981 Messages. I wish all on the mailing list to again hear Our Lady's words, as there is much that many still need to hear. Much of that information is contained in those four Messages. Now you will listen to Rosa. Also, don't worry, as Rosa speaks her Italian. It will be translated in sound for you."

Rosa: "Make known the fact that the waters of the Fountain Well are truly miraculous. The waters will bring many cures in the Faithful who use them. Dear children of our Holy Mother, go back and read some of the Messages given to me by Our Queen and Mother. Goodbye."

Seer: Now that they are vanishing, Jesus is coming to join Our Lady, St. Francis, and St. Therese. He is dressed in the usual garments, (so I will not explain His looks anymore). St. Francis now is saying something.

St. Francis: "We now need many new vocations to the religious life. Pray much that these vocations come into existence, for I cannot stress enough how they are needed."

Seer: He and the two ladies have now vanished from the area.

St Michael says: "My children of earth, you must read and re-read the past Messages from all the true Seers. You have not prayed enough to even-off the scales."

Seer: St. Michael is now holding the scales and they are heavily tipped to the left. They must be evened somehow.

St. Michael: "Many do not wish to believe the Messages, due to their own vanity. My children of earth, I tell you now, you have little time left. The Horn is ready to be blown, and then the Warning shall be upon you.

"In the past, We warned you that there would be many minor Chastisements in your nation and on foreign soils as well. From East to West, North to South, your nation has been minor-Chastisement struck. Without prayer, conditions that are already bad, will get worse. I shall list just eight minor amounts of the unpleasantness you have brought upon your nation through sin:

      1.) Eight inches of snow in Aspen Colorado in mid-June, 1984.
      2.) Winter Park, Colorado: 23 degrees (temp.) in June, 1984.
      3.) Denver and Lakewood, Colorado: softball size Hail in mid-June, 1984.
      4.) Kansas and Illinois: heavy rains and flooding, June, 1984.
      5.) Nebraska: dust storms stop traffic, mid-June, 1984.
      6.) 81 miles per hour winds in Minnesota, mid-June, 1984
      7.) Mid-June, 1984, 50 tornadoes, 29 in North Dakota alone.
      8.) Vermont: Flooding, mid-June, 1984
      9.) Connecticut: Flooding, mid-June, 1984
      10.) Massachusetts: Flooding, mid-June, 1984
      11.) Nebraska: Flooding, mid-June, 1984

"Many more things have happened; however, you must pray now, many times a day, or the list shall grow, My children of the world. My child, Jesus now wishes to speak to you, and through you, to the world.

"Goodbye now."

Seer: St. Michael now has vanished and Jesus is coming forward.

Jesus: "My son and My children, I tell you now, you must pray hard for your world leaders. There is a plan enroute from Libya to remove your President, using Libyan-trained American terrorists. Not only is your President in danger, but also any who run against him in the forth-coming American election.

"Your Pope, Our Vicar upon earth, he too is in danger, especially between September 28, 1984, and January 1, 1985. Pray for him. Should you lose him, things can do nothing then but get worse.

"My son, pray now one Ave and one Gloria."

****

Message given to a privileged soul by Our Lady, August 6, 1984, Feast of the Transfiguration of Our Lord Jesus Christ

Our Lady: "My child, you shall be visited by two saints whom you shall not be able to see with your eyes tonight.

"They will be invisible to your eyes, yet their work through you will be quite visible, as they guide your hand in sketching a Map of the World Land Masses, and then indicate, in red, the position of all of the submarines carrying Submarine Launched Ballistic Missile, from Russia, or from Red China. Also you will be indicating, in blue, the position of all of NATO"s SLBM launching submarines.

"You will, My child, by this map, be quite surprised as you see the great number of submarines now surrounding much of the world. My child, you will now allow Saint Francis and Saint Maria to use your hands for the sketch. It shall be quick, and it shall be simple. I will rejoin you shortly."

Seer: I was amazed by the Map that St. Francis de Sales and St. Maria Goretti used my hands to draw. Our Lady now wishes me to repeat after Her, in print:

Our Lady: "My child, you shall not find the last Message that I gave to you. You were given warning not to leave it in your possession; however, you did not listen to Me. If you had mailed it, as I had requested you to do, you would not have lost it in your last move. The information from that Message, however, will be given out to you in future Messages. The Messages will be few, and slow in the near future, My child, as We cannot burden you with a cross larger than you can carry.

"My child, while I was on earth I suffered many times, yet never once did I complain. Just as such, should you be, in your life. Accept your small sufferings as a Grace because they are just that. You, My child, are afraid of suffering, but yet, you must suffer for others' salvation. There are many who have become Great Saints by their suffering.

"My children of the world, pray now, a series of Rosaries. Send them up as a solid link of prayer. Bead to bead, link to link, chain to chain, the prayers must go, until there is a Balance to the Scale again. The Scale, of which St. Michael carries, is almost irreversibly tipped to the left. It is now dangerously close to this point. Soon shall come the take-over, if you do not pray now.

"Goodbye for now, My child."

The circled x's are submarines of the USA and its allies. The x's are submarines of Russia and Red China.

****

Message given to a privileged soul by Our Lady and by St. Michael, August 19, 1984, 2:00 PM, Eve of Feast of St. Bernard, Abbot

Saint Michael is coming forward and he is wearing a green skirt-like piece of clothing about his waist, and has on a golden colored shirt of armored plates. In his left hand is the Scales. They are hung heavily to the left, and that means that evil is strong in the world at this time. In Saint Michael's right hand is a sword with a long, pointed at the tip, blade

Now the loud voice of Saint Michael is booming out in the Heavens and the words he is saying are almost too loud to be able to understand. Oh, now the words are reverberating softer so I can understand them.

St. Michael: "Repeat. my little one: '"Woe, Woe, Woe to the inhabitants of the earth; Woe, Woe, Woe! Soon, my little one, I shall go forth and bind down in the fires below all of the lesser demons of ages past. Shortly after this shall I, then, bind the Legion of Dark Angels themselves, also into the fires of Hell.

"My little ones of earth: I speak now to you all. I bring to you all a Message from the Father of All Creation. He demands that the people of your world stop sending back to Him the children that He gives to you.

"Doctors of the world: Many of you have used the knowledge given to you by the Father, for the intention of murderous acts of abortion and euthanasia. As such, you have chosen to no longer find face with The Father. You Doctors and Nurses, who perform abortions, know now that you have chosen the Dark Angel Lucifer as your Father of Death. Just as you now claim the earthly lives of children yet unborn, so shall Lucifer claim your souls in the end. Repent now, while you still have a chance, and you will again find face with the Father of Heaven, and you will be forgiven.

"Women of the world: The same goes for you. You must not kill your unborn children. Many of you are vipers. You go forth seeking all forms of carnality and pleasures of the flesh, then you are afraid to bear the child. If you continue in this procedure, you are guilty of murder, and without repentance, you shall be guilty of mortal sin at death, and Lucifer will be waiting for your soul to join his in the Kingdom of the Damned and Condemned.

"Goodbye, now."

Our Lady: "My child, your Pope will travel soon; be sure that all pray for him. He will be in need of many prayers. My child, remember the Poem Theresa gave you in 1983 during the month of March. The poem titled "Satan's Plans for John Paul II." This, My child, you shall now put in print again, for it is necessary.

"Pray now, My child, for I shall return in exactly one-half of an hour."

Satan's Plans for John Paul II - Pope

Your Holy Father must not come or go,
The danger before him, he does not know.

He must not, right now, in another country show,
Planned is an Ambush from the forces below!

Your Holy Father will deal with the anger never greater in any earth-age.
The Head, Luciel, shall attempt to turn his page!

Not only him, but all of the forces of Hell
But, with prayers, We will cause them to quell.

That day, for him, will begin as just any other,
Except for the entity that attempts to smother~

Everywhere along his travel will follow the Forces of Hell.
They shall attempt to attack him wherever he may dwell.

The attack may be by day among a big crowd,
Or by night, in a dwelling of which he'll be proud.

Daily now you must all remember to pray
That on the throne your Holy Father will stay.

Upon this Son our graces now all do fall
But you all must help him stand up real tall.

Unless you wish him under Satan to now fall.
Send all your prayers to Heaven to call.

Jesus will hear them with all Heaven too
Your prayers may save him as well as you.

Part Two of [the] Message:

Our Lady: "My child, you shall now be viewing the Image I wish to have placed on the front of My Medallion that shall grant many Graces to all. After a brief moment you will view the back of the Medallion. Then you will draw what you see, below, and have the Image struck somewhere.

"The Image must depict Myself standing upon a hilltop and the snake beneath My feet. I am to be with folded hands and I am to have My Rosary in My hands. There is to be a three-pointed crown upon My head. There are to be 14 rays of light emanating from My right side and 14 rays of light from My left side as well. Around Me are to be the words "Our Lady of All Holy Titles Pray for Us." On the back the Image is to be of the world. It is to depict the United States of America, and a dot will be where Connecticut is. The Image will have a crucifix upon the globe. Around the edge of the back will be the words "The Cross of Martyrs over the U.S. and the World."

"The front of the medal is to have a transparent blue plastic over the Image. The back will be either a stainless steel or copper alloy, of either silver color or copper color.

"The Medallions are to be cast, then the cost, divided by the number of the Medallions, and the donation price is then available. There is to be no profit afforded to the Workers of Our Lady of All Holy Titles for this Medallion. My child, the donation system for the Medallion will allow for reimbursement for the funds of the apostolates which are used for the Medallion. Thus will funds still be available for printing the Messages.

"Goodbye for now, My child."

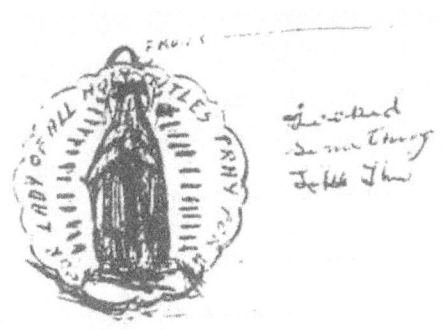 

****

Message given to a privileged soul October 2, 1984. Feast of the Guardian Angels, Eve of St. Therese, the Little Flower

Our Lady: "My child, you have been lacking in your responsibilities recently. You must pay more attention to your Mission. You did not check with Me before telling your assistants you could not answer so much mail anymore. You will again begin to answer your mail or you will be given a heavier burden to carry. Remember, My child, you were not given the Mission for glory or fame; nor for personal gain or satisfaction, but yet you were given it for the reason you have a big mouth and love to spread everything you are allowed to tell everyone in general. However, remember you must limit who you tell some of the private visions to.

"For Shame! My child, you did not answer the request of the Australian Seer. You will write to this Seer, My child; do you understand?"

Michael: "Yes, I do, my Mother and Queen."

(Mary has vanished, then Jesus appeared, and spoke.)

Jesus: "My children: You must find a way to again outlaw abortion in your land, the nation of America, and the world. Abortion is Murder of the Holy Innocents. Shortly after a celebration period, coming near the end of the twelfth month, there will be a time none of you should wish for. This time, as all others, may be halted, for a period, by prayer, but it is highly unlikely, unless you all begin to pray far more than you do now. Hear Me now, My children: All things that are to happen, their time is conditional upon mankind's response in Prayer.

"Pray the Rosary when you are sitting idle at home. Doing nothing but watching your television sets, is part of why your world is today. You watch sensuality, sexuality, carnality, lustful shows, shows full of Murder, yet you wonder why your children run about, doing all manner of rapings, murderings, and all other forms of sin purely from the Abyss and Satan. No family is safe from these shows if they watch them as the shows are from Satan and the Abyss. Instead of watching this sinful box, pray instead. Pray the Rosary of My Mother. Your Queen, who is My Mother, gave this to you all, long ago, to pray, for She is not only My Mother, but also the Mother of all Mankind, too. Will you pray the Rosary for peace? Or do you prefer destruction and death in the streets?

"If you do not all pray, then soon there shall be death and destruction in the streets of Shore-Line cities, such as Long Island, New York, and cities in Massachusetts. There will also be great destruction in Canadian cities if you don't all pray now, and continue praying."

(Jesus vanished and Theresa gave me a personal Birthday Poem, but I chose to share it with everyone.)

Theresa:

"You have the name of He Who Is Alike Unto God;
He who stands with spear- tipped Rod.

Call on this, your Patron Angel much;
For he has requested that I tell you such.

Pray that his statues again are placed in the Church;
That in every town they are found on at least one Perch."

****

Message given to a privileged soul (Michael) December 7, 1984, Eve of the Immaculate Conception

Our Lady: "My child, your attitude tonight will gain you naught but sorrow. If you were to attempt 'that', you would only be stopped, My child."

Seer: "Please tell me, Mother, how would I be stopped? I don't wish to come across as a brat but my attitude is affected by 'that" which is around me."

Our Lady: "First, I would tell someone, whom I would cause to be standing near you (in their sub-conscious mind) that you were planning self-abuse. They would stop you. My child, don't you comprehend and, or realize, that you have personally failed a great test of Faith, a test that was designed specifically for you at this time in your Mission?

"My child, you were what We had thought of as resistant to Luciel's workings. We allowed him to work on your spirit to see if he could break your will, My child, and, as you can see, he did almost succeed. My child, your testing is now all past you at this time. However, be aware that you will be tested again in the future. Things will continue to be hard for you, until you learn not to be so stubborn and obstinate, and you stop being so resistant to Our advice. Times will be easier on you for a while. When you least expect it, you will find out that Luciel is again testing you. Asmodeus* will also be testing you. You will know them by their tests. Rebuke them in My Son's Name, My child, and their testing of you will end. I removed this last test from you, My child, because you had gone to the point of non-prayer. Did you not realize that this was exactly what Satan-Lucifer, the Prince of Darkness, wanted?

"Be light-filled now, My child."

Note: Brief moment of silence while Our Holy Mother became so bright that I had to close my eyes, and still I could see Her clearly!

Our Lady: "Open your eyes, My child. Allow the light to enter you. Become strong of spirit - do not worry, the light will not hurt your eyes, for it is a mystical light, not an ordinary light.

Note: I obeyed Her command. She was beautiful. The only way I can explain it is She was like a white-hot pure white star. She was dressed in white from Her robe top to Her mantle to Her tunic. Yet still She had a blue sash. Her girdled fine chain-link belt was like pure spun gold.

Our Lady: "My child, and My children of the world, soon the week of Christmas shall be here. During that week I give this wish to you all now: Remember My Son's Birth. Do not just live through Christmas as a holiday, but remember it for, and as, a Holy Day. Christmas has become paganized, My children, so put My Son, Jesus Christ, back into Christmas. This is My first request to you all today.

"My second request is that you all pray extremely hard from December 23, 1984, to February 28, 1985 for, without extreme prayer, on, or shortly after the Feast Day of the Holy Innocents, shall be a most extreme event.

"My child, Jesus' Message to you will not be open to the public (first part), nor to your assistants and workers. His Message (first part) which is soon to follow, will be for you as a puzzle to figure out.

"Only the last part of the Message shall be given out, for it does not have to do with the first part. Blessings to all who are praying on plastic, wood, cord, or seed and metal Rosaries at this time. Many wonder if they are all just as good as each other. The answer is Yes, provided they have been properly blessed.

Peace, My child, and My children"

(End of Message of Our Lady.)

*Asmodeus: An evil demon mentioned in Jewish and Persian literature – Tobit, Chapter 3, Verse 6.

Message (second part) of Jesus' Message (public part)

"Many of you out there among My fold, are daily murdering babies. This must end now, as My hand may, and will soon, come down upon you, and the destruction shall be great. Remember, I am a Loving God, however, your generation has incurred My Wrath. The Father of All is hurt deeply by the murder of babies through abortion. What I have created I can destroy just as easily, and soon I shall, unless some changes are made.

"Your world is a cesspool of evil. The number of vipers is great. Never have We seen greater evil than in your world now. The Antichrist shall soon take Rome in his hand. When the Host, which is My Body and My Blood, is replaced, know then that the End is near, and that the Church has then, for a brief period, become Satan-Lucifer's. Know now, My children, Luciel knows all of the things contained in My past Messages and in My Mother's, as well.

"There will be one more false seer soon, out of Africa. He will be joined among all of the false seers in your world. He will be led by Luciel, the Prince of evil."

Jesus to Satan: "Luciel, Prince of Darkness, your time is short. Soon you shall return to the Pit."

****

Message given to a privileged soul (Michael) Tuesday, December 18, 1984, Advent Weekday

Our Lady: "My child, how can I smile and be happy when I am losing so many of our children We send to earth? Too many now live lives of which are filled with sin. Greed, My child and My children, is brought on by one of Lucifer's own army. Demons exist in the spirit realm, which exists coinciding, side by side, with your world. They can reach into your world to cause evil beyond anything seen before. They are doing so every day. Do you not recognize the accidents that are not accidents in your world now, My children? There are many of them. Look about you. Look about you!

"My child, there are many now, who are through demonic spirit, agents from Hell, trying to remove you. They have contacted, through one who was possessed, the Prince of Evil, himself. Lucifer has, at this very moment, sent out a major demon with [a] mission to tempt you. Know ye this, My child, this demon will be allowed to tempt you, as the test We mentioned to you in the last Message.

"We were going to allow you time before you were tested, but remember - you did pray to us, for another chance to prove thyself. We give you this warning, My child, because We, in Heaven, know you would have no chance to fight the demon Asmodeus' temptations, if you did not know his name. Asmodeus, as you know, My child, is the demon of lust, sexual perversion, and major lasciviousness. He also, as you well know, is one of Lucifer's top demons, having come from the Angel Choirs, as Lucifer himself once did.

"As in Lucifer's case, Asmodeus' Angelic Abilities were never taken away from him. While in past times he tested you from afar, he now tempts and tests you from right where you are. He will be with you as soon as We leave you, My child, since you have just now, in your thoughts requested this, you will be allowed the Grace of seeing Asmodeus when he tempts you. You also will see all of the other demons who are about you now, My child. This will help you to combat them all now. Now is the time to remove the three others.

"Goodbye now, My child. Pray when tempted. Pray the Rosary"

In conformity with the Decrees of Pope Urban VIII and the Second Vatican Council, without wanting to anticipate it in an undue manner, we accept gladly the judgements of Holy Mother Church concerning these Messages.

****

Message given to a privileged soul (Michael), Christmas Eve, December 24, 1984

Our Lady: "My child, I am now going to give you a brief Message tonight. There is very little time before you will be needed by someone else, My child.

"My children of the world: Soon you will have yet another of the small prophecies to you in the past actually happen. Soon there shall be great tremors striking your land, the United States.

"At Lourdes I called Myself the Immaculate Conception, and here I called Myself Our Lady of All Holy Titles. I have many beautiful titles, My children, so remember Me by them. Invoke Me by My titles. I will bless you for it. Honor My Son. He died for your sins. Do you not remember this? The way your world dishonors Him now, there is little that can be done to halt the approach of the coming Chastisement.

"You were warned at Fatima, you were warned at Lipa, and you were also warned at La Salette. You were given countless warnings at San Damiano, Bayside, Necedah, and at this apparition. You have in your hands now, the full power to either let fall, or hold back, the hand of My Son, before it comes down upon you.

"Pastors, remember My Son, in His Churches during Services. Many of you do not even pay attention to the words you are saying. You have no idea what you are doing to yourself by not putting your heart into the Mass. You are losing many Graces. You will be in need of them when you come over the veil. Sadly, many of you have already, or will, fall. O Pastors of the world, I ask you this" 'Why have you, the Shepherds of My Son's parishes on earth, disregarded the Rosary in your Ministry? What has happened to the Holy Hours of Adoration?' My Son is in the Blessed Sacrament. You are keeping needed Graces away from many of My children throughout the world. It is because I love you all that I come to you, and speak to you through My Seers. Listen to them. They are here for you, as well as for the lay people. Also, you must teach the children about the lives of the Saints. Many children cannot tell you who St. Anthony is, or St. Joan, or St Monica or a numerous list of the other Heavenly Court of Saints. Teach them, O Pastors, for they are your responsibility.

"My children, not enough of you pray The Rosary. There must be a complete reversal of the new trends in the Church, in which My weapon, the Rosary, given to you, is no longer used. You must all pray hard and devoutly. If you knew the value of just one Hail Mary, all your day would be spent in prayer. There are 53 in My Rosary. Can you not spend even the time for one Rosary with Me, My children? I am truly the Mother of Sorrows. My Heart is given freely to you all, and yet, many of you turn your back upon Me. Do you know what it is like to have to travel and speak constantly? I'm sure you all do, to some degree. I do it because I love you all with a Mother's Heart. I don't wish to see even one of My children fall. There are so many of you who would be lost if I did not follow you all about and tell you all of the errors that I see.

"My children, remove all the pornography from your homes. This is a great thorn in My Heart when I see the impurity of heart that results due to pornography. You who are addicted to pornography: Find My Son's Grace and you will need not the earthly pleasures in the photos of this evil from the minds of the Abyss. Only Satan knew man would find pleasure in the photos of a naked female. Women: keep your bodies covered. Do not fall to the maw of the viper, by placing yourself in the hands of a man who prints pornography.

"Goodbye, My children. My child, pray much for those about you. Pray to My Son's Sacred Heart for them all."

****

Message given to a privileged soul (Michael), Holy Family Day, December 26, 1984

Our Lady: "My child and My children, I come to you to give you a Message of great importance. I come to warn you to change your ways now in the short time left to you, before it is the end. You are going in a path led by the Abyss. Many of you are seeking bodily pleasures, lusting after thy brother, or thy sister. Homosexuality has been, and still continues to be, the downfall of the nations. Too much time is spent trying to amuse the human body. And what of Babylon? Shall We hasten the destruction? You do not realize what your sins of lewdness and depravity are calling down upon you.

"My children, you cry up to Me in Prayer, saying: "And when shall this all come to pass?" I tell you now, you do not want to be on earth when the destruction does actually come upon you. Since first I began to plead to you all, I have not ceased. My Heart is torn, for so few listen to Me. See My Heart, covered with thorns. I am truly a Mother of great sorrow. My Heart still longs for the conversion of even one of Our lost children. I would offer every last drop of My blood for the conversion of one of you, My children. Do you not realize how much that We, in Heaven, love you all? The Death Angel, Exterminatus, is still wandering about, plotting the deaths of many of you. Go nowhere after dark, if you have sins upon your soul. Exterminatus is seeking out specifically, you, who have sinned, and are out after dark.

"Do not take this warning too lightly, My children.

"Many of you ask for a time of peace. How can We give you peace? You have, in your own hands, the power through the Rosary, to obtain your peace. Pray the Rosary and you will find this out. Now, My child, you will begin your Prayers.

"I will be back again soon.

"Goodbye for now."

In conformity with the Decrees of Pope Urban VIII and the Second Vatican Council, without wanting to anticipate it in an undue manner, we accept gladly the judgements of Holy Mother Church concerning these Messages.

****

1985 Messages

Message of Heaven to a chosen soul (Michael), February 14, 1985, Valentine's Day, Feast of St. Cyril and of St. Methodius

Our Lady is now present. She is wearing a different garment tonight. I have never seen Our Holy Mother in almost solid pink before. Her robes are a light pink with luminescent sparkling golden trim. Her tunic, or inner dress, is a lighter pink, almost a white color. She has a deep blue cloth-like belt about Her waist. Her hair is covered by a long flowing white mantle. She is not crying tonight. This is a good sign, for She is smiling.

Our Lady: "My child, you wonder about the color; it is for those of the world who have listened to Me and prayed. I come as a living Valentine of Grace. All who have prayed all of this time: continue to pray, for there are many more Graces and answers to your prayers in store for you.

"You, My child, are well to believe that you will not lose your Mission over the small problem you have. You must accept the fact that your Mission will now be going much slower. You will cause a need for more prayers to be said to make up for your lack of prayer. You have neglected to pray for yourself. You have the gift of discernment of spirits – you are to use it tonight. My Son (Jesus) gave you this gift so you could do a clearing out of ills brought on by the demons.

"Your main concentration will be upon those who are suicidal or have the tendency to be suicidal. My Son, (Jesus) is the person you should fear, My child, not I – for I come to warn you often of the things you do wrong. Your fear should be of My Son because He is the one who will, one day, be your Judge.

"You are to stay in contact with My 'Little Pebble'. I feel it would be of benefit to you both. My child, because of your decision about your problem you will not be allowed to have your own, open to the public, prayer and apparition site. In this area you must now add to the small amount of prayers that are being said."

Our Holy Mother has now vanished. Now I must pray.

It is now 5:00 AM on Friday, the 15th

Our Lord says: "You are all to [be] examples to those about you. No single one of you should consider yourself better than any other. You were all put on earth with one purpose in mind: that purpose was, and is, to get back to Heaven. You will do this in whatever way you can.

"My little one, pray much now."

****

Message of Heaven to a chosen soul (Michael), March 13, 1985, Wednesday (Lenten Weekday)

A bright blue luminescence is now coming towards me from the ceiling of the room I am in. It is Our Holy Mother coming towards me now. She has the most beautiful colors of white, gold and blue on today. Oh, She is so pretty. She is wearing beautiful white tunic, or gown-like garment. It appears to be made of a garment like silk or some other expensive cloth. About Her waist is a belt of spun gold. I do not remember seeing Our Queen looking so beautiful in any place (that) I have seen Her Image on earth. No sculptor could ever place Her beauty on a piece of clay. Her robe is like the color of a cloudless sunny blue sky in the summer. Her mantle is white and it is covering a beautiful Head that is radiating out the most beautiful light. She is nodding to me that She wants to speak.

"Yes, Mother, I now am paying attention to what You have to say."

Our Lady: "My child, you have done very well in describing Me. You have touched My Heart like I wish you would when you pray to Heaven.

"My children of the world, you all must pray hard until after the new Synod of Cardinals and Bishops in

Rome this year, as the Dark One now seeks to remove him (Pope). You all must continue to pray your Rosary with deep reverence. With My Rosary about your neck, you can save yourself from some of the turmoil ahead. My Rosary should be used as the only weapon in your world. I tell you, My children, it is a weapon, and it causes all of Hell to tremble when you pray it. Will you not help Me in the battle that is now on about you all? I grow tired of coming to you all in this manner each year, yet I come back out of My love for you all. I do not wish to lose even one of you. Yes, My children, you all tell Me in your prayers, about how you are discouraged; what then do you think that We, in Heaven, are, when We see even one of you, who were among the true fold at one time, fall? My tears now fall for you all, My children of the world.

"I tell you now, this secret that has been kept from you by the fallen angel, Lucifer, the Prince of Evil: Discouragement is his tool against you all. If he places one bit of it in your path, you seem to all lose your way. You must learn to fight this discouragement with prayers, My children, for, only in prayer will your problems in life lessen. And you, My child, this goes for you too. Your problems would lessen greatly if you but prayed hard enough.

"Pray now, My child, and await St. Joseph. He will be with you soon."

St. Joseph: "My little son, please pay attention now, as I wish to speak through you now. You will finish your Rosary later.

"My sons and daughters of earth, I speak to you all now. There have been some small victories in the fight against abortion, yet you must keep a steady fight going against abortion, as it is Murder. Listen now, My child, and hear the voice of one known to you."

"Yes, St. Joseph" St. Joseph now says "Listen"

"Woe, Woe, Woe to the inhabitants of the earth. Woe, Woe, Woe!"

"The voice you have just heard, My child, is St. Michael's. My child, you are to listen to the advice from Australia. You will use the advice from him, as it is the truth. On the Feast of St. Patrick, you will have another of those of Us who are in Heaven visiting you. After all, it is his Feast Day and he does have a Message for you. You will pray again now, My son. You were on the second decade at the 3rd Hail Mary."

****

Message of Heaven to a chosen soul (Michael), March 17, 1985, Sunday, Feast of St. Patrick

St. Patrick is now coming forward, and he is dressed in a green colored robe. His tunic is white in color and he is carrying a kind of a cane, or something made out of a golden colored wood in his hand. The wooden object is called a staff, according to St. Patrick. Oh, he is so regal looking.

St. Patrick: "My child and my children: you must all chase out the vipers in your lands, as I chased out the vipers in Erin (Ireland). When I ask you to do this now, I also ask you to forgive your neighbors who have wronged you. Only in forgiving one who has wronged you can many of you exhibit a form of charity.

"If charity is too hard for you to see in this way, then let us explain it in more depth for you all: maybe then, some of you will understand it. In the case that one has wronged you, there is no greater a charity than to forgive him of the wrong that he has done.

"This, my children, is the Message that I came to bring to you all today. Now, my son, you will pray much."

****

Message given to a privileged soul (Michael) by Our Lady, Tuesday, May 21, 1985, Easter Weekday

Our Lady: "My child, you will tell the workers of the Shrines of the world that they must keep up the good work!

"One of the reasons that the Messages are so far apart in the Shrine apparitions is because that they have been used as a test to the believers of My Messages from Heaven. This was a test to see who would be discouraged, to forget about the Messages when they did not have a Message. I, The Mother of your God, have done this test, and you would be surprised if you knew the numbers of people that have fallen away, due to the lack of a Message.

"Describe Me now."

Our Holy Mother is wearing a beautiful white garment or tunic today. The outer ½ inch of Her garments, at the edges, is all a glittering golden color. Her head is covered in a white veil that is almost clear enough to see the shadow of Her hair through. Her feet are bare today. About the waist of Our Lady is a blue sash. On the right side of the sash She has something dangling. She is reaching to pick it up from Her side. Ohh, it is a beautiful Rosary. This Rosary is smaller, by far, than any I have ever seen Our Lady with. However, it is a beautiful Rosary. The Rosary is made of wood and the links in between are made of gold. She is speaking now.

Our Lady: "My child, you will now pray and be happy with the fact that I will be back again soon. No, I shall not tell you when as of yet. You must wait.

"Now you will pray."

****

Message given to a privileged soul (Michael), June, 1985, Eve of the Feast Day of the Sacred Heart

Our Holy Mother is with me now, and She has asked me to briefly describe how that She looks. She is all radiant with light tonight, and I am having a terrible time discerning the color of Her garments. Oh, now She says She will now allow my eyes to pierce through the light about Her, so that I may describe how She looks. She is beautiful, so beautiful that I must say that never have I seen this kind of beauty on earth before. Our Holy Mother is dressed in a tunic of the purest colored white that I have ever seen. She has a deep blue colored robe on, this evening, and the colors of it are the deepest blue that I can say that ever seen. The borders of both the tunic and the robe is lined with a designed trim that is stenciled in pure gold. About the waist of Our Holy Mother is a small thin golden mesh-like belt. Attached at Her waist on the belt is Her Rosary. The Rosary is a wooden Rosary with large wooden beads. Her feet are just barely showing under the edge of Her tunic.

Oh, She says:

Our Lady: "All women should wear clothing that covers below the knee and preferably to the ankle. Continue describing, My son,"

Our Lady is wearing a white covering over Her head but about an inch or so of Her hair is not covered and is blowing in the wind. This covering also is lined with gold on the edges of it. Now She is speaking again.

Our Lady: "My child and My children of the world, I wish you all to know of the suffering that was endured for you all, since April 15, 1975, by a very courageous girl, then only 21 years old. She agreed to suffer for you all when I asked her if she would like to save souls, and free souls from Purgatory with her own form of suffering. She was aware of many things, in the comatose state, that she agreed to stay in, for the past ten years. When she first lapsed into a comatose state, 1 came to her in a dream-like state and met with her soul and asked her if she would suffer that way if I guaranteed her immediate entrance into the Kingdom of My Son. She agreed.

"If you all knew of the number of souls that she saved, you would realize why I have placed her among the great Saints of the Kingdom of Heaven. Now, My child, you will describe what you view as I show you what happened two days ago at approximately 7:03 your Time-Zone time. Describe it now, My child."

All about me now I see figures illuminated with bright light. They all seem to be too bright to see. Now I see these little balls of light that must be cherubs carrying what appears to be a banner. I cannot see the banner. Oh, oh, I do not know if I should read this.

Our Holy Mother says: "You will read the banner." It says: "Welcome to Karen Quinlan who suffered a living martyrdom until her last breath." Now a female-shaped figure surrounded by tremendous light is rising out of a portal in the area below where this is all at. The other side of the portal has flames behind it and I truly do not understand the purpose of the flames. Our Lady says that Karen spent one minute in Purgatory, as she made her way up to Heaven. This figure is dropping roses all over the place and they seem to be falling right out of Heaven. Now it seems like thousands of people who are surrounding her and it seems like the common word is 'thank you' that they are saying to her, and I really do not understand, at this time, what exactly that they are thanking her for. Now Our Lady says that they are the ones whom Karen has saved by her suffering. Now everything is fading away as if I were to be alone with Our Holy Mother again.

She is saying: "Now that Karen is gone and no longer is suffering for mankind, many trials and hardships that were kept back from New Jersey and New York will begin to happen with more rapid pace with each succeeding day. There will be many more of the accidents that are not accidents.

"My child, you will now pray on your Rosary with Me." I prayed one Rosary with Our Holy Mother.

"Now, My child, you will continue to pray the Angelus on your own."

I would like to add that, when I began to be more aware of the room around me again, I found a large number of wild tea-roses around the room, and the odor of the roses was strong, and still is, on this, the day after the Message.

****

Message given to a privileged soul (Michael), Friday, July 26, 1985, 1100 PM, Feast Day of St. Ann and St. Joachim (Mary's parents)

Our Lady: "My child, and My children, you must all pray for your President now. There is a plan underway to remove him from among you. I tell you now that Satan had planned to remove him by causing the surgeon to blunder. I averted this due to prayers rising up all over this great nation. However, even more prayers are at this time needed if you are to avert the next planned attack upon the life of your President.

"My child, and My children of the world, there is a series of three other topics I wish to warn about tonight.

"Do you not all realize that those of you on earth who use the beaches are responsible for each other in many ways? There are swimsuits that are only but underwear. My children of the world, do you not realize that these are sinful and the cause of sin? Women of the world: when you wear the suits you call a bikini do you not realize that you are naked in a man's eyes? As he lusts after you, you are guilty, just as much as he, for you caused him to lust by dressing in such a manner of nudity.

"Worse yet, My children of the world, are the nudist beaches. Do you not realize that when the Ball of Redemption, the Wrath of the Father, comes upon you, you will burn in all spots of lustful nudity that are exposed? You live in pure sin, My children. Turn back before it is too late. You are approaching now the point of no return.

"Parents of the world, I give you a guidance now: As a Mother, My heart aches when I see, in your world, the children who are not cared about enough by you parents. Why do you parents keep pornography? Do you not realize what it is doing to your child? Even worse: Many of you do not realize until it is too late, but the phone is a source of filth for many of the children among you. Many of the children see Mommy and Daddy call to these places for words of sexual nature, so they imitate them, but most of them do not realize it is evil and wrong.

"O My child and My children, the last thing that I have come about is the most important at this time and of most dire concern to many. Many young children shall soon be lost to Satan's Maw. Pray, My children, pray hard and devoutly. Your devotion and prayer could well save your child or your next door neighbor's child. Pray much, as your children will be the victims if you do not. The Angel of Death now walks among you, in a human form, and his members are numbers of Legion. They are Legion 666.

"Now, My child, you will offer your prayers."

****

Message given to a privileged soul (Michael) by Jesus and Mary to the world, Wednesday, August 28, 1985, Feast of St. Augustine

Our Lady is here now and She is wearing pretty, clear-glass, slippers upon Her feet tonight. Her robe is a yellow color. The edges are trimmed in a golden metallic trim. Her mantle is totally covering Her hair. She is now putting Her finger up to Her mouth and motioning for me to listen to Her and repeat.

Our Lady: "My children of the world, and you, My child, there must be much prayer for your nation and for the world. In the recent years, the Soviet Bear has hidden its true desire for a full scale war behind a mask of peace. A child from your nation, the United States of America, was a Martyr recently. She was fooled by the Bear into believing that the Bear was seeking peace. With her was fooled a great many people among the population of the world.

"The plane in which this child was, had been flying toward the homeland of the United States. While still on the ground, prior to liftoff, the plane had a small veer-device placed in the plane. This device caused the plane to veer, while near the coast, still. Then over-near the sight of landing, they were thus caused to both veer off course and crash as well. The Bear has thus caused the Martyrdom of the child who sought peace between the nations. The Eternal Father allowed her to be martyred because if He did not, she would have been exploited by the film industry of your nation. She now is a saint in the flower gardens of Heaven.

"The Ogre of Satan's creation is now living in human form in the State of California. Luciel, Prince of darkness: Your time is short. Your kind were all murderers in the beginning, and they are all so existing now." Our Lady chanted the quote to Luciel.

Our Lady: "My child, you must pray that the Angel of Death and the Ogre of Destruction do not destroy your nation, the once proud United States of America. Mothers, Daughters, and Children: you will go no place after dark, for you are the primary targets of the dark ones. If you must go somewhere after dark, then you should wear your cross clearly showing on the base of your neck. The Cross must be blessed so that it will protect you from the. Ogre.

"Parents of the world: you are responsible for teaching your little child to go to Confession. So many children are afraid of the Confessional. Your Church does not truly educate the children anymore.

"My child, you will pray for mankind now, as you await My Son"

Jesus is here and Our Lady is gone now.

Jesus says: "Luciel, you shall soon be vanquished. My child, you will pray that your world finds peace.

"Pray now, My child."

****

Message of Our Lady to the World, Wednesday, September 18, 1985, given to a privileged soul (Michael), Eve of Feast of Our Lady of La Salette

Our Lady is wearing a blue robe that is trimmed in ½ inch of gold trim. Her tunic is a pure white color. Our

Holy Mother's hair is just barely visible under Her mantle. She is now looking down to Her feet and She is saying:

"My child, describe My feet." Our Lady's feet are covered by nothing tonight. They are bare. They are dainty and small."

"My child, and My children of the world, I have a Message of dire concern for the world today. Did I not warn you of what happened when the continent of Atlantis was on your earth? You were warned that the earth is now doing as poorly as it did when your earth housed Atlantis. You must pray and pray unceasingly. Do not give lip-service, but give full concentration to Thy Lord and God. He died for you, so now remember Him in all you do.

"He is with you always, but He will not be in you until you ask Him to enter unto you as His Temple. Pray the Rosary daily. Carry it with you. And you non-Catholics: remember your Lord in the Stations of the Cross. Remember His Passion, His Death; remember His Love for you. He loves all His children and He is a Merciful God. Parents: bring your children unto Jesus. He desires their presence.

"My child, your Holy Father in Rome needs your prayers, and the prayers of all of you. My children of the world, if the amount of prayer in the world does not triple, the Supreme Pontiff of Rome, Our Son, your Vicar, John Paul II, will die a Martyr's death in a bloodbath in a time prior to the Synod.

"The Synod must happen, My child, and My children. Much of the world's fate depends upon it. If it does not occur, there will be a great deal of your small amount of time that is left removed from you all. Luciel, Prince of Darkness: you may seek to remove him now, but your time is short, and you will fail to remove Faith in My Son from mankind's hearts.

"Now, My child, you will describe what is about to happen here."

"Yes." Our Holy Mother is opening Her arms wide and, I do not know where, but there are many rose petals cascading down from Her! She is saying: "They are to be used for cure and conversions, My child. You too, My child, are to keep one with you. Yes, you know why, My child. Out of love for you, My child, I will not say why.

"Also now, My child, I will give the last part of this, today's Message to you. Out of Africa, Russia, China, and Cuba will come World War III.

"My child, you will pray now a Rosary with Me. My child, you will keep your Rosary with you at all times, for there is a plan of Satan to remove you. I have averted one plan to remove you from the world. You will keep this (first plan) a secret, My child.

"Pray now, My child."

****

Message given to a privileged soul (Michael) on the Feast of St. Wenceslaus, Martyr, Saturday, September 28, 1985, Eve of the Feast of the Archangels

Our Lady: "My child, and My children, at this time there is still a need for at least one third more prayers in the world. Your Holy Father's life hangs in the balance. There must also be prayers for your country's leader. My children, again soon there shall be an attempt upon him. It is from the forces of darkness.

"My child, you know of the need for prayer in the world. Also, you know of the need for Sacrifices, Atonement, and Suffering in the world. Yes, My child, due to the lack of Sufferings and Atonement being accepted upon earth, Gloria the Hurricane was allowed to fall upon your country in the Eastern United States of America. The severity of the storm was tempered by the lack of prayers in your world, My children.

"O My children, when will you listen? When will you realize that all the carnage could be prevented if your world would just turn back to prayer and love of God? Soon, if you do not turn back, your shores will be filled with a full scale invasion while your leaders themselves will be toppled from rule by the Communist National Party within your country. Is this what you want? Africans, trained by Russia, are already upon your seacoast. The only thing holding them back is that they are awaiting an order from the Kremlin to invade.

"Pray now, My child."

****

Message of Jesus and Mary to a privileged Soul (Michael) on Saturday, December 7, 1985, Anniversary of Our Lady of All Holy Titles, Eve of the Immaculate Conception of Mary Immaculate

Seer: There is a presence of Heavy scent of Italian Cigar tobacco in the air now. There are now two men before me. They are quite old. One is saying:

St. Padre Pio: "My son, you must identify us as St. Benedict and St. Padre Pio."

St. Benedict: "I, St. Benedict, am here to warn my followers the Benedictines, to wear my Medal. Almost none of you do wear it now. It will soon come to a time when they, who follow my Mission, will be unable to get my Medal, as there will be no lead or aluminum to cast my Medal in. I urge all of you to wear the Medal I am upon. It is a major weapon feared by the Prince of Darkness.

St. Padre Pio: "I, Padre Pio, have come to tell you that the good Italians, and non-Italians alike, who are praying to the (Eternal) Father through me: I, and the Father and the Son Jesus and the Holy Ghost, along with all of Heaven, have heard your prayers. San Giovanni Rotundo in Foggia, Italy, shall be considered as a Sacred Site in my name. All who pray with mention of my name, shall have their prayers joined to those of my good women of San Giovanni Rotundo. Ask much in my name. I will present it to Jesus and Mary in your names."

Our Lady: "My children of the world, this is a very short Message I have for you tonight. It is short but sad news, My children. If there is not more love and reverence given unto My Son this Christmas Season, the Father will let a major catastrophe come upon your world. This catastrophe is the catastrophe I mentioned to you, My child, in private some time ago. You ask: "Shall it happen?" It is in the hands of mankind, My child.

"My children: Pray and adore My Son as you go throughout your Christmas Season, and remember to put My Son, Jesus Christ, back into Christmas. Pray now, My child."

Seer: Our Lady left at this point.

Prayer to obtain the Glorification of Padre Pio

O Jesus, full of grace and charity, victim for sinners, so impelled by love for us that you willed to die on the Cross, I humbly beseech you to glorify in Heaven and on earth the Servant of God, Padre Pia of Pietrelcina, who generously participated in your sufferings, who loved you so much and laboured so faithfully for the glory of your Heavenly Father and for the good of souls.

With confidence I beseech you to grant me, through his intercession, the grace of ... which I ardently desire.

Glory be to the Father...(three times).

Imprimatur - Manfredonia, 12-3-1971 + **Valentino Vallat**, *Archbishop*

****

1986 Messages

Message from Heaven given to a privileged soul (Michael), Monday, March 3, 1986, 10:00 - 11:00 PM, Eve of the Feast of St. Casimir

Our Lady: "My child, and My children of the world; I come to you this night to bring you a new Message. It has been some time since I have come to you, My child; but it is a test that was performed by the lack of Messages. How many of you are presently thinking: "How long till there will be another Message?" Have you not learned from the past Messages when I have said that, if you obeyed the Messages, We would be helping you more often?

"My child, St Monica desires to speak to the World through you, now. You will listen and repeat what she says, starting now."

St. Monica: "Parents of the world: what has become of so many of you? You are neglecting your children. You say that you love them; but do you? Do you really love them, or are those just words? Some of you do truly love your children; yes, this is known to us. However, the majority of you do not love your children. How many of you can say that you, daily, take time to be with your child and do something with your child that he, or she, actually likes to do? How many of you actually take care enough to wonder, and question, what your child does with their free time? Neglect leads to crime and street terror.

"How many wives and husbands in Society don't love each other anymore, and take it out on your children? How many of you try to blame a child for your lack of love for your husband or your wife? How could you blame a blameless child for your desires of divorce? Do you, parents of the World, know the ramifications of the harm that is caused psychologically by your misplaced blame? And yet those of you who do this, when asked, would say: "Oh, yes, I love my child." Do you? How many times have you sat down and asked your child: "How their day went?" "What did they do?" "How do you feel today?" These are all thing you need to do.

"How many times do you, at least, say: "I love you"? Can't you tell them you love them? How many of you, right now, think: "They know I love them; what need is there for me to really tell them that I love them?" How many children lack self-expression these days because you parents are afraid to express yourselves? Some of you say: "I don't have the time - I'm too busy." But, I tell you, if you loved them, you would find the time.

"Remember, the children are both the innocent victims of you all - and the future of your world. It is up to you to share your world's future. Will it be good or bad? Many of you spend hard-earned money on doctors, such as psychiatrists and psychologists, but to no avail. Why, you then ask, is there seemingly no help for your child? The answer is to love them; to share your life with them; to communicate at all times with them. If you do this, you then could say: "I have tried." How many of you have failed to try to communicate?

"The scourge of disobedient children is a scourge because you failed to be an adequate parent. In your society, many children turn to drugs off the streets, never being quite sure of what they are taking, all due to feeling unloved. It is not too late for your child's future. My family was converted by years of prayer and constant love. If I had not loved him, and prayed for him so much, the world would not even know of St. Augustine the Great, my son. So remember, your world's future is in your hands. Will it be good or bad?"

Our Lady, "My child, this now concludes tonight's Message You will pray now with Me and you will remember long enough to include with the Message all the words of My prayer for the Parents. You will later pray for the fellow Mission in Australia. My Little Pebble will need your prayers while he travels in your nation."

Prayer for Parents

"O Father, may you grant to all parents the Gift of Your Grace, touching their hearts and minds. May they be open to Love You alone are. May Your Love burn in their breasts till they are able to share it with family, friends, and even with their worst enemies."

Next, say:
Four: Our Father's;   Seven: Hail Mary's;   One: Glory Be…   One: Apostle's Creed
Four: Jesus, Mary, Joseph, I love you, save souls!
Two: Eternal Father, share Your all-consuming Love with all Parents.
Four: Thank you, Father.

****

Message of Heaven given to a privileged soul (Michael), Saturday, March 22, 1986, Eve of Palm Sunday

Our Holy Mother is now coming through Her portal and is standing before me. She is actually floating in midair before me. She is wearing a very odd outfit tonight. The tunic, or inner robe that She is wearing, is of a canary yellow, while the outer robes are purple and blue color. The blue is almost a purple. The sash about Her waist is of a deep blue shade. She is now putting Her finger to Her lips and kissing a bead from the big wooden Rosary in Her hands. Her Rosary is like the ones that the nuns in olden days used to carry at the convents with them. Now She is speaking.

Our Lady: "My child, you have many questions on your mind. Let Me say this first before We begin." (In private She discoursed with me.) "Now My child, you may speak publicly in repeating what I shall now say. You wonder much about the Bermuda Triangle, My child. I tell you this now - there is a need at this time for this information in your world. While many will leave My apparitions to you behind because of this Message, there is a small group of scientists who need to be made aware of the truth behind the relative Time and Space magnetic flux fields of the triangle.

"My child, in the past I told you that there were five Arks that escaped from the destruction of Atlantis and Lemuria. The total survivors of the lost continent were numbered at 160 in all. This Lemurian race, after intermingling with Noe's race, some 700 years later, had constantly been trying to move the technological developments of your world up to where they are at the point of this present day. They had a need for the equipment made in your present time era. The plan of the descendants of Atlantis and Lemuria was, and still is, to use present technology to build great ships your world calls UFO's to bring the Atlantian/Lemurian descendants back to the days prior to Noe, in an attempt to stop the events which caused the continent to sink below the ocean's waters. However, since it is impossible to change time-events, as they have already passed, they have failed so far.

"Many people from your Time-era have vanished from your Time by being brought aboard these ships. Some aircraft had to be destroyed because they flew too close to the ships of the Atlantian /Lemurians while they were going into a "Time-Window." They will do practically anything to keep the knowledge of how the Time-Windows work from your society. No, My child, worry not, as you are not in personal danger from them as long as you wear My Scapular that I have blest for you. It will make you as invisible to their eyes, should they seek you out.

"The Windows of Time were used by Atlantis and Lemuria on quite a lot of occasions while the continent was above the water. The Time-Windows are all caused by the relation to the magnetic lines of the earth in its position in the Solar System. Any magnetic or electrical impulse of great voltage is enough to open a Time-Window in the triangle. All that is needed for proof is to look at the fact that watches, on every passenger in a plane, will, on occasion, be up to ten or fifteen minutes slow at touchdown of the plane, while, at liftoff, they were all accurate. A Time-Window would affect these clocks.

"My child, this is all for now. I will return in fifteen minutes to give you yet a different Message to go with this Message in print.

"My child, I have returned again. You will now repeat: Priests of the world, you will honor My Divine Son, or you, too, shall suffer for your irreverence. Remember, even your own office as Priest of My Son is not too high to be showing the best of reverence to My Son. You as a priest above all else, are required to show reverence by the office that you hold. Were it not so, I would tell you.

"Lay people of the Church should never handle My (Divine) Son, your Lord and God. Have you no respect, any longer, for My Son? O Pastors, you are whittling away at your Church's foundations from within. Should you turn to the light and realize your mistakes, the Church you're responsible for will be the better for it.

"Daughters of the Church: whatever has become of you? Have you lost your convictions? The full habit must be brought back. It is necessary to wear it. I tell you now that you, O Mother Superiors, are responsible for your nunneries. Run them well and follow the wishes of Heaven, and I will send more daughters of the Church to your doors"

****

Message given to a privileged soul (Michael) by the Blessed Virgin Mary and Her Son Jesus, Our Lord, Sunday, June 1, 1986, Feast day of Corpus Christi

Our Lady: "My child, and My children of the world, you are fast, now, approaching the time when it will be too late for many of you. I have, at some places, spoken of a great cold which is to strike your earth. My child, tomorrow you will discover a small sample of this cold in a much smaller degree. It will be, to many, a cause for a cold. You will be protected from this fate, My child. My (Divine) Son, your God, desires to bring you a public short Message. Before He does so, however, there is something that I must have you describe. Describe now what you see, My child."

Seer: Our Holy Mother is now opening the outer edges of Her robe, wide open. Until now She has had the edges held tightly shut. Oh, how beautiful! There are rose petals now falling down in front of me. She is now descending to just in front of me, and is handing me a handful of very fragrant rose petals. She has Her hands full with these rose petals. I do not know where they came from, but they are here now! I have never smelled more fragrant rose petals. "Thank you, Blessed Mother, thank you."

Our Lady: "You must use these petals that I have just handed you, very wisely. These petals are the ones that I told you (in private) about, last week. You will tell no one what that these ones (I have just handed to you) are to be used for. The other petals, however, are for use with conversions and cures."

Jesus: "My children, you will hear many rumors about that I have returned. Know you this: When I return, it will be in the clouds, and all will know. So, while I do at apparition sites, believe no man who says: "I am Jesus." for he is not I.

"Also, My children, the abortions in your world must cease if you are to gain any more extensions on time. Present time has almost run out.

"Pray now, My child."

****

Message given to a privileged soul (Michael) by the Blessed Virgin Mary and Her Son Jesus, Friday, June 6, 1986, Feast Day of the Sacred Heart of Jesus, Eve of the Feast of the Immaculate Heart of Mary

Seer: Our Lady has come down in Her usual blue and white robe and tunic, tonight. She is now motioning with Her finger to Her lips. I must listen and repeat what She is ready to say.

Our Lady: "You will, My child, skip the description. You need to only let them know that you have seen My feet and My Rosary. It is made of large gold links and wooden beads. My child, I thank you for placing the pillow on the floor beside you. If you would move it toward Me one foot, I will then stand upon it. The floor is cold, My child.

"My children of the world, I come to you this evening to bring unto you this Message of instructional guidance. This Message is directed to those of you who are between the ages of ten and thirty years of life. Your parents are to be loved and respected. Sons and daughters of the world, your parents brought you into this world. How can you dishonor them with your disobedience? You may not like some of the things that your parents may be standing for, but you must still love them for who they are, not what they are. I have seen much evil lately among you all, My children. I say "you all" as a general term to mean that, among you all, there are many of you who are in a state of doing much evil.

"What do you seek, My children? Do you know the fast, wide-open road that you are traveling? Do you know unto where that it leads? It leads you unto the path of Hell. How few of you there are who truly know the way to Heaven. You must not hate anyone. Hate comes directly from Luciel, the Prince of Darkness. You must love thy enemy as thyself. This is the way of My Son Jesus, your Lord and God.

"And how many of you are daily, going to the so-called doctors of your world to end the life formed in your wombs? It is a murder that you commit, when you have an abortion. My children, abortion is one of the most wide-spread breaking of the Ten Commandments in your society today. Thou shall not kill! Remember this commandment.

"Many of you lie about anything and everything. Are you not aware that you are traveling the road to Perdition when you lie? My children, you must return to the Sacraments. A Confession is a good step to the return to My (Divine) Son, your Lord and God. Pray the Rosary, as it will help you to realize how to better your life in the path to Heaven. The road to Heaven is short and narrow. Without My Son, you cannot enter Heaven. If you deny My Son's existence, you must confess this to enter the State of Grace within your soul. My child, you will now pray a bit with Me on your Rosary till Jesus comes to give you a Message."

Seer: I have just prayed with Our Holy Mother. Now Jesus is before me. I can hear, in my mind, the words that He wishes me to repeat. He has just told me that I am worried about my fellow-mankind. I had not said this, so I know that this is definitely Our Lord before me now.

Jesus: "My son, you will receive a Message from Me on Monday, 9th of June, 1986, Feast Day of St. Ephrem. I wish you now to pray the Sorrowful Mysteries of the Rosary. Beware of the evil one's temptations toward you, My son, as he plans to keep causing you trouble.

"Good night."

Seer: Jesus now is rising up through the roof of the room and is gone. The room suddenly feels so empty. Oh well, I must pray the Rosary now.

****

Message given to a privileged soul (Michael) by Jesus on Monday, June 9, 1986, 1:00 AM, Feast Day of Saint Ephrem, Doctor of Divinity

Seer: Jesus is now here, as He told me (on 6th of June) that He would be. He is very stern looking, tonight. However, I sense a feeling of calm and peace every time that He is before me in an apparition of this nature. Our Lord now wishes to speak.

Jesus: "My children, I, your Lord and God, now give you all the command to pray more.

"Make your every action into a prayer. You must tip the (scale) balance back soon or I will be forced to allow your present time to run out. There is far too much evil in your world now. O little sons and daughters of the world, what do you seek in the reading, and in the printing of pornography? This vile material, of which the vipers of your world produce, is from nowhere else but the Pit. Pornography is depravity and defilement, and pure sin. Many are on the road to Hell because of it.

"Pick up your Bible and read it. In this book you will find your strength and guidance for these last days, as you know them. We constantly are asked in Heaven, by the Saints: "How long, O Lord, shall You wait?" How much do you think that We will wait, I ask you, My children?

"I, your God, give you the Directives of Heaven, both Myself, and through My Mother. How many of you, there are, who choose to disregard these Directives. Those of you who do not listen, and take heed, to Our

Directives, will find it hard when you come to Heaven, for your judgement before Me, for you have been warned, but have not listened. It would be far better for those of you who this will happen with, it you had never left your mother's womb alive, for you have been given a Mission to make your way back to Us in Heaven. You must choose your path. It will not be chosen for you.

"The images of the Saints must be brought back within your Church life and your family life. O Parents of the World, teach your children about your known saints. If this knowledge is out of sight, it will be out of mind. Where would you be today in knowledge of your Saints if no one told you about the Saints? It is a Command from Me, as your Lord and God, that the Lives of the Saints must be known of by your children, so that they will be aware of their intercessors with Us in Heaven. Many favors may be obtained through the Saints.

"My son, you will pray on your Rosary now. I request the Joyful Mysteries at this time be said by you. Thank you for being ready, and waiting, for My Message, My son."

****

Message given to a privileged soul (Michael) by the Blessed Virgin Mary and St. Theresa, Friday, June 13, 1986, 5:30 AM, Feast Day of St. Anthony of Padua

Our Lady: "My child and My children, We have come this night to bring you Theresa's Poetic Message for the world. Yes, My son, the words will be automatically translated for you."

St. Theresa:

> "The Atlantians come, and the Atlantians go;
> They hope that mankind does not learn what they know.
>
> It is the Bermudan Triangle from whence they are coming;
> It is the Bermudan Triangle from whence they are going.
>
> In the dark of the night they hover;
> The vast Triangle they cover.
>
> They travel. in lines of displaced time;
> These words are clear in form of rhyme.
>
> I tell you of fact, within the rhyme;
> Radar cannot penetrate through the Windows in time.
>
> And into these Windows the Atlantian craft do climb;
> Your radar will lose them within years of time.
>
> The Atlantians are clever - united with one theme;
> To stop Atlantis from sinking, has been their scheme.
>
> Thus the ships and planes will disappear;
> Near Atlantis, years-ago they will reappear.
>
> The men are hypnotized - and then are taught
> To destroy a bomb-control, they try - but are always caught.
>
> Time cannot be within their grasp to change;
> It is out of even the Atlantian's range.

Our Lady: "My child, this is the Message for this night. You wil now say a Hail Mary and then sleep will come at once, for you have a long day yet ahead of you shortly. Be at peace of soul, My child.

"Good Bye for now."

Seer: With this, Our Lady rose through the ceiling of my room and, in the absence of the light She made with Her presence, I said a Hail Mary and, as She said, I fell asleep as soon as I said Amen.

****

Message given to a privileged soul (Michael) by the Blessed Virgin Mary, Saturday, June 21, 1986, 8:00 AM, Feast Day of St. Aloysius Gonzaga

Seer: Our Holy Mother is before me now. She is requesting that I now be in silence, waiting, as She wished to show me something. Then I am to describe (pause). Oh, Our Lady is emitting a vast amount of Graces. She says I must now repeat after Her.

Our Holy Mother: "My child, and My children, the Graces I have just sent out are to all who have believed in the Message of Heaven and have listened to the words of Heaven. They are receiving these Graces. There are still many, to whom, of which this Message is unknown. It must be given to all who ask.

"Soon, on a day in July, your country, the United States of America, will have a celebration around the fine statue that has been the symbol of your nation. At this celebration will be much of the ships of your nation. Because of the type of celebration that it will be, We will guard all of your nation at this time.

"Know you this: It was the plan of satanic groups in your country to call in the foreign armies to invade your proud country. If it were not for the prayers of the few, your country would have already been overrun by the time that this Message will reach most of you.

"My child, I wish it to be known that there is little that We, in Heaven, are not able to change with the power of the prayer of mankind. The only problem is that Mankind is not willing to offer the prayer. The Rosary is the weapon of Heaven. Mankind must learn to use this Heaven-sent weapon. With the power of each bead, a person could make major miracles if God so Willed to allow the miracle. Many miracles will happen at the few true Shrine-sites left. The miracles will be of major potential. Some who, in their skeptical mind, think there is no miracle, will be astounded to see a cripple walk freely. Some will be astounded to see the blind suddenly have their sight for the first time in their life. These miracles will happen if there is enough prayer. The Rosary is your source of peace. If there are the needed amounts of Rosaries, the peace your world seeks will come to pass. I will tell you, of fact, that sadly your world is far from the needed amount of requested prayers.

"Luciel, the Prince of Darkness, is removing many of you who have [been] chosen for Missions due to lack of Prayer, not on the part of the believers, but on the part of the Seers themselves. My child, you will repeat what I now say, also.

"Luciel, Prince of Darkness, your time is short to do your evil. You may remove many of My voice-boxes, but I will spring-up new apparitions in other place when you do.

"My child, Luciel has tried to remove you as well. I have protected you, this far, due to the prayers of your workers and your faithful flock. You, as well, are in danger from the Prince of Darkness now, if you do not pray more.

"I now wish you to pray on your Rosary this night coming, for two hours longer than your usual time. If you feel sleepy, you will ask M. and M., the two guardians We are now assigning to you, to awaken you if you begin to fall asleep. You will now begin your morning prayers.

"Goodbye for now, My son."

****

Message given to a privileged soul (Michael) by Our Lord Jesus Christ and St. Monica, Wednesday, August 27, 1986, Feast Day of St. Monica

Jesus: "My little son, this is to My children of the world. You will see that it is printed. My Mother's agony was very great. Her Martyrdom was a living Martyrdom. The Queen of Heaven suffered for mankind almost as much as I, Myself, suffered for you. You will remember this. You will honor My Mother when She comes to you all in the Shrines of your earth. You will not go about to and fro talking and making merry among yourselves. You are there (called there) to pray. You will do so or you may find the means to visit the Shrines of My Mother will be removed from you.

"Pastors, Brothers, Sisters, why do you not honor the Queen of Heaven anymore? She is there daily to guide, comfort, and protect you, if you will but ask for Her guidance, comfort, and protection from darkness.

"There are many of you, My faithful children of the world, who are repentant at this time of your past transgressions into sin. I wish you to read in your Book of Life and Love the 8th verse through the 10th verse of the 15th chapter of St. Luke. You will find knowledge of consoling need within this chapter's verses. There are a number of you who question if there is truly a life over the Veil for you. To find this answer you will again turn to your Book of Life and Love, and you will read the 15th chapter of the 1st to the Corinthians. (Paul's first letter to the Corinthians.)

"My child, you will now pray a Rosary with your second favorite Saint in Heaven."

Seer: Oh, now St. Monica is coming forward and she (is) making the Sign of the Cross with her Rosary which is made all of wood and gold.

St. Monica: "My brother, you will now pray fifteen decades of the Rosary with me for your brothers and sisters of Earth. You may describe later if you wish."

I desire not to describe the visit of St. Monica as I am now extremely tired.

****

Message given to a privileged soul (Michael) by Our Lady, Monday, September 29, 1986, Feast Day of Sts. Michael, Raphael and Gabriel, the Archangels.

Our Holy Mother is now coming out of Her portal of light. She is all light at the moment. I know it is Her even while I still cannot see Her. Now She says my eyes will pierce the light to see Her. Oh, Our Holy Mother is dressed differently tonight. She desires me to describe Her, so I will obey.

The tunic is white as fresh snow. Her belt is made of fine miniature mesh links of solid gold. The belt has a tassel hanging from it. It hangs about two inches from Her belt. Her mantle is of blue with a golden trim of one-half inch thickness. The blue is deep blue like new denim's navy blue shade. Our Holy Mother's feet are in golden brown leather sandals. They are only visible about one-half inch above the ankle. However, the straps of the sandals tie somewhere above the hem of golden trim on her tunic. The neckline of Her tunic is lined with one-half inch trim of gold braid trim.

"Mother, is it true gold" She is nodding "Yes."

The Rosary (fifteen decades) is of large wooden beads. The crucifix and centerpiece of Our Holy Mother's Rosary are also of wood. The corpus (on cross) is skin-colored; it shows the actual wounds of Jesus. The Rosary is dangling from Her hands as She is praying for us all even while I describe Her. She is now holding it out so I can see all fifteen decades.

Now She is looping it back around Her arms and is saying: "This is how the statue will look, My child, folded hands in prayer and the Rosary wrapped in loops around My arms. The corpus of My Lord and God on My Rosary will be skin-tone, but there is no need to show the wounds. No human artist could duplicate them very accurately."

Our Holy Mother has a green cape on and it comes down on Her back to the back of Her knees. The cape is trimmed in gold leaf also. It is billowing with the wind. Her robe is of blue, like the denim color of Her mantle. Her cape is joined together at the neck by a one-fourth inch thickness fine gold chain. She is standing upon a snake's head with Her left foot, and Her right (foot) is upon his body, which is coiled beneath Her feet. Now the full image is upon a globe for the base of what will be the statue's image. The globe is to picture North America beneath the snake and the feet of Our Lady. South America's top will also show and any of the rest of the geography towards the back of the globe beneath Her would show on the sides and the back of the statue. Our Holy Mother's hair just barely shows on the sides of Her head under Her mantle. The edge of Her mantle is trimmed in gold.

Now Our Lady is speaking: "My child, you now will know why I come dressed as such. I am showing you that I am truly Of All Holy Titles. I represent all of My Shrines in this image. You may cast the statue in this image."

(Pause) Rose petals are given from Our Lady.

Our Lady: "My child and My children, how often must I come to your earth and plead with mankind for the removal of the laws that allow the murder of the innocents sent to the wombs of your nation? How many times We send children down to the wombs of your nation and the world, and how many are returning to Us daily? The daily rate in your nation alone is nearly one half of the children conceived daily. They are being returned to Us through murder. Murder of the young, as unborn, was condemned by the (Eternal) Father in the days of King Herod, and so it is today. To those of you, My children, who do care enough to fight the battle in your nations to end abortion, I say you must continue this battle and more fervently.

"During this coming winter many will suffer if there is not more prayer. The Centers of Light around the world are growing very dim, My children. They must get brighter or your nation will collapse, as well as many other nations of the world. Both monetarily and materialistically, they too shall collapse.

"Pray now, My child."

****

Message given to a privileged soul (Michael) by Jesus and Mary to the World, Saturday, November 1st, 1986, Feast Day of All Souls and of All Saints

Seer: Our Holy Mother is before me now and is with a worried look upon Her face. She is very sad looking at this time. I truly wonder what She is worrying about. I am, at this moment, quite sure that She will tell us. Her mantle is yellow in color and this is usually meant to signify the Papacy. Our Lady is now nodding, "Yes." The robe upon Our Holy Mother at this moment, is of such a dark blue that it is almost a purple color. I am not quite sure which color that it, in truth, is. It is trimmed with a border of golden trim. Our Holy Mother is barefoot tonight. Her feet are so delicate looking that I would be very surprised that She was not cold if I did not know that the personages of Heaven are able to be warm in the middle of the coldest rain even! The belt about Our Holy Mother's waist is of a golden color also, and is made of small golden links of spun gold. Our Lady is now beginning to speak.

Our Lady: "My child, your time to vote on your representatives will be here in a few of earth's sunrises. My child, and My children, when you vote on these people, it is on you to decide who will best represent your nation. You must pick the ones who will not keep the allowance of Abortion on Demand in your nation. If you pick enough of the people who are correct to govern your nation it will be possible to change this law. Thus, many of the babies sent down to your earth would live to be born into your world.

"Each one of you has a Guardian Angel sent to you at the time of your conception in the womb. Call upon your Guardians. Ask for their guidance. It (guidance) is there for you if you will but ask for it. My child, Jesus wishes to speak to the world through you now. I will return at a later date to give you yet another Message."

Jesus: "Upon your earth now, My children, is an army of the darkest angel of all time. They are wandering about, among you. They seek to destroy all that is good in the world before My Return. Ask your Guardians, daily, to help you decide on any actions, as you do them, as the Dark One is always there to try to influence you to do the wrong thing.

"He still has most of the abilities he had while he was one of My angels. Say your Saint Michael Prayer daily as this will remove him from you for a brief period of time. My child, you will now recite the Saint Michael Prayer as I leave you. I, too, will return at a later date to give you a new Message."

Seer: "Saint Michael, the Archangel, defend us in the battle. Be our protection against the wickedness and snares of the devil. May God rebuke him, we humbly pray. And do thou, O Prince of the Heavenly Hosts, by the Divine Power of God, cast into Hell Satan, and all of the Evil Spirits who wander throughout the World, seeking for the ruin of souls. Amen."

****

Message given to a privileged soul (Michael) by the Blessed Virgin Mary, Sunday, December 7, 1986, Eve of the Feast of the Immaculate Conception

Our Lady: "My child, the name of the Seer you seek is Teresita Castillo. She is now in the Carmelite Order. My child, and My children, long ago at Lipa, in the country of the Philippines, I appeared to Teresita in seeking to guide you all. In 1948 there were many things I asked Teresita to bring forth to you all.

"Luciel, Prince of Darkness, you won over there, but you shall fail over here. You may have caused the child to be forced by [her] Vow of Obedience to be silenced by the Bishop. In order to fulfill her vows to My Son, she was forced to disobey My requests. Thus she was allowed to stay in the convent, and My words be forgotten, but you have not silenced Me. I have revealed My words to many other Seers and shall continue to do more of revealing My words. You shall never stop Me.

"There are many Shrines in the world where I appeared and was once honored; yet now sadly, many of My Shrines are Shrines, but are unknown of, due to you bishops of the world who are not faithful enough to Me to promote them. Sadly, even those Shrines that are authorized by you bishops, cardinals, and My (Divine Son's) representative, Pope John Paul II, are unknown by most children. O Bishops and Cardinals of My Son's Church, I, the Queen of Heaven, Our Lady of All Holy Titles, request of you that you allow your peoples to visit My Shrines. Remember that you will have to explain your actions when you come before My (Divine) Son in your Judgement.

"My child, Richard is known of by Us. My (Divine) Son and I see all that ever happens on your earth. He will know that he has been heard (question) by Us, and our answer is: "There is always room for more prayer."

"My child, you will now join Me in one Hail Mary and one St. Michael Prayer."

****

Message given to a privileged soul (Michael) by Jesus and Mary, Wednesday, December 24, 1986, 11:30 PM till 2:30 AM, Thursday, December 25, 1986, Eve and Feast of the Birth of Jesus, Our Lord.

Our Lady: "My child and My children, in your world now, there is much abortion. The abortions must not continue. There must be much prayer, much prayer. Pray, Pray, Pray! It is needed now, My children, for no matter what your world, your nation, or each of you shall do in actions, the actions must be prayers, or they (actions) are meritless. Every letter that you write, every action that you make, it must be a prayer in these Latter Days. I have told you on numerous occasions, My child, that everything you do must be a prayer, for if it is not with prayer, it is meritless, and you know what meritless fruits are. They are naught before the Father. At all times, My child, wear your crucifix. Do not remove it, My child. It is necessary for you."

Seer: "Yes, Mother."

Our Lady: "Repeat the following Poem."

> "Think always of your God and Lord;
> Then you never have excuse to be bored.
>
> Remember always to Honor My Son;
> It is Treasures of your life that you've won.
>
> Remember always, the Church is for Prayer;
> Then your life's Prayer will always be fair.
>
> Think always of the true Glory of God;
> Without Him, mankind would still be sod."

Our Lady: "My child, at this time I wish you to repeat the prayer that you always love to say for Me in Latin, and it will go on the printed Message the same."

Seer: "Yes, Mother, I know you are referring to the Ave Maria, the Hail Mary."

"Ave Maria, gratia plena. Dominus Tecum. Benedicta Tu, in muleribus. Et benedictus fructus ventris Tui, Jesus. Sancta Maria, Mater Dei, ora pro nobis. Recatoribus nunc, et in hora mortis nostrae. Amen."

Our Lady: "My child and My children of the world: Soon to come upon you will be the destructions. The destructions which have been mentioned in the past. I do not say that they will come in the beginning of the next year, in the middle of the next year, in the end of the next year. Nor do I even say that they are in the next year; nor do I say that they are in the ending of this year. I only say that they are soon. A date will not be given, My children, unto you at this time. But, My children of the world, you must be aware. You must be aware of the fact that in your nation the Bomb, which had been mentioned in the past, and shall be mentioned again, will, one day, go into a large explosion that will set off a major earthquake and much shall be destroyed. Much of New York shall be destroyed. California in most parts shall be destroyed; parts shall sink below the ocean. You, My child, will pause and listen as I speak to you but this must not go in print. (Private Message was given concerning dates.)

"Continue repeating, My child. "Japan shall sink below the water. Hawaiian Islands: You, too, shall sink below the waters."

Seer: "Blessed Mother, do you mean the bomb will set the San Andreas (fault) off, and then San Andreas in turn, set the other fault lines off and it will cause California - North, South, and West of the line, to sink?"

Our Lady: "Yes, My child, it shall sink very low below the waters. It will not be able to be considered as part of the United States after that point. When this bomb goes off, many bodies will be burned beyond recognition, charred to the bone. You will think that it is the day that your God has returned and that He is destroying the evil, but it will not be He. He will return, but much will happen before that, much will happen, and My children, you can add more time before this happens, if you pray hard. Prayer, prayer, prayer is your only weapon that you have now. It is the only weapon against the demons which will be loosed again within your nation, within the world. They will begin in full force, and the only weapon that you will have, I repeat again, is your prayers.

"Pray the Rosary; the Rosary is your weapon. Each little bead that you pry is a bullet in the heart of each of the demons. They cannot stand to hear the prayer. When you pray, each little prayer that you say will pierce their heart. You will send shivers of fear through every demon by simply praying.

"My children, is it much to ask you to pray? Every action that you do you can pray. Some of you run in the morning or jog in the evening. During this time is it not easy to pray? Prayer need not always be verbal. You can pray in your heart. You can pray in your soul. Meditate upon My (Divine) Son. Meditate upon Him in the Sorrowful, the Joyful, or the Glorious Mysteries. Meditate upon the Way of the Cross. He died for you - now remember him. Remember your Lord and God. My child, My Son, your Lord, will be with you real soon, and when He visits you, and St. Michael visits you, you will await the next Message before sending the Message on to your workers for printing, as they must be printed together.

"My Heart is saddened, My child, saddened by the evils already in your world. We, in Heaven, look upon your nation now and We see pornography rampant in your nation. The children view this. And it is not just viewing it, far too many now are being forced into it. O mankind, My children, what have you done? Why do you read the literature of these vipers, My children? Are some of you actually unaware that it is sin to even view the sick so-called works of art?

"Why have you taken the children (the purity of your nation) and made it impure? Continuously, you have been taking more and more children, discarding their immortal souls, by picturing them in perverse pictorials in your magazines. Yes, My child, I am crying - you should let them know. Do not be ashamed to let them know that I am crying, they should know. It is due to the pain to My Son's heart that I am crying, for My heart too, suffers greatly. My heart is saddened to the point where it seems un-useful for Me to continue with My various Messages to you all around the world, through various Seers, Stigmatists, Mystics, and Visionaries. Yet I will continue, for there are still many who must be saved. These Messages in these Latter Days will save many. Many will be saved that would never have ever had a chance prior to the Message reaching them.

"See, My child, My heart; Each of your prayers, My children, eases these thorns. But the sufferings are great. Were it not for My suffering and the suffering of My Son, and the sufferings of many upon your earth who have offered their suffering up to Us in prayer, your nation would already have fallen. All of the nations of the world would, as such, now be communistic. My Son's Return would come quicker. Many would die and would not be saved, that should be saved, that could be saved, and that must be saved.

"My child, do not repeat again, until I say repeat. Repeat:

"Now, My child, you will bring forth the small amount of Rose Petals I have brought to you. You will have these laminated, and they will be given out as all of the other rose petals in the past have been, to the people.

"Quite a long time ago I spoke to you, My child, about the danger to many people of your earth through assassination. I spoke to you of a planned attempt of assassination upon your Vicar, John Paul II, upon Prince Charles, and Princess Diana, and Queen Elizabeth and your President of the U.S.A. Nothing has changed. There are still plans for the attempts. My children, there must be much prayer. It is now, My children, that prayer must come out in multiple force, or your nation, as you know it, shall fall. My child, you will now await My (Divine) Son. You must now pray in silence."

Jesus: "You will repeat: Much Grace was given this evening to those in your nation and around the world, who have prayed at the same time as you, in union. By asking for all people who were praying throughout the world, to have their prayers joined with you, you have made it for them as if they were all here praying with you at that moment. In some small ways, part of your world is getting better, but still the balance is being far tilted to the left, and Luciel's (Prince of Darkness) reign will begin soon.

"Luciel, Prince of Darkness, your time is short!

"When you pray, My children, We ask that you not only give lip-service, but actual heart and mind, along with your prayer. My heart is grieved that I must say: war is approaching, and you are in a time where no peace will be coming. Again, My children, I repeat My Mother's words – Prayer, prayer. This is all you have to do. Remember to pray the Rosary, the weapon My Mother gave to you ages ago.

"Describe, My child."

Seer: "I see before me a large Asiatic-skinned hand and arm. Upon it is a ball of flames. The flames are licking about, in red, yellow, and orange hues. It is a night or early morning sky. It would be hard to say; it is other than the Ball of Redemption."

Jesus: "Repeat, My child: My children, it is insanity for all of the people who are committing the acts against society – Murders, Adultery, Pornography, these acts are all insanity of the mind, insanity of the heart. Our hearts are saddened. Soon Our hearts will be saddened no more. Soon your nation, and all of the nations of the world will fall. My Return will then be imminent, but you can slow this happening if you will all pray.

"Do not repeat (private Message).

"Repeat: I say unto you now, children: Mankind, you are becoming perverse. You must repent before My hand is forced to come down quicker than you would expect. When My hand comes down upon you, the Chastisement will be great upon earth. Again, I repeat, only one thing will save your earth now: Prayer, Atonement and Sacrifice. I am a Just God. I do not like to see fights and quarrels between My Creations quarreling over what Religion is correct. You will all be nowhere without Prayer, Atonement, and Sacrifice. All Christians must line themselves together in this battle of Armageddon. My child, you will now await St. Michael. You will pray in the meantime while you wait."

Seer: "I understand."

Seer: Before me now is a Large Angel. He said:

St. Michael: "Do not describe me. There are not enough funds to print the descriptions at present. I say this because I understand how your normal descriptions are. You go into too much detail. I say unto you now, a Servant of the Mother of the Lord, you must never remove this crucifix. This crucifix, which you have, with the relics of the Saints, is your weapon at this time, against Lucifer. He shall try to attack upon you in body and in spirit. In spirit he will succeed, upon occasion, with temptation. Yet, you must never let him attack your body.

"Thus, this crucifix must never from you part!

"Goodbye for now.

"The Queen will again see you soon. And, do not forget to pray."

****

Message given to a privileged soul (Michael) by Our Lord, Saturday December 27, 1986, 11:48 PM till Sunday, December 28, 1986, 12:04 AM, Eve and Feast Day of the Holy Family.

Jesus: "My little son, the coming year will be a very different experience for many. There will be many who will leave your earth this year through unnatural deaths. Pray for them, as they need prayers, as they may not attain Purgatory even. The Miracle you are thinking of, My son, is truly the sign that you question it to be. It is a sign concerning the Monarchy I've spoken, along with My Mother, to you of, in the past. You know now who you are to pray for, as it [is] that time now, My little son.

"In your United States now is being planned, the attack upon the democracy of your nation. During the next election, within the next few years, in the planning is to put a Communist Party representative on the presidential ballot. He would be unknown in regard to his connection to the Communist Party. Should he become president, the Red Bear's forces would enter your nation's shores. When this happens, you will find it is too late, for you will be on your knees to send your Messages, in your prayers to Me after your nation will already be sentenced to communism. The strategy for this is already active in your present country of the Eagle, also known as the U.S.A.

"The winter will grow much colder if the prayer does not increase. Your country has only experienced the tip of the cold so far. Your prayers, My children, will temper the winter's cold and storm."

****

Message given to a privileged soul (Michael) by Jesus to the World, Wednesday, December 31, 1986, Eve of the New Year, and Eve of the Solemnity of Mary Immaculate

Jesus: "My little son, there are many diseases now, that are spreading rampantly through your nation. If you wear your Sacramentals, and add a drop of Holy Water to your liquids and solids, you will have less chance of catching those passable through the food. The chance will depend upon your faith in My words to you all, and how you act upon My words.

"My little son, any liquids you drink, you will bless with your Miraculous Crucifix and all ill - natured items, such as harmfulness due to poisons, or toxins, will be rendered null for you. Pray now."

****

1987 Messages

Message given to a privileged soul (Michael) by Our Lady, 19th, 20th of March, 1987, Feast Day of St. Joseph

"My children, you must all remember to pray your Rosary daily. It is the weapon against the Enemy of God. It is the second most feared weapon against the Enemy of God. The first weapon is your brown Scapular which is your armor and protection at this time. More and more there is need for prayers in your world now. You must remember prayer before you leave your home each and every day. Every Hail Mary, Glory Be, or Our Father that you say, could help your day start off in a much better way. Every decisive action throughout your day should be done in prayer.

"There must be much more prayer for John Paul II, your Vicar on earth. He needs your prayers. Without your prayers he cannot continue to Shepherd the Church of My Son. Which wolf shall you gain if you lose your Shepherd? Pray much now for the failure of a plot within. You cannot afford to lose your Vicar. You will be lost without him.

"My children, there is much need for you to pray, also, for a change in the pharmaceutical company's policies. Pray very diligently that the drug Mifepristone does not enter the open market for sales in the United States. This drug, also known as RU486, the chemical abortifacient, will, if it enters your country of the United States raise the abortion murders so high that My Son will be forced to chastise you sooner than you would expect. This drug was brought into existence by vipers of the Swiss Hoechst-Roussel Pharmaceuticals Company. Pray, My child, that these 'doctors' as they are called, go back to doing what the License of Medicine states that they are to do. They should save, not destroy lives.

"My children of the United States of America: the AIDS virus is spreading so rapidly among you all because of how your young people are having sex outside of marriage, against the wishes of the (Eternal) Father. So I say again: Pray, My children, Pray."

****

Message given to a privileged soul (Michael) by Archangel St. Michael, March 25, 1987, Annunciation Feast Day

Before me is an Archangel named St. Michael. I was praying before, and, as such, he told me to continue until I was done, as I was making music to his ears. Now he wanted me to finish my Rosary and since I have, he is here to tell me the following Message that he will give in a moment or two. He just said: "Annunciation Day". That was the answer to the question I was thinking. This means that this is the authentic St. Michael. "Praise to you, St. Michael!"

"Do not praise me. You must praise the Queen of Heaven and Her Son. I am but a servant of the Lord and the Queen. You will now bow your head to your Lord." He is holding up a Host to the Sky.

"You are not yet worthy of the Lord's Body and Blood. Now behold."

Suddenly I am nowhere. Now, all around is the odor of both Roses, and then cigars. The scent comes in waves: first, cigars, then roses, then cigars, and then roses. Now before me is a Monk, a Priest. He is nodding to me to come forward. "Kneel: How long since last Confession?" Padre Pio gave me Confession.

Then St. Michael returned me to where we started from, where he had brought me to, was half-way into the Spirit World. Upon return he said, "Open thy mouth young one." I did so. "Corpus Christi. Amen." I received Our Lord. Next, he held out a Chalice to me to drink from. I do not know where he got it from. "Anima Christi. Amen." I received the sweetest wine I've ever tasted. Of course this was Our Lord in Host and Wine. I must pray now. (Pause)

"Now, Young One, repeat: "In your world now is a great evil known as Cryogenics - freezing of humans for revival in the future. I bring you this Message that all of Heaven wishes you to know that there will be no way ever for man to revive you if you are cryogenically frozen in nitrogen. What will be revived will be an agent of the Antichrist and do you think you will be okay for this act of suicide, should you be alive while you are being bodily frozen? You will, as such, be accountable for your actions.

"The newer evil in your world is computerized credit between your banks and your food markets. Soon all will be on computer and without your having a chip placed in your forehead, you will not be allowed to purchase food items. Is this what you want? The Mark of the Beast via computer chips that will read your value, money wise, like a storage cassette? They will then move up to mind control computer chips. Is this what you want? Pray, children of the world. Pray hard. You, little Seer, will now pray your Rosary."

Then I prayed the Rosary.

****

Message given to a privileged soul (Michael) by Our Lady, April 2, 1987, 2:00 AM, Feast Day of St. Francis of Paola

"My child, you have done well to think the question of the water. In fact I came here this day to give you a Message concerning your weather and the flooding waters in the North East.

"My children of the world, the weather of the world is controlled by Luciel, the Prince of Darkness. He seeks to destroy much. The (Eternal) Father is allowing the turbulent conditions of the weather to go on, because of the lack of prayer from you all. It is the way of a punishment from the Father toward a sinful world. All you need to do, as a nation, as a group, as in small groups, is pray, pray, pray. This is not much to ask of you. Many people receive the Message, and read My words. They see the request for prayers and say: "Mary or Sue will pray - I don't feel like it today. I will pray tomorrow." Now is when the prayer is needed, not tomorrow, but now! Tomorrow may be too late. If you do not pray, your fruit crops and vegetables and grain crops in the South will suffer a frost and you will have famine in your United States greater than has ever been before. Is this what you want? It will come upon you if you do not pray. Your prayer must be more than lip-service. You must mean what you say with your heart and mind and soul.

"Soon there will be a contamination of the soil of the growing fields in your nation. The salt-level in your reservoirs of the United States is rising monthly in some spots. Is this what you want? You all must realize the war going on around you in the spirit realm, the war of good and evil. Luciel, the Prince of Darkness, seeks to destroy. It is your choice: death and destruction and famine, or prayer and prosperity of your nation. It is your choice of good and its benefits, or the other way about."

Note: One day later, the crowd at his (John Paul II) visit, was fired upon by [the] Government.

****

Message given to a privileged soul (Michael) by Our Lady on Palm Sunday, April 12, 1987

Our Lady: "My child, you will await Me on Good Friday with your Rosary in hand. There will be much prayer, and I have much to tell you on Friday. There must be prayer now for Our Vicar, your Holy Father on earth. There must be prayer for him until he ends his visit in the United States which will soon occur. If there is not enough prayer, his life will be forfeit in the United States of America during this upcoming visit.

"My child, you will pray now."

At this point, Our Lady was gone. I prayed a Hail Mary and then I wrote this short Message, from Her down onto paper.

****

Message given by Our Lady on Good Friday, April 17, 1987

Our Lady is wearing Her blue regal robe. Her belt is of golden links that are woven and unlike no earthly metallurgist could ever have made. She has a tassel, like the Necedah Apparition, today. Her tunic is of a white that is purer than that of actual snow. Our Lady's hair is not showing through Her mantle at all today. The mantle is a slightly darker shade of blue than the robe is. Our Lady seems to be in sorrow. As She gives us Her Message, I'm sure we will understand why She is sorrowful, as such.

Our Lady: "My child, describe the area of My feet."

With a curious look, She is nodding for me to look down. "I obey Your wishes, Blessed Mother." (It was hard to look down from Her, but since it was Her wish, I did so.) Our Lady is barefoot, but floating in the air. By Her feet are miniature rosettes. They are of reds, pinks, yellows, and whites. Now She is holding Her finger to Her lips and asking me to repeat.

Our Lady: "I will be known not only as **Our Lady of All Holy Titles**, but I wish to be known that I still come as **Our Lady of the Roses** as well. Many think that My Shrine at Bayside has fallen. It has not fallen yet, My child and My children of the world. My child, you will pray with Me now."

(At this point Our Holy Mother had me pray the Our Father, Hail Mary, Glory Be, and the Saint Michael prayer.)

The Our Father

Our Father, Who art in Heaven, hallowed be thy Name. Thy Kingdom come; Thy Will be done on earth as it is in Heaven. Give us this day our daily bread; and forgive us our trespasses against us: and lead us not into temptation, but deliver us from evil. Amen.

The Hail Mary

Hail Mary, full of Grace. The Lord is with you; blessed is the fruit of your womb, Jesus. Holy Mary, Mother of God, pray for us now and at the hour of our death. Amen.

The Glory Be to the Father

Glory be to the Father, and to the Son, and to the Holy Spirit, as it was in the beginning, is now, and ever shall be, world without end. Amen.

Prayer to St. Michael

St Michael, the Archangel, defend us in battle. Be our defense against the wickedness and snares of the devil. May God rebuke him, we humbly pray; and do thou, O Prince of the Heavenly Host, by the Divine Power of God, thrust into Hell Satan, and all the evil spirits who wander throughout the world, seeking the ruin of souls. Amen.

Our Lady: "My child, you will now repeat. In your world now there is a new great sin, a sin done by the surgeons of your land. In this sin, great evil is committed, for man seeks to recreate his own life at the expense of another. Man seeks to take his life and extend it beyond that of which the (Eternal) Father wishes. The Father has not yet intervened. He will allow man to do as he is now doing. He will not stop you all until it is too late.

"This new lease on life that man seeks [is] in concern of Parkinson's Disease and such related diseases. In some cases, mankind is taking glands from a fetus to produce a substance in the brain. This is not right, and is not in the Will of Heaven [to] take life from one and supply it to thyself at their cost. O mankind, whatever shall become of you? You seek evil and even try to hide it to make it to seem as good.

"Do you even know right from wrong anymore? Do you not wish to do the Will of Heaven? Some of you do, yes, but there are many who do not. O Man of Science, I speak to you now. You have gone too far to the left. You must return. You must return to Us now before it is too late. You seek to recreate your life over and over again. It shall not be. It shall not be! There must be much prayer said in your world now, My child and My children. There must be much prayer. The Rosary - it is your weapon. You must pray it daily. You must not pray with just lip-service but you must pray with your heart, with your mind and with your soul.

"And those of you Christians who are not Catholic, the Way of The Cross will be just as efficient to all Christians. I say now, you must unite in Prayer, Atonement, and Sacrifice. We ask this of all of you daily. Is it too hard to pray? When you wake up in your morning, is it too hard to remember your Lord and God along your way? He is there; if you but ask of Him, He will be there to comfort you in prayer. You may not see him with your physical eyes, but your Lord and God is there. All of Heaven's Angels are at your disposal, My child, at any time you need them to help you to pray for everyone, everywhere. You must all remember that We seek Prayer, Atonement, and Sacrifice daily. My child, you will again pray with Me, for We need many prayers now. We need many prayers. My (Divine) Son is in sorrow and I, myself, am in sorrow. Console Me now, My child, console Me."

"Yes, Mother, I will pray with You now." As I was praying a decade of the Rosary I noticed She was crying. I asked Her why as follows: "Why do You cry now Mother?" (Her tears were streaming.) All about me the scene suddenly is changing; now I'm not alone with Our Holy Mother. John is holding her up. Mary Magdalene is present and other women as well, at a distance with the Roman guards.

I am now at the foot of the Cross, and the sky is overcast, almost dark with clouds. I am afraid to look upon Our Lord Who is bleeding even now before me on the Cross. I am moved to tears, myself now, at all this suffering I see about me now. Now I must look up and see Our Lord upon the Cross. I am wretched in the stomach. Were it that I had just eaten I would have nothing left in my stomach from the sight of all of Our Dear Lord's wounds. I want to just go to Him and kiss His feet and tell Him how sorry I am for not loving Him even more. Yet I'm frozen where I am, in this position. I cannot move.

This is a sight no man would like to see. There is Our Lord's Sacred Precious Blood, all over the place. There is hardly a small strip of flesh that has not been torn. Everyone here, except the guards, is crying. John is helping Mary to stand, here at the foot of the Cross. Jesus now is speaking to John; I do not understand. Now I do understand. Jesus is telling John to behold thy Mother, and telling his Mother (Our Lady) behold thy son. In this it is imparted that Our Lady is now to be regarded as the Mother of the world. John is regarded as a representative of all mankind, as children of Mary. That they must take care of each other is also imparted unto them.

Now Jesus is looking up to the clouds. He is yelling out something, I do not quite understand. The words sound like "Eloi, Eloi, Lama Sabacthani." Now I understand - He is saying: "My God, My God, why hast Thou forsaken Me?"

Now everything seems to be tragic, as the guards are saying something, and pointing to Jesus. Our Lady is saying that they are stating that Jesus is calling for Elias to help Him. Now all is fading except for Our Lady. We are now back where we were before. Our Lady is now telling me that this is the reason She cries. For yearly, this death of Her (Divine) Son, Our Lord, is reviewed by Her, and Her Motherly Heart is yearly rent asunder by the daggers which pierce Her heart in pure sorrow. Yearly He dies, descends, and rises again. Not in the physical sense, but in the spiritual sense.

Our Lady: "You must all remember this. You must remember it. He died for your sins; now you must remember Him."

And now we are going back again to another scene. We are back at the Cross. Jesus is asking me if I wish to know of His suffering.

Now, I am sure: A lot of you will not believe this, but as I said "Yes" to Jesus. I spent three minutes nailed to His Cross, bleeding, and the pain tore at every nerve ending in my body. It was as if every nerve was on fire; and even worse, at that moment of the end of the third minute, I began to wish for death. Then Jesus, Who was standing looking up at me, said: "Enough." And He was again upon the Cross. I was now upon the ground again and weakly looking up at Him. I now understand the suffering Jesus is, and has gone through for us all. I even felt the great love He had for me. There was not one nerve in His Body which did not feel pain. His complete body was pained. While I was on the Cross, my voice was as naught. My throat was dryer than desert sand. I felt like I had not a drop of blood left. Yes, I do now understand His suffering better than I ever have in the past. Our Lady is now taking me back to where we started from.

Our Lady: "Remember Him, My child, daily. You, yourself, do not pray enough. You must pray more. You must pray daily, and you must pray your Rosary. You have been lax in your prayer. There are many people who have requested your prayer. You must remember them daily. It is not enough that you should say to your guardian angel to pray for you in your place. You must pray. It is true that your prayer is powerful, My child. This is why We request your prayer. Without your prayer, many will fall, many who need not fall if you will pray enough. Is this too much to ask of you, My child?" "No, Mother, it is not."

Our Lady: "Then you must pray more. And you, O mankind, you must all pray more too. Yes, all of you, My children, must pray much more. It is not enough to pray only once a day. You must remember your Lord in your way. As you daily go about in your businesses, in all of your actions, take a moment to think of Him. Think of His sorrows. Think of His Crucifixion, the Death, the Burial in the Tomb. Then think of the Resurrection. He died for your sins, now remember Him! Yes, My child, this is repetitious, but it is necessary, for you and many others do not remember your Lord, Our God. It is necessary now, My child. You will pray one Hail Mary with Me."

After this one Hail Mary, Our Lady nodded to me. I am to pause and wait.

Our Lady: "'You will now hold out the palms from Palm Sunday, for Me."

From Her hands are coming blue rays with glass-like white Graces intermittently among the rays. From above Our Lady, through a Hole in the sky, is coming a pink Ray of Light with clear white filaments floating into the palms.

"You will understand soon, My child. You will understand soon. You will take these palms, My child, and you will cut them into small segments and these will be laminated and given to the people of earth. All who do request, will be given one until they are diminished. But, as you will see, My child, these two palms will make more than you could ever imagine. Yes, My child, you will understand soon. Even though you do not yet understand. Remember My (Divine) Son and the loaves and the fishes; then you will understand.

"Yes, Mother, I now understand you. They will divide and multiply; although I do not understand how. It is not for me to understand. It is Your Will."

"Yes, My child, it is in the Will of Heaven."

At this point Our Lady rose into the sky further and was gone. I heard Her voice saying: "Pray now, My child, until I return at a later date. You will pray and you will pray more, until you can pray no more.

"Good-bye now, My child."

****

Message given by Our Lady on Easter Sunday, April 19, 1987

Our Lady: "My children, the mentally ill of your land are almost all treated with medications that could be dangerous to them. The chemicals in their brain are off, slightly, so, rather than correct the chemical deficiencies with synthetic chemicals, you treat them with dangerous medications. O men of science, called doctors, you have done your profession wrong. You should help your fellow man, not cover the problem with medication.

"Yes, My child, this is different than what I spoke of on Friday to you.

"You will pray now, My child."

****

1988 Messages

Message given to a privileged soul (Michael) by Our Lady, Holy Thursday, March 31, 1988, 11:00 PM - 12 Midnight

Our Holy Mother is now appearing in a bright opening of light. She is the source of the light. The light is coming from Her in soft pastels of deep blue and of pink. With this is pure white light coming from behind Her. Our Lady has on a purple-hued mantle and robe. Her feet are bare and are very dainty. Her tunic is of a yellowish shade of white. Not the usual ecru color, but of a yellowish white. The outer edges of all of Our Lady's garments are lined in pure spun-gold leaf. It is designed almost like little links of chain. Our Holy Mother's hair does not show this evening. It is completely covered by Her mantle/ veil. The heartache She is feeling is quite apparent on Her face this evening as She is crying. She h silently crying. She is speaking:

Our Lady: "My tears fall, My child, because it is deafened ears that My words seem to fall upon. Mankind has closed himself to the truth. Were it not for the few who care , the few who pray for Mercy, the few who offer their small part in reparation, the time would be up and My (Divine) Son's hand would be upon you all. The murder of the innocents must stop! My Son's heart is breaking. He is filled with pain for all those in the world who still send His gifts (unborn souls) back to Him.

"It is not only for pleasure that the sexual intercourse exists, My children. It is only made pleasurable because The Father (Creator) did not want you all to think it laborious to follow His directive to "go forth and multiply". Chastity is a virtuous thing. If you do not desire more children, then Chastity is the Way of Life for you. The so-called doctors and men of science, who produce items called birth control are only, in truth, disguising their acts of murder under the name of science. Those who have used the womb-destroyers, called by science inter-uterine devices, are alone at fault for the destruction of their womb. They also are guilty of the murder of each child they would have had if the IUD had not made their womb hostile to life. The men of science are just as guilty for each child who dies. This hardly mentions as well, the millions each year that are aborted via doctors (with devices) entering the womb and removing the child.

"We, in Heaven, daily hear the cry of the many saints, as they ask My Son: "When, O when, O Lord, shall You stop this murder?" Soon there will again be a time for your nation to pick its leaders. If you elect those who support abortions, then you have not done your part to stop the carnage.

"My child, you will pray now. I will return to you tomorrow night."

****

Message given to a privileged soul (Michael) by Our Lady, Good Friday, April 1, 1988, 11:00 PM to 1:00 AM, Holy Saturday, April 2, 1988

Our Lady is before me already; while praying She materialized behind me and told me to turn around. Tonight She is almost looking the same as yesterday except She is crying more still, and Her tunic is ecru, like it usually is. Our Lady's robe and mantle are a deep shade of bluish purple, more purple. Today She has slippers made of what appears to be rose petals. They are all purple as well (the rose petals were purple). Our Holy Mother is speaking now:

Our Lady: "My child and My children, you must love My (Divine) Son! You must not mock Him. The veils must be brought back upon the heads of the women in My Son's Churches. The offense to the Angels offends My Son as well. O Pastors, you do not teach your flock of the offense to the Angels caused when a female enters a house of My Son without a veil as a head coverage. You, O Pastors, are guilty if your flock members do not know. Many of you say: "The Law was abrogated long ago." It is a Bible writing that they change if they seek to change this law. Since when are the priests above the disciples who wrote the Book of Laws, [the] New Testament? Come down from your proudness, O shepherds of My Son. Proudness leads to the fall of a soul. How can you shepherd My Son's flock if you are, yourself, not obeying the word to teach My Son's flock? The statues must be returned in the homes of My Son. Remember the saying of St. Theresa: "Out of sight - Out of mind." The Host, once consecrated, must be placed upon the tongue, not in the hand. When placed in the hand it is a sacrilege.

"My child, you will pray now for those who don't realize these errors in the Church of today."

With this, Our Lady slowly went up into the source of light She always enters when She leaves.

****

Message given to a privileged soul (Michael) by Our Lady, Saturday, June 18, 1988, Feast of St. Ephrem - Traditional

Our Lady: "My child and My children, you have forced the hand of My (Divine) Son upon you all. How long your weather pattern will be abnormal for, will be up to each and every one of you. I have asked for prayers from each and every one of you for years. Now My words fall upon deaf ears!

"Your once proud United States of America - what has become of it? The Eagle has been plucked. Unless you pray, all of you, as a nation, pray like you never have before, the trials and tribulations will increase upon each one of you three-fold! You are in a war of the Spirits. You can only join one side - God or Evil. If you do not pray, and you do not ask for help from your God, then you have already made your choice. In this war you have one all-powerful, all-good weapon of peace. It is not guns, bullets, lasers, bombs, or bacterial weapons. It is the Rosary. The Rosary is your weapon.

"Behold, My child, and describe now what you see."

I see an area filled with castles and moats, and long stretches of open land. I believe it is Old (ancient as in the far-past) England. Our Holy Mother is nodding 'Yes'. Now I see a war party marching from across open land. They are being met by a war party from the largest castle. In the war party are, let me count, 1, 2, 3, 4, 5 nuns in full habits. They are kneeling at the edge of the great expanse of the battlefield. Now the king is saying to them to go back and pray for them. They are not listening to his order to leave. They are, however, now kneeling to pray the Rosary. At this moment; each is taking the Rosary from about her neck. The Rosaries are all wood on what appears to be solid silver links. The Mother Superior's looks golden in the links. They are now praying: "In Nomine Patris, etc." (Our Lady says to translate.) "In the Name of The Father, and of The Son, and of The Holy Ghost, Amen." (Our Lady had me [to] do the translation so anyone not knowing Latin would not be confused by the words in Latin.)

As they are praying, the clear sky is suddenly becoming covered in clouds. Oh, it is almost completely dark, the way the sky has become covered. Now the two parties are fighting with swords and spiked hammers. Now the lightning bolts are coming down from the sky. They seem to be striking and killing each of the attackers, one at a time. Many of them are fleeing now. The ones who remain are now dying one at a time. The nuns are now chanting.

"Holy Mother, I do not understand what they are saying."

"Listen and in a moment you will understand." (Somehow I knew then what they were chanting.)

"All Hail the power of the weapon of Our Holy Mother and Queen, Mary." Everything is now fading. There is a mist that is enveloping all. Now it is thinning.

Now I am in a chapel, a rather large one. I am floating with Our Holy Mother above a group of monks or priests. They are praying the Rosary. We must be in the 1900's now as I hear an airplane flying high above. Our Holy Mother is saying: "World War II - Japan. Now behold." Suddenly I hear a high pitched whistling sound. Oh, there is a sudden flash of light outside.

"This is the Atomic Bomb." Our Lady is saying. The Monks are not even aware of it. It is clear the Rosary is saving their lives. Now I am being brought outside by Our Holy Mother.

"Behold and describe."

The area is like a pool of glass. There are shadows cast upon the ground. They appear to be human shadows but there are no bodies in this spot. It is as if the bodies burned up but photo-printed their shadows on the ground first. "Nagasaki and Hiroshima, both are the same, My child." Now as I look around, all buildings except the Chapel are destroyed for a good distance. The monks inside are still fine.

Now again Our Holy Mother is speaking: "There are many more scenes I could show you, but I will avoid doing so now as this Message already shall be a long one for you."

Our Lady: "There are some of you who pray the Rosary unceasingly. You few are as stars here in Heaven. If only the majority of people would join you in the praying of the Rosary, your nation would be restored to its former glory. Your nation is but a skeleton of its former self."

"You must all pray for the bishops of the world that they gain the insight to pray for the conversion of Russia. The Bear will only be converted when every bishop prays at the same time for the conversion. Then the Russian Orthodoxy will unite with the Church of My Son, led from Rome. There is a plot again against Our Vicar, your Holy Father upon Earth. The evil one's minions are again seeking to remove him. Pray that he does not travel far from Rome at this time. Should he travel, you will all have to pray to Our Angel of Protection We call Golden Boy, better known to you as Saint Michael. He will protect him from danger if enough of you pray for him.

"Soon an election will be held for a new leader for your country. You must pray that your country elects a proper leader. Only if you get a proper leader will your nation again become more than a skeleton of its former glory. There is a plan to invalidate some electoral votes in your country. Pray that this plan fails. Prayer is a need in your world today, more than in any age of the past. I cannot stress the need for prayer any more than I now have done. is the thought of many people now, but I shall stress prayer until the Last Day.

"Soon your earth will begin to experience another Ice Age. The new weather patterns are a pre-requisite to this time of ice. Only prayers can stop this Ice Age. Without this prayer, once fertile fields will become too hot and dry to support any life. They will become as the desert now is. Much of the Northeast and Middle of the United States will become too cold to support plant life. Again only prayer can avert and hold back this situation.

Already there are samples of this in your in your nation now. Soon the prices of all dairy and plant foods will rise above what can be afforded by anyone of you. Your nation will experience the famines of which Africa already knows and experiences on a daily basis. Is this what you want? My (Divine) Son's hand is falling upon your nation. He is plucking the Eagle's skeleton because of lack of Prayer, Sacrifice, Atonement, Reparation and Repentance made in the Eagle's land. And what of the daily murder of the Innocents? Abortion will have to cease in your nation, or it will suffer this boil from the hand of My Son. It is your choice. The few victim-souls have held this situation back from happening so far, but now it has increased beyond the point their sufferings make up for.

"Bishops and priests of My Son's house upon earth: Why do you not demand the head cover back upon the heads of the women? The Angels and Saints are offended by this action of the women in not covering their heads before My Son (in the Tabernacle) during Mass and in Church in general. The immodesty before My Son must cease or your nation will suffer an even worse Boil upon it.

"Pray now, My son."

Note: The rule (tradition) regarding the need for head covering on women is found in [the] New Testament, St. Paul's first Letter to the Corinthians, Chapter Eleven.

****

Message given to a privileged soul (Michael) by Our Lady, July 1, 1988, Feast Day of the Most Precious Blood of Jesus Christ.

Our Lady: "My child, and My children, your weather both is, and shall be, very different in the future from what you have in the past known. It will bring the famine that is soon to come upon you to take the proudness from your nation, America the Beautiful. What has become of it? Your nation boasts of its wealth before the world, yet you have people starving in your streets. There are many in your nation who are boasting of their material and monetary greatness. Soon, because of your proudness, those of you who I speak of shall soon join the starving of your nation in the streets. And why? [On] account of your lack of prayer, lack of love, for My (Divine) Son, thy Lord and God. You do not love Him. You do not honor Him. You mock Him. You scorn Him. Charity is lacking among you; and so as such, all of your material wealth will shortly avail you naught. You have had warning after warning on these offenses to My Son. Some of you heed them. Some of you listened to My guidance, but the vast majority of you do not.

"Pastors, bishops, and cardinals: You hold a good part in the failure of My Son's flock. Of all of you, only ten percent obey the directives of My (Divine) Son. You, yourselves, must pray for the light. Ask for guidance of the Holy Ghost, and you shall receive it. You are supposed to be as fishermen. Your job is to be as fishermen for the souls of mankind. Who do you now fish for souls for? You can only obey one master. How many of you have given up your fishing for the ways of the world? How many of you have prayed the long hours of prayer that your forefathers, the Saints of Old prayed?

"Bishops: the statues must return in your parishes. If the likeness of Heavenly figures is removed, then the only thing that happens is that since We are out of sight, We are out of mind. Do not let the minions of Lucifer convince you that the likenesses are as in Idolatry. You do not worship a statue. You venerate it for whom the figure represents. There is in this a difference. Do not confuse the meanings left by your forefathers, the Apostles of Old. What has become of the Prayers after Mass? (Last Gospel and St. Michael Prayer). What has become of the veneration of My Son in the Blessed Sacrament?

"Bishops: if you truly love My (Divine) Son, your Lord, then show it. Bring back the Holy Hours and the veneration of My Son in the Blessed Sacrament. Only in this way will you prove your true love for My Son.

"My child, you will pray now. I will return with the second half of this Message shortly.

"My child, and My children, many months ago I spoke of Atlantis and Lemuria. I left their exact positions as a puzzle for the men of science to piece together. Since mankind has not found these once large land areas, which are now below the Atlantic (Ocean), I give you now more information. My child, you will now take a blank sheet of paper and a pencil. Now you will follow the outline of the Image you see on the paper."

I did so and came up with the Map of the World in the Age of Atlantis.

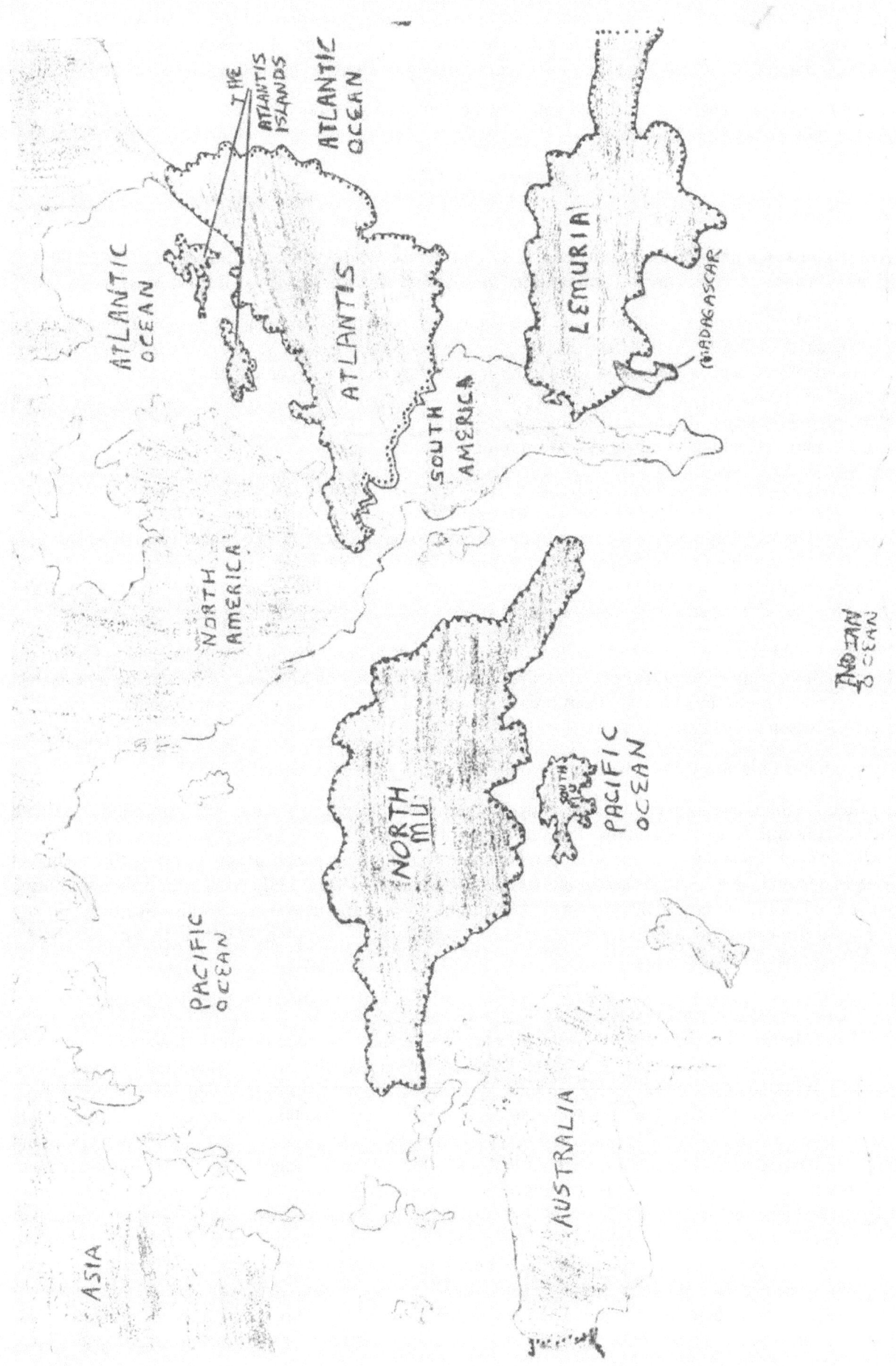

"This will be as more information for mankind to use in finding those parts of the world which destroyed themselves at the hand of the Father Eternal. In finding them, you men of science should learn to better yourselves and to find the way of peace as you learn from those mistakes made by past civilizations."

Explanation of Map: The land areas and small islands outlined with dots are the land masses which have fallen beneath the oceans.

****

Message given to a privileged soul (Michael) by Our Lady, Wednesday, December 7, 1988, 12:00 AM till 1:30 AM, Eve of Feast Day of Immaculate Conception, Anniversary Day of First Message in 1982.

Our Lady: "My child and My children, there are many souls who thirst for your prayers. You must begin an unceasing chain of prayers around the world for the poor souls in Purgatory, My children. In this day and age all too many of you neglect them. You seem to forget that they are there. Would that I were able to show you how many of you have family ancestral members in Purgatory, you would not forget. You would never want to stop praying for them. My child, I ask you now to prepare thyself to describe what I will very shortly show you of Purgatory. Continue to repeat (My words) for now.

"Our Holy Vicar upon earth, John Paul II, has instructed you all to pray more. Why do you not listen to him? We, in Heaven, see the numbers of you who disregard what he has instructed you to do. When you come before My (Divine) Son, what will come of you? If you do not merit Hell, due to sin, you will spend time extended in the purging fires of Purgatory due to your lack of compassion for those already there. Many of you, as you read My words, will think that these words are too stern to have come from Me, but what shall I do? Not warn you of the consequences you shall suffer for your own neglectful ways?

"Mothers: would you allow your children to suffer in your jails of earth if you knew beforehand of what was to become of your child? My children, you know you would not. As the Mother of All, I can do no less than to warn you and try to save you. My heart breaks at the sufferings that many souls must endure before they can view My Son's Kingdom.

"My child, it is time now (to go). Reach out your hand to Me and come. Describe now."

Seer: I am reaching out my hand and Our Holy Mother is now holding my hand. She is so gentle. I feel so calm and peaceful. She is crying now. I can tell it is for the sight I am to view in a moment or so. I don't know how, but I just know I am correct. It is almost like Her emotions are so strong in sorrow that I can feel Her emotions with Her. It is a peaceful and compassionate sorrow. Our Holy Mother is walking with me now. She is leading me up a stairway which seems to be evaporating below us. It is also like the stairs are going down from above to raise us up quicker than we could walk on our own. We are in an area surrounded by just bright blinding white light.

Our Holy Mother: "Do not let go of My hand, My son, or your body till die in this state of Limbo."

Seer: "Yes, Mother - I understand." Now the area around Us is like a cloud opening up above Us and now swallowing Us up. Now all around Us is a sea of flames. This area is almost like when I viewed Hell. There is one big difference here. There are no demons or devils. There are, however, people everywhere I look. They are not 'burning' themselves, but they feel the pain as if they were burning physically. All the people are see-through like a ghost or a wraith in a ghost story on earth would be told of looking like. Now the stairs are raising upward again. We are not walking upward. They are just raising Us up, up into darkness now. Here it is very cold and dark. I hear the screams of the people as I did below, but here I can't see them beyond the light of which Our Holy Mother's presence is emitting. The people below and here, I notice, seem very much unaware of Our presence here. It is as if We are not here to them. Again, we are raising upward on the stairs. Now there is light everywhere about like on earth during a day in the summer at 12 noon. Everyone here seems to be unaware of Our presence. Oh, above Us there are angels. Someone is now being taken out of this place to somewhere by an angel. There are angels everywhere. This seems to be the Purgatory just before Heaven. The souls here are aware of the angels. They are praying for the people on earth here. The angels are carrying their prayers to Heaven.

Now We are dropping fast lack to my room on earth. We are now back in my room. Our Holy Mother is now saying:

Our Lady: "My child, you will now pray. I will return on December 12th."

With this She was gone.

****

Message given to a privileged soul (Michael) by Our Lord, December 12, 1988, Feast Day of Our Lady of Guadelupe

Our Lord appeared to me today in His Ecru-white tunic. His royal robe was a scarlet color of red trimmed with golden edges. I quote Him now as He gave the Message to me.

Our Lord: "My little son, there must be more prayer in the world. The many times My Mother speaks to the world, and has spoken to the world in the past, seems to have fallen upon deafened ears. At Fatima She warned you all of the condition of the changes I never approved of in My house (Church). What has been done with Her warnings of Fatima? Man has cast them aside. The red berets (cardinals) in Rome have chosen to cast this Message of warning aside. They do not pass it on to the laymen of the flock.

"Red Berets: how do you expect I will look upon you when you do not inform My flock of the warning My Mother gave for them? You must, from Rome, have it sent out for the world's shepherds in My houses around the world to read off to My flock. This is My last warning to you, red berets. My hand is still descending shall soon be on the world. The revelation in My houses, of the warnings given by My Mother, will slow the fall of My hand upon the world.

"My little son, I tell you now to still be prepared for the Message of My Mother on the 15th of December.

"You will pray now."

****

Message given to a privileged soul (Michael) by Our Lady, December 15, 1988, Feast Day of St. Herman of Alaska

Our Lady: "My child and My children, there is a lack of prayer still in your world. The Rosary is the prayer the Catholic should pray unceasingly. If you knew the value (that) each little prayer within the Rosary prayers holds, you would not cease praying. Your prayers may consist of other forms as well.

"Non-Catholics: remember to pray the prayers of your Church. Prayer is your weapon. Storm your earth's cities with forces of Faithful and True. Under the banner of Faithful and True you can still save many of your cities from the coming tribulations in this time of Lucifer's reign upon earth.

"Luciel, Prince of Darkness: your time is short. I shall soon crush your proud head back to the land of eternal darkness. You have removed many of My voice-boxes from Me, but you will never succeed in silencing My voice!

"My children, you must continue to have a voice against abortion. Senators, Congressmen, you must change your laws of the land. Abortion must be ended. You are as responsible as the butchers who call themselves doctors. When My (Divine) Son sends a soul to earth to live its life out, He does not wish it to be sent back.

"Parents: let Me warn you now - you must cease the senseless return of these souls. The saints cry out to My Son - "How long, O Lord, shall You allow this carnage to continue?" I tell you His hand is almost upon you. Many of you shall be turned away, and spit out, when you come before My Son. You do not seem to understand that it is because you have rejected those (souls) we have sent to you. You have sent them back to Us. As you are all My children, can you not understand why We must warn you? I cannot stand to see the many (persons) who are being lost to Heaven because of the murder of the unborn. My children, My Heart breaks at this loss of souls.

"Solace Me. End the murder of the unborn and I will convert Russia and usher in the time of world peace.

"Pray now, My child."

****

1989 Messages

Message given to a privileged soul (Michael) by Our Lady, Tuesday, April 4, 1989, Feast Day of St. Isadore

Our Lady: "My child, and My children, there must be more prayer in your nation and the world. You should realize by now how much that Man of Evil has encroached on the lives of all of you. Many of your children are out of control - and why? Because of the lack of prayer; because you have left them to the worldly ways of the Evil One. They run about in your streets causing all manner of wrongdoing to be brought about.

"Yet many of you only say: "What can we do?" You can pray for them. Pray that they leave the drugs behind. Pray that they seek out My (Divine) Son. Pray that they turn away from following the Evil One's teachings. Teach them of the Saints of My Son's Church. The adage of Old is still true - "Out of sight, Out of mind.""

****

Message given to a privileged soul (Michael) by Our Lady, Saturday, April 29, 1989, Feast Day of St. Catherine of Siena

Our Lady: "Now orbiting the earth is a satellite that has some men of science worried. They shake their heads about it, in closed circles. The Eagle blames the Bear and the Bear blames the Eagle or the Dragon (China) for its launching. Some men of science even say it is from another world with no earthly origins. O men science, when will you learn? The facts surround you, yet you are blind to their validity. You have been told of the time windows of the Atlantian Race. You were told of how they destroyed their own continent with Atomic Warfare. You were told of the Arks which survived the destruction of Atlantis and Lemuria. Now I will give you another piece of the puzzle that you should have unraveled already.

"By now the Atlantian Race has brought the world up to just below where their level of technology was on the day of the reign of Atlantis as a world superpower. The Atlantians have even increased their own knowledge by leaps and bounds through the long years. It is they who placed the satellite into orbit. They placed a defensive sphere of pure neutrino and positrino flux fields around the satellite. No energy force can penetrate it. It is powered by ionic and magnetic flux fields. Its mission is to learn all of the details in a recorded record about earth's defensive weapons and forces. It also learns, and records, all details of day to day life in any given spot that it is orbiting above. It beams a signal at above light speed, which is far superior to your present technology and capacity to understand. Thus, men of science, you believe it to be from non-terrestrial origins. There are more details to this puzzle, but you must find some of them on your own."

****

Message given to a privileged soul (Michael) by Our Lady, Thursday, May 4, 1989, Feast Day of the Ascension of Our Lord to Heaven

Our Lady: "O My child and My children, work in prayer and actions must never cease in the cause of ending abortions in this nation and the world. You have before you, the chance to end all abortions in America. Pray as never before. If there is enough private and public prayer, then this offense to My Son's Kingdom will end. My Son has granted you reprieves upon reprieves. Time has run out for reprieves. This brutal murdering of the unborn must end. Each day there are more deaths than there were when the murder of the Holy Innocents happened 1989 years ago.

****

Message given to a privileged soul (Michael) by Our Lady, Thursday, May 29, 1989, Feast Day of Corpus Christi, Eve of St. Philip of Neri Feast Day

Our Lady: My children, pray the Rosary daily. It is your weapon of peace and hope. My child, bless you for the Rosary Group that you have started: They would never have begun praying if not for you. My children, start prayer groups during the evenings, at your local hospitals and health care centers for the elderly of your local communities. You would be surprised at how much love and peace and joy a prayer group will bring in these places of sorrow. There are so many who long to pray but do not remember how. They have no one to teach them how. All Christians must take more interest in the elderly in their community. With their added prayers, the destructions of the enemy upon your nation and the world will be slowed. Pray hard and devoutly upon this matter and you will receive the Grace to persevere, and begin the groups. Do not say: "I cannot be involved with this." Many Graces have been lost to the nation and to the world because too few would be involved, too few would take time for prayer. It is your only weapon in this time of the reign of the Antichrist."

****

Message given to a privileged soul (Michael) by Our Lady, Monday, June 12, 1989. Eve of the Feast Day of St. Anthony of Padua

Our Lady: "My child, and My children, there must be much prayer for the Red and the White (robed) Fishermen of My (Divine) Son's house in Rome. They must consecrate Russia (the Bear) soon or it shall be too late. Since 1917, I have cried at various sites. I cry because man, in his stubbornness, will not listen to Me. O Bishops and Cardinals within My Son's house, Wake Up! Do you not see the coming of the Dark One towards Rome? Will you not awaken and bring forth the light which is My (Divine) Son out unto the flock? Your Mission is to fish for the souls of mankind, and you have grown lackadaisical in doing so. If you were to come before My Son today, what reason would you give for not consecrating Russia? For removing the statues of the Saints? For not ordering the teachings of the children with the proper Church teachings?

"Bishops: have you ordered your Shepherds to make sure the children know the Way of the Cross, and the Rosary? How many children, today, are actually taught the Rosary? Sadly, all too few. How many parents know how to pray the Rosary? All too few. I repeat again: Shepherds, Wake Up!"

Our Holy Mother was crying during this whole Message. She was dressed in a yellow Robe. Her tunic, as well, was of a yellow color. Her belt was a deep blue, almost a purple. The edges of all Her garments were trimmed in gold.

****

Message given to a privileged soul (Michael) by Our Lord, Thursday, June 29, 1989, Feast Day of Sts. Peter and Paul, Apostles, Eve of the First Martyrs of the Church of Rome. Pagan Emperor Nero burned Christians in Public Fire in 64 A.D

Seer: I am sitting in my room, praying at about, oh, it must be 11:00 PM at night. I am awaiting the appearance of Our Lord Jesus. It will be at any moment that He will be here. I am starting to get that feeling of peace and serenity. It is like – all around me the room is becoming filled with, I can only describe it as crackling electricity. It is so pretty. It is in bright reds, yellows, blues, and whites, mixed with tones of hot pink. This electricity is now settling down to rays of solid bright pink and white light. It is filling the darkness of my room. Now I see Jesus, Our Lord, coming forward. He is not speaking but I hear Him anyway. He is saying:

"Repeat, My little son, what I am about to say."

Our Lord: "Purgatory is filled with the souls of those who have not made it to Heaven yet. Many will be there for years if you do not pray for them. One prayer said for a soul in Purgatory is worth so many Graces. Store your Graces up while in this life you are now in, and you shorten your eventual stay in this place of suffering.

If you pray for these souls you will have them praying for you in return. While they cannot pray for themselves, their prayers for you will gain many Graces for you. You gain their entrance into My Father's Kingdom, and you will have saints praying for you and shedding rays of Grace upon you in return.

"You can never completely comprehend the strength of your prayers for these souls. Shepherds within My houses on earth: Remember to teach your flock to remember to pray for these poor souls. My little son, you will describe Me now, and then finish your Rosary."

Seer: Our Lord's tunic is of ecru white. It is trimmed in a golden weave at the edges of the neckline where the cape meets it. The cape is of a scarlet red. His feet just barely show under his tunic. They have the wounds still visible in them. And His hands, as well, have the wounds visible. Neither of these four wounds are bleeding. They are just like reddened holes in His hands and feet. His hair is long, but it is very neatly kept. It looks like how shiny a girl's hair gets when they brush their hair a lot. His face is surrounded now in a very bright light. I can no longer see His facial features.

Now Jesus is saying: "You will pray now." He is gone, just like that.

****

Message given to a privileged soul (Michael) by Our Lady, Thursday, July 6, 1989, Feast Day of St. Maria Goretti, Patroness of Chasity.

Seer: Our Lady is before Me now with a bright light emanating from within Her. Her mantle and robe are both of a deep blue; Her tunic is of a white color that resembles new fallen snow. The belt about Her waist is of links of spun gold. About Our Lady's back is a cape of deep green. She has Her beautiful golden crown on tonight. Her hair is covered by Her crown. (Same as our statue of **Our Lady of All Holy Titles**). She is not smiling nor is She frowning or looking sad. I would say Our Lady's facial features are more of a serious look. Now, from behind Her, She is being joined by a very beautiful girl dressed in solid white and carrying a white lily-branch or stalk in her hands. Our Holy Mother is raising Her large wooden Rosary up and blessing this girl with it: "In the Name of The Father and of The Son and of The Holy Ghost." Now She is saying:

Our Lady: "This young lady, during her short life on earth, exemplified all the standards of chastity and purity that all young people should strive to copy. On this day, the Feast of St. Maria Goretti, I bring her to you, My child. She has a Message for the youth of the nation."

Now Our Lady is stepping back and is sending St. Maria Goretti forward. While I do not understand what language she is speaking in, I do however know through the Grace of Our Holy Mother what she is saying.

St. Maria Goretti: "My brother in Jesus, I come to you to speak through you to the youth of the nation. It is terrible how many of today's youth do not know the value of chastity before marriage. How many Graces are lost by each person who does not maintain the state of chastity. I faced death by butchery at the hands of young Alessandro, a victim of pornography, rather than give up my virginity.

My brother, ever since you obtained my bone-chip (relic), I have been with you, helping you in your Mission. Why do you not call on me for assistance in removing Asmodeus (demon) from tempting you when he bothers you at night? When he tries to tempt you to view those things of the world that you should not, why do you just sit there and let him send to you these thoughts? I beg you not to try to resist him on your own. Soon you will not be strong enough to do so. Unlike humans, Asmodeus is never in need of sleep. Call upon me, my brother. I cannot help you if you do not ask for my help. Do not be too proud to ask for my help. Remember, vanity and proudness always preceded a downfall."

Seer: "I will remember to do so."

St. Maria Goretti: "Dear brothers and sisters of the world, when you feel tempted to lust, ask for assistance from Heaven. There are many armies of Angels waiting to assist you to rebuke that which tempts you and to restore peace to your mind. Dear Holy Father in Rome: do not neglect the youth. Send a decree to the shepherds in the world to speak to the youth in their flock. Too few are now maintaining their state of purity.

Too few know the value of modest dress. Too few have ever been taught these values. Your shepherds do not listen to you. Whatever shall become of this generation of lust-filled youth? Now my brother, you will pray the prayers of Faith, Hope, and Charity. When you finish, We shall both have left you and you will retire for the night."

****

Message given to a privileged soul (Michael) by Our Lady, Wednesday, July 26, 1989, 2:00 AM, Feast Day of St. Joachim & St. Ann (Our Mother Mary's Parents)

Our Lady: "There must be much prayer for Our Vicar, your Pope in Rome. There is a new plan in the works to remove him from among you. There is a large group of persons who do not want him to speak to the world. My children, pray as never before that he remains in Rome till after October, 1989. Should he make his planned travel, he may die via Commando Tactics. This group of persons seeks to remove, not only him, but his envoys as well."

****

Message given to a privileged soul (Michael) by Our Lord, Monday, August 14, 1989. Eve of the Feast Day of Our Holy Mother's Assumption into Heaven

Our Lord Jesus: "My children, you must remember to honor. My Mother. She loves you and cares for you as Her own. You can best honor Her by remembering to pray your Rosaries daily. She has been given the flock as an Intercessor with the Eternal Father. Do not forget to ask Her to intercede for you."

(Brief private Message, then Jesus continued to speak to me but said the public could hear the rest of what He had to say to me.)

"You will repeat again now:

"My little son, you will now issue the Messages We have had you hold for so long. It is now time for them to go out.

"Pray now."

****

Message given to a privileged soul (Michael) by Our Lady, Sunday, December 24, 1989, Christmas Eve

Our Holy Mother has just arrived in the room with me. I have placed a pillow on the floor, but Our Holy Mother is just floating above it. Oh, Our Holy Mother is giving off light that is so brilliant that I think that, if the light were coming from any other source, that I would be blinded. Our Holy Mother's tunic is whiter than the snow. Her mantle is a deep blue. About Her back tonight, Our Lady has on Her green cape (like our statue of Our Lady of All Holy Titles). Upon Her head She is wearing Her golden crown. About Our Lady's waist is Her belt of golden mesh links. Our Holy Mother's Rosary, tonight, is made of wooden Hail Mary beads, and crystal Our Father beads. The crucifix is made of wood with a life-like figure of Her Son, Our Lord Jesus. The effigy has all of the wounds as Our Lord Jesus had them. Now Our Holy Mother has no shoes on Her feet. She is holding Her finger to Her lips now which is the signal for me to listen and to remember, or repeat.

Our Lady: "My child, it has been quite some time since I have come to you to have you give a Message to My children, but the time is slowly closing in on the return of My (Divine) Son. We have warned all who have read Our words, but have they listened? Have they listened? Sadly, all too few choose to heed Our words. I bring you this Message today because it is necessary that man be aware of the time that he is living in. I cry tears of sorrow for you all, My children. You do not see the signs of the times that you are living in. You are in the time when communism is rapidly losing its hold on many countries and nations of the world.

"The Time of Peace is rapidly coming upon you. You must all pray as never before, if you wish the Time of Peace to come to the world. If there is not enough prayer, the Time of Peace will be delayed. Facing the idea of the Time of Peace being soon, can you not all pray harder? Is it so hard to offer a simple prayer during your daily life? Consider the other side of the picture. If there is not enough prayer, then the situation could change again for the worst. Communism would then be allowed to spread in the world again.

"Is this what you want?

"All Christians must pray now. Worship in your Churches. Obey your pastors and priests. O Pastors: lead your flocks to My (Divine) Son. Teach them to read the writings of the Apostles in the Book of Love and Life. My children, remember My Son, your Lord in all you do. In this Season, it is clear that you must remember the reason for the season. Without My Son, there would be no Christmas. Put My Son back into your lives during this season, and always.

"My Son is grieved by the sinful state of abortion that is prevalent in your country and world .Many times have We told mankind of the horror that abortion is. What right do so-called doctors have to end the life of children? Mothers, We send your children to you to raise, that they in turn may raise more children. Why do you send them back to Us? Abortion is Murder! Pray, My children, that this legalized murder of the Holy Innocents is ended in your nation and in the world. My child, you will now pray your Rosary."

At this point Our Lady instructed me to pray, so that is what I did. At this point, Our Lady departed in a light-filled mist.

****

Litanies and Prayers

A New Litany of St. George (Message of Christmas Eve, 1983)

Lord, have Mercy on us. *Christ, have Mercy on us.* Lord, have Mercy on us. Christ, hear us. *Christ, graciously hear us.* God, the Father of Heaven, *have Mercy on us.* God, the Son, Redeemer of the world, *have Mercy on us.* God, the Holy Ghost, *have Mercy on us.* Holy Trinity, One God, *have Mercy on us.*

Holy Mary, *pray for us.* St. Joseph, *pray for us.* St. Michael, *pray for us.* St. Benedict, *pray for us.*

St. George, Thou who drove out the serpent-dragon, *pray for us.*
St. George, Full of Patience, pray for us.
St. George, Most Just, *pray for us.*
St. George, Most Prudent, *pray for us.*
St. George, Most Courageous, *pray for us.*
St. George, Protection against the dragon, *pray for us.*
St. George, My Protector, *pray for us.*
St. George, Guardian of Cities, *pray for us.*
St. George, Guardian of virgins, *pray for us.*
St. George, Guardian of the sickly, who were caused so by Satan, *pray for us.*
St. George, Terror to the demons, *pray for us.*
St. George, Protection for Holy Church, *pray for us.*
St. George, Illuminated from On High, *pray for us.*
St. George, Silent and eloquent, *pray for us.*
St. George, Shining, as a Star, into Eternity, *pray for us.*
St. George, Learned Expounder- of Mysteries of God, *pray for us.*
St. George, Fragrant blossom of Heaven's Garden, *pray for us.*
St. George, Powerful in word and work, *pray for us.*
St. George, Refuter of Luciel's Errors, *pray for us.*
St. George, Model of Holy Death, *pray for us.*
St. George, Solid rock of Hope and Help, *pray for us.*
St. George, Mighty Defender of the Faith, *pray for us.*
St. George, Bright Mirror of Temperance, *pray for us.*
St. George, Protector of the Persecuted, *pray for us.*
St. George, Unshakable Pillar of Fortitude, *pray for us.*
St. George, Defender of Justice, *pray for us.*
St. George, Trumpet of Eternal Salvation, *pray for us.*
St. George, Conqueror of Devils, *pray for us.*
St. George, Companion of Angels, pray for us.
St. George, Protector of those who invoke thine aid, *pray for us.*
St. George, Cherished by Jesus, *pray for us.*

Lamb of God, who takest away the sins of the world, *spare us, O Lord.*
Lamb of God, who takest away the sins of the world, *graciously hear us, O Lord.*
Lamb of God, who takest away the sins of the world, *have Mercy on us, O Lord.*

Pray for us, St. George, *that we may be made Worthy of the Promises of Christ.*

LET US PRAY:

O God, who has sent St. George to remove the devil-dragon from breathing out his pestilence upon the city, send him again upon earth to cast out Lucifer from our cities, as in the days of old. Answer, for us, the petitions we send up to You through St. George, our Intercessor. *Amen.*

Litany of St. Anthony (Message of March 7, 1984)

Lord, have Mercy on us. *Christ, have Mercy on us.* Lord, have Mercy on us. Christ, hear us. *Christ, graciously hear us.* God, the Father of Heaven, *have Mercy on us.* God, God, the Son, Redeemer of the World, *have Mercy on us.* God, the Holy Ghost, *have Mercy on us.* Holy Trinity, One God, have Mercy on us.

Holy Mary, *pray for us.*
Holy Father Francis, *pray for us.*
St. Anthony of Padua, *pray for us.*
Glory of the Order of Friars Minor, *pray for us.*
Martyr in Desiring to Die for Christ, *pray for us.*
Pillar of the Church, *pray for us.*
Worthy Priest of God, *pray for us.*
Apostolic Preacher, *pray for us.*
Teacher of Truth, *pray for us.*
Terror of Evil Spirits, *pray for us.*
Comforter of the Afflicted, *pray for us.*
Helper in Necessities, *pray for us.*
Deliverer of Captives, *pray for us.*
Guide of the Erring, *pray for us.*
Restorer of Lost Things, *pray for us.*
Chosen Intercessor, *pray for us.*
Continuous Worker of Miracles, *pray for us.*

Lamb of God, who takes away the sins of the world, *spare us, O Lord.*
Lamb of God, who takes away the sins of the world, *graciously hear us, O Lord.*
Lamb of God, who takest away the sins of the world, *have mercy on us, O Lord.*
(Christ Hear us. Christ Graciously Hear us.)

V. Pray for us, Blessed Anthony
R. That we may be Made Worthy of the Promises of Christ.

LET US PRAY:

Almighty and Eternal God, You glorified Your faithful Confessor and Doctor, St. Anthony, with the gift of working miracles. Graciously grant that what we seek with confidence through his merits, we may surely receive through his prayers. Through Christ, Our Lord. *Amen.*

V. So, if your need be great, if even Miracles you seek, remember, death, disease, and devils fled. The sick and ailing rose up cured.
R. Those of Padua have told well the help of Blessed Anthony, the power of his prayer.

V. Seas obeyed, bonds were broken, weak limbs grew strong, lost things were found.
R. Those of Padua have told well the help of Blessed Anthony, the power of his prayer.

V. Dangers vanished, needs disappeared. Those who saw told all the world.
R. Those of Padua have told well the help of Blessed Anthony, the power of his prayer.

V. Through Holy Anthony our prayers be given. For glory to Almighty God. To Father, Son, and Holy Ghost. R. *Those of Padua have told well the help of Blessed Anthony, the power of his prayer.*

Pray for us, St Anthony, *that we may be made worthy of the Promises of Christ.*

LET US PRAY:

God, let your Church always rejoice in the memory of St. Anthony and, strengthened spiritually by his help, come to eternal happiness. *Amen.*

Litany of St. Joseph (Message of March 18, 1984)

Lord, have Mercy on us. *Christ, have Mercy on us.* Lord, have Mercy on us. Christ, hear us. *Christ, graciously hear us.* God the Father of Heaven, *have Mercy on us.* God, the Son, Redeemer of the World, *have Mercy on us.* God, the Holy Ghost, *have Mercy on us.* Holy Trinity, One God, *have Mercy on us.*

Saint Joseph,

Illustrious Son of David, *pray for us.*
Light of Patriarchs, *pray for us.*
Spouse of the Mother of God, *pray for us.*
Chaste Guardian of the Virgin, *pray for us.*
Foster Father of the Son of God, *pray for us.*
Watchful defender of Christ, *pray for us.*
Head of the Holy Family, *pray for us.*
Joseph, most just, *pray for us.*
Joseph, most chaste, *pray for us.*
Joseph, most prudent, *pray for us.*
Joseph, most valiant, *pray for us.*
Joseph, most obedient, *pray for us.*
Joseph, most faithful, *pray for us.*
Mirror of patience, *pray for us.*
Lover of Poverty, *pray for us.*
Model of workmen, *pray for us.*
Ornament of the domestic life, *pray for us.*
Guardian of virgins, *pray for us.*
Safeguard of families, *pray for us.*
Consolation of the poor, *pray for us.*
Hope of the sick, *pray for us.*
Patron of the dying, *pray for us.*
Terror of the demons, *pray for us.*
Protector of the Holy Church, *pray for us.*

Lamb of God, who takest away the sins of the world, *spare us, O Lord.*
Lamb of God, who takest away the sins of the world, *graciously hear us, O Lord.*
Lamb of God, who takest away the sins of the world, *have mercy on us, O Lord.*

V. He made him lord over His house.
R. And the ruler of all His possessions.

LET US PRAY:

O God, who in Thine ineffable providence didst vouchsafe to choose Blessed Joseph to be the spouse of Thy most Holy Mother, grant, we beseech Thee, to have him for our Intercessor in Heaven, whom on earth we venerate as our Holy Protector, Who livest and reignest world without end. *Amen.*

Prayer:

We turn in our trouble to thee, blessed Joseph, and after praying for aid from thy Holy Spouse, we seek with confidence thy patronage also. By the affection that united thee to the Virgin Immaculate, Mother of God; by the fatherly love wherewith thou didst surround the Infant Jesus, we beseech thee to help us to the possession of the heritage that Jesus Christ conquered for us by His blood and to aid us by the power and succor in our need.

Foster, O thou most wise guardian of the Holy Family, the elect people of Jesus Christ. Keep us, O thou most loving father, from every spot of error and corruption. Be favorable and help us, from the heights of Heaven, O thou our most mighty deliverer, in the fight we must wage against the powers of darkness. And even as thou didst snatch the Child Jesus from the danger of death, so now defend the Holy Church from the snares of the enemy and from all adversity, through Jesus Christ, Who with the Father and the Holy Ghost, lives and reigns, world without end. *Amen.*

Litany and Other Prayers for A Happy Death (Message of February 14, 1985)

Lord, have Mercy on us. *Christ, have Mercy on us*. Lord, have Mercy on us. Christ, hear us. *Christ, graciously hear us*. God the Father of Heaven, *have Mercy on us*. God, the Son, Redeemer of the World, *have Mercy on us*. God, the Holy Ghost, *have Mercy on us*. Holy Trinity, One God, *have Mercy on us*.

Holy Mary, *pray for us*.
All ye Angels and Archangels, *pray for us*.
Holy Abraham, *pray for us*.
St. John the Baptist, pray for us.
St. Joseph, *pray for us*.
All ye holy Patriarchs and Prophets, *pray for us*.
St. Peter, *pray for us*.
St. Paul, *pray for us*.
St. Andrew, pray for us.
St. John, *pray for us*.
St. Jude, *pray for us*.
All ye holy Apostles and Evangelists, *pray for us*.
All ye holy Disciples of Our Lord, *pray for us*.
All ye innocents, *pray for us*.
St. Stephen, *pray for us*.
St. Lawrence, pray for us.
All ye holy Martyrs, *pray for us*.
St. Sylvester, *pray for us*.
St. Gregory, *pray for us*.
St. Augustine, *pray for us*.
St. Basil, pray for us.
St. Ambrose, *pray for us*.
St. Francis de Sales, *pray for us*.
St. Vincent de Paul, *pray for us*.
St. Aloysius, *pray for us*.
St. Stanislaus, *pray for us*.
All ye holy bishops and confessors, *pray for us*.
St. Benedict, *pray for us*.
St. Dominic, *pray for us*.
St. Francis of Assisi, *pray for us*.
St. Ignatius, *pray for us*.
St. Philip Neri, *pray for us*.
St. Camillus de Lellis, *pray for us*.
St. John of God, *pray for us*.
All ye holy Monks, Hermits, and founders of Religious Orders, *pray for us*.
St. Mary Magdalene, *pray for us*.
St. Lucy, *pray for us*.
St. Scholastica, *pray for us*.
St. Teresa, *pray for us*.
St. Catherine, *pray for us*.
St. Clara, *pray for us*.
St. Ursula, *pray for us*.
St. Angela Merici, *pray for us*.
St. Jane Frances de Chantel, *pray for us*.
St. Barbara, *pray for us*.
All ye holy Virgins and Widows, pray for us.
All ye saints of God, *intercede for us*.
Be Merciful unto us. *Spare us, O Lord*.
Be merciful unto us, hear us, O Lord.
From Thy anger, *O Lord, deliver us*.
From the peril of death, *O Lord, deliver us*.
From an evil death, *O Lord, deliver us*.
From the pains of Hell, *O Lord, deliver us*.
From all evil, *O Lord, deliver us*.
From the power of the devil, *O Lord, deliver us*.
By Thy nativity, *O Lord, deliver us*.
By Thy cross and passion, *O Lord, deliver us*.
By Thy death and burial, *O Lord, deliver us*
By Thy glorious Resurrection, *O Lord, deliver us*
By the Grace of the Holy Ghost, the Comforter, *O Lord, deliver us*.
In the day of Judgement, *O Lord, deliver us*.
We sinners beseech Thee, *hear us*.
That Thou wouldst spare us, *we beseech Thee, hear us*.
That Thou wouldst vouchsafe to bring us to true repentance, *we beseech Thee, hear us*.
That Thou wouldst vouchsafe to grant eternal rest to all the faithful departed, *we beseech Thee, hear us*.

Lamb of God, Who takest away the sins of the World, *have Mercy on us*.
Lamb of God, Forgive us our sins. Grant that we may die in thy love and Thy Grace.
Lamb of God, by thy precious Blood, we *beseech Thee to Hear us and lead us to Life Everlasting*.
Lord have Mercy on us. *Christ have Mercy* on us. Lord have Mercy on us.

LET US PRAY:

We beseech Thy clemency, O Lord, that Thou wouldst vouchsafe so to strengthen Thy servants in Thy Grace that, at the hour of death, the enemy may not prevail over us, and that we may deserve to pass with Thy angels into everlasting Life. Almighty and most merciful God, Who, for Thy thirsting people, didst bring forth from the hardness of our hearts tears of compunction, that we may bewail our sins, and receive forgiveness of them from Thy Mercy! O Lord Jesus Christ, Redeemer of the world, behold us prostrate at Thy feet. With our whole heart we detest our sins of thought, word, and deed, and because we love Thee above all created things we steadfastly purpose, by the help of Thy grace, never more to offend Thee, and rather to die than to commit one mortal sin. *Amen*.

Litany of St. Michael (Message of March 13, 1985)

Lord, have Mercy on us. *Christ, have Mercy on us*. Lord, have mercy on us. Christ, hear us. *Christ, graciously hear us*. God the Father of Heaven, *have Mercy on us*. God the Son, Redeemer of the world, *have Mercy on us*. God the Holy Spirit, *have Mercy on us*. Holy Trinity, One God, *have Mercy on us*.

Holy Mary, Queen of Angels, *pray for us*.
St. Michael, *pray for us*.
St. Michael, filled with the wisdom of God, *pray for us*.
St. Michael, perfect adorer of the Incarnate Word, *pray for us*.
St. Michael, crowned with honor and glory, *pray for us*.
St. Michael, most powerful Prince of the armies of the Lord, *pray for us*.
St. Michael, standard- bearer of the Most Holy Trinity, *pray for us*.
St. Michael, guardian of Paradise, *pray for us*.
St. Michael, guide and comforter of the people of Israel, *pray for us*.
St. Michael, Splendor and fortress of the Church Militant, *pray for us*.
St. Michael, honor and joy of the Church Triumphant, *pray for us*.
St. Michael, light of angels, *pray for us*.
St. Michael, bulwark of orthodox believers, *pray for us*.
St. Michael, strength of those who fight under the standard of the Cross, *pray for us*.
St. Michael, light and confidence of souls at the hour of death, *pray for us*.
St. Michael, our most sure aid, *pray for us*.
St. Michael, our help in all adversities, *pray for us*.
St. Michael, herald of the everlasting sentence, pray for us.
St. Michael, consoler of souls detained in the flames of Purgatory, *pray for us*.
St. Michael, whom the Lord has charged to receive souls after death, *pray for us*.
St. Michael, our Price, *pray for us*.
St. Michael, our Advocate, *pray for us*.

Lamb of God, Who takes away the sins of the World, *spare us, O Lord*.
Lamb of God, Who takes away the sins of the World, *graciously hear us, O Lord*.
Lamb of God, Who takes away the sins of the World, *have Mercy on us, O Lord*.
Christ hear us. Christ graciously hear us.

V. Pray for us, O glorious St. Michael, Prince of the Church of Jesus Christ.
R. That we may be made worthy of His promises.

LET US PRAY:

Sanctify us, we beseech Thee, 0 Lord Jesus, with Thy holy blessing and grant us, by the intercession of St. Michael, that Wisdom which teaches us to lay up treasures in Heaven by exchanging the goods of this world for those of eternity. Thou who livest and reignest, world without end, *Amen*.

Almighty and eternal God, You in Your own marvelous goodness and pity for the common salvation of men, chose the glorious Archangel, Michael, to be the Prince of Your Church. Make us worthy, we beg You, to be delivered by his beneficent protection from all our enemies so that at the hour of our death none of them may approach to harm us. Rather, grant that, by the same, Archangel Michael, we may be introduced into the Presence of Your Most High and Divine Majesty, through the merits of the same Jesus Christ, Our Lord. *Amen.*

St. Michael, glorious Prince, chief and champion of the Heavenly Host, guardian of the souls of men, conqueror of the rebel angels, steward of the palace of God under Jesus Christ, our worthy Leader, endowed with super human excellence and virtue, free us from every ill, who, with full confidence have recourse to you. By your incomparable protection, enable us to make progress every day in the faithful service of our God. *Amen.*

Litany of St. Patrick (Message of March 17, 1985)

Lord, have Mercy on us. *Christ, have Mercy on us.* Lord, have Mercy on us. Christ, hear us. *Christ, graciously hear us.* God, the Father of Heaven, have Mercy on us. God, the Son, Redeemer of the world, *have Mercy on us.* God, the Holy Ghost, *have Mercy on us.* Holy Trinity, One God, *have Mercy on us.*

Holy Mary, Mother of God, *pray for us.*

St. Patrick, *pray for us.*
St. Patrick, Apostle of Ireland, *pray for us.*
St. Patrick, vessel of election, *pray for us.*
St. Patrick, model of Bishops, *pray for us.*
St. Patrick, enemy of infidelity, *pray for us.*
St. Patrick, profoundly humble, *pray for us.*

St. Patrick, consumed with zeal, *pray for us.*
St. Patrick, example of charity, *pray for us.*
St. Patrick, glory of Ireland, *pray for us.*
St. Patrick, instructor of little ones, *pray for us.*
St. Patrick, our powerful protector, *pray for us.*
St. Patrick, our compassionate advocate, *pray for us.*

Lamb of God, Who takest away the sins of the world, *spare us, O Lord.*
Lamb of God, Who takest away the sins of the world, *graciously hear us, O Lord.*
Lamb of God, who takest away the sins of the world, *have mercy on us, O Lord.*

V. Pray for us, O Holy St. Patrick,
R. That we may be made worthy of the promises of Christ.

LET US PRAY:

O God, Who didst send among us Thy blessed servant, St. Patrick, to instruct and save us, and didst infuse into his heart so great a share of Thy own tenderness, Charity and zeal, listen, we beseech Thee, to the prayers, which we now offer up in union with the prayers of our glorious patron and father in Heaven, and grant us, through his intercession, the intentions of Thy faithful, and the grace rather to die than to offend Thee. *Amen.*

The Breastplate of St. Patrick

I rise up today, God's power guiding me, God's might upholding me, God's wisdom directing me, the eye of God looking before me, the ear of God listening for me, the word of God speaking for me, the hand of God defending me, the Way of God stretching out before me, the shield of God protecting me, the Hosts of God guarding me from the snares of demons, from the seduction of vice, from the wicked desires of my nature, from every man who plots against me, near or far, alone or with others.

Christ be with me, Christ be before me, Christ be after me, Christ be within me, Christ be beneath me, Christ be above me, Christ be at my right hand, Christ be at my left hand, Christ be in the fort, Christ be in the chariot, Christ be in the ship, Christ be in the heart of every man who thinks of me, Christ be in the mouth of every man who speaks of me, Christ be in every eye that sees me, Christ be in every ear that hears me.

> Hail, glorious St. Patrick! We honor thy name,
> Tho' Erin may claim thee, the world knows thy fame.
>
> The faith of our fathers is our treasure too,
> How holy the thought, that they learned it from you.
>
> Thru crosses and trials, its fires burning bright,
> They show us the way, and the truth, and the light,
>
> Great Saint! Intercede, that we always may be
> Devoted and loyal, true children of thee.
>
> Our love and devotion be ever like thine,
> Our thought be of Jesus, our heart be His shrine.
>
> And when to the end of life's Path we have trod,
> Be near us, Great Bishop, anointed of God!

Litany of St. Sharbel (Message of May 21, 1985)

Lord, have Mercy on us. *Lord, have Mercy on us.* Christ, have Mercy on us. *Christ, have Mercy on us.* Lord, have Mercy on us. *Lord, have Mercy on us.* Christ, hear us. *Christ, graciously hear us.* God, the Father of Heaven, *have Mercy on us.* God, the Son, Redeemer of the world, *have Mercy on us.* God, the Holy Ghost, *have Mercy on us.* Holy Trinity, One God, *have Mercy on us.*

St. Sharbel, *strengthen our faith.*
Athlete of the spiritual life, *strengthen our faith.*
Partaker of the Fountain of Life, *strengthen our faith.*
Beacon enlightening the Church, *strengthen our faith.*
Voice inviting sinners to conversion, *strengthen our faith.*
Hermit filled with the Holy Spirit, *strengthen our faith.*
Petitioner for the faithful, *strengthen our faith.*
Hearer of the Word of God, *strengthen our faith.*
Living hymn of praise, *strengthen our faith.*
Follower of the Way of the Cross, *strengthen our faith.*
Servant of the Virgin Mother, *strengthen our faith.*
Lover of solitude and prayer, *strengthen our faith.*
Priest of the reconciling Altar, *strengthen our faith.*
Instrument of the Divine Physician, *strengthen our faith.*
Model of monastic life, *strengthen our faith.*
Precious fragrance filling the world, *strengthen our faith.*
Servant of the Holy Mysteries, *strengthen our faith.*
Healer of bodies and souls, *strengthen our faith.*
Precious crown of religious life, *strengthen our faith.*
Example of humility for mankind, *strengthen our faith.*
Great Mystic of this century, *strengthen our faith.*

Lamb of God, Who takes away the sins of the world, *spare us, O Lord.*
Lamb of God, Who takes away the sins of the world, *graciously hear us, O Lord.*
Lamb of God, Who takes away the sins of the world, *have mercy on us, O Lord!*

V: Pray for us, OP holy hermit of God.
R: That we may be worthy of the promises of Christ.

LET US PRAY:

O Father of Truth, you continue to send us saints to remind us that we must complete what is lacking in the sufferings of Christ's body, the Church

You called Sharbel to the top of a mountain and asked him to offer himself as a sacrifice pleasing to you. Drawn by the Fire of Your Love, his life was consumed with prayer and penance. In Your Mercy You accepted his offering through Your Only Begotten Son, and granted him life.

Father, we are confident in Your Mercy. Let Your Spirit come and deepen our understanding of penance and sacrifice. If we desire to live in, and with You, we must offer ourselves with Christ, as oblations pleasing to You. Dying with Christ, we will then live with Him and share in His glory forever. Amen.

Lord of Salvation: we know that only prayer and sacrifice will enable us to follow You to accomplish deeds pleasing to your Majesty, and to be united with You. Grant us, through the intercession of the Hermit, Sharbel, to follow You in the Way of the Cross, a path of self-sacrifice which leads to our eternal glory and the Glory of Your Heavenly Father. *Amen.*

Litany of The Blessed Virgin (Message of June, 1985)

Lord, have Mercy on us. *Christ, have Mercy on us*. Lord, have Mercy on us. Christ, hear us. Christ, graciously hear us. God, the Father of Heaven, *have Mercy on us*. God, the Son, Redeemer of the world, *have Mercy on us*. God, the Holy Ghost, *have Mercy on us*. Holy Trinity, One God, *have Mercy on us*.

Holy Mary, *pray for us*.
Holy Mother of God, *pray for us*.
Holy Virgin of virgins, *pray for us*.
Mother of Christ, *pray for us*.
Mother of Divine Grace, *pray for us*.
Mother Most Pure, *pray for us*.
Mother Most Chaste, *pray for us*.
Mother Inviolate, *pray for us*.
Mother Undefiled, *pray for us*.
Mother Most Amiable, *pray for us*.
Mother Most Admirable, *pray for us*.
Mother of good Counsel, *pray for us*.
Mother of our Creator, *pray for us*.
Mother of our Savior, *pray for us*.
Virgin Most Prudent, *pray for us*.
Virgin Most Venerable, *pray for us*.
Virgin Most Renowned, *pray for us*.
Virgin Most Powerful, *pray for us*.
Virgin, Most Merciful, *pray for us*.
Virgin Most Faithful, *pray for us*.
Mirror of Justice, *pray for us*.
Seat of Wisdom, *pray for us*.
Cause of our Joy, *pray for us*.
Spiritual Vessel, *pray for us*.
Vessel of Honor, *pray for us*.
Singular Vessel of Devotion, *pray for us*.
Mystical Rose, *pray for us*.
Tower of David, *pray for us*.
Tower of Ivory, *pray for us*.
House of Gold, *pray for us*.
Gate of Heaven, *pray for us*.
Morning Star, *pray for us*.
Health of the Sick, *pray for us*.
Refuge of Sinners, *pray for us*.
Comforter of the Afflicted, *pray for us*.
Help of Christians, *pray for us*.
Queen of Angels, *pray for us*.
Queen of Patriarchs, *pray for us*.
Queen of Prophets, *pray for us*.
Queen of Apostles, *pray for us*.
Queen of Martyrs, *pray for us*.
Queen of Confessors, *pray for us*.
Queen of Virgins, *pray for us*.
Queen of all Saints, *pray for us*.
Queen Conceived without Original Sin, *pray for us*.
Queen assumed into Heaven, *pray for us*.
Queen of the most Holy Rosary, *pray for us*.
Queen of Peace, *pray for us*.

Lamb of God, Who takes away the sins of the world, *spare us, O Lord*.
Lamb of God, Who takes away the sins of the world, *graciously hear us, O Lord*.
Lamb of God, Who takes away the sins of the world, *have mercy on us, O Lord*.

Pray for us, O Holy Mother of God, *that we may be made worthy of the Promises of Christ*.

LET US PRAY:

Grant, we beseech Thee, O Lord God, that we Thy servants may enjoy perpetual health of mind and body and by the glorious intercession of the Blessed Mary, ever Virgin, be delivered from present sorrow and enjoy Eternal happiness. Through Christ, Our Lord, *Amen*.

Prayers to St. Ann (Message of July 26, 1985)

Most august St. Ann! Heaven admires you; earth blesses you; God the Father loves you as the mother of His cherished daughter; the incarnate Word loves you as the parent of His well-beloved Mother. The Holy Ghost loves you as the mother of His perfect Spouse. The angels and the elect honor you as the tree producing a flower, the celestial perfume and beauty of which charms them, and whose divine fruit is their life and their joy; Repentant sinners look on you as their powerful advocate with God, the just, through your intercession, hope for an increase of grace, and penitents the expiation of their faults. Be propitious to us, O most merciful mother; unite with Mary, your dear and admirable child, and by Her intercession and yours, we shall confidently expect mercy from Jesus, to whom you were so intimately allied; also the intentions of this devotion, every grace during life, and above all, the grace of a happy death. Amen.

****

O God, Who didst on Blessed Ann, confer the signal grace
Of meriting the motherhood of Her who gave our grace

Thine Only Son to be our All, O hear our lowly prayer
And deign to place us in her arms - surrounded by her care.

May we who celebrate her name O grant it graciously,
Be aided by her patronage, acceptable to Thee.

We ask it through the same, Our Lord, This Jesus Christ, Thy Son,
Who lives and reigns, One God with Thee, while endless ages run.

In the Eternal Unity.
Of God, the Holy Ghost,
To Whom be every creature's praise,
Our Hearts' Adoring Boast.

(Roman Missal-Collect, of Feast of St. Ann.)

****

With my heart full of the most sincere veneration, I prostrate myself before thee, O glorious Saint Ann. Shield me with thine effectual patronage and obtain for me from God the power to imitate those virtues wherewith thou was so plentifully adorned. Grant that I may know and weep over my sins in bitterness of heart. Obtain for me the grace of most active love for Jesus and Mary, and resolution to fulfill the duties of my state of life with faithfulness and constancy Save me from every danger that confronts me in life, and help me at the hour of death, so that I may come in safety to paradise, there to sing with thee, O most happy mother, the praises of the Word of God made Man in the womb of thy most pure daughter, the Virgin Mary. Amen.

If we devoutly say some prayers in honor of St. Ann on Tuesday of any week, we are granted a plenary indulgence (on usual conditions) of seven years. (The Raccolta - No. 493, 4)

Litany of the Mercy of God (Message of August 28, 1985)
(for private recitation only)

Lord, have Mercy on us. *Christ, have Mercy on us.* Lord, have Mercy on us. Christ, hear us. *Christ, graciously hear us.* God, the Father of Heaven, *have Mercy on us.* God, the Son, Redeemer of the world, *have Mercy on us.* God, the Holy Ghost, *have Mercy on us.* Holy Trinity, One God, *have Mercy on us.*

Mercy of God, supreme attribute of the Creator, *we trust in Thee.*
Mercy of God, greatest perfection of the Redeemer, *we trust in Thee.*
Mercy of God, unfathomable love of the Sanctifier, *we trust in Thee.*
Mercy of God, inconceivable mystery of the Holy Trinity, *we trust in Thee.*
Mercy of God, expression of the greatest power of the Most High, *we trust in Thee.*
Mercy of God, revealed in the creation of the Heavenly spirits, *we trust in Thee.*
Mercy of God, summoning us to existence out of nothingness, *we trust in Thee.*
Mercy of God, bestowed upon mankind in the Sacraments of Baptism and Penance, *we trust in Thee.*
Mercy of God, granted in the Sacraments of the Altar and the Priesthood, *we trust in Thee.*
Mercy of God, shown in calling us to the Holy Faith, *we trust in Thee.*
Mercy of God, revealed in the conversion of sinners, *we trust in Thee.*
Mercy of God, manifested in the sanctification of the just, *we trust in Thee.*
Mercy of God, fulfilled in the perfecting of the saintly, *we trust in Thee.*
Mercy of God, font of health for the sick and suffering, *we trust in Thee.*
Mercy of God, solace of anguished hearts, *we trust in Thee.*
Marcy of God, hope of souls afflicted with despair, *we trust in Thee.*
Mercy of God, always and everywhere accompanying all people, *we trust in Thee.*
Mercy of God, embracing the whole universe, *we trust in Thee.*
Mercy of God, bestowing upon us Immortal life, *we trust in Thee.*
Mercy of God, shielding us from merited punishments, *we trust in Thee.*
Mercy of God, raising us from the misery of sin, *we trust in Thee.*
Mercy of God, justifying us in the Word Incarnate, *we trust in Thee.*
Mercy of God, flowing from the wounds of Christ, *we trust in Thee.*
Mercy of God, gushing from the Most Sacred Heart of Jesus, *we trust in Thee.*
Mercy of God, giving to us the M t Blessed Virgin Mary as Mother of Mercy, *we trust in Thee.*
Mercy of God, shown in the revelation of the divine mysteries, *we trust in Thee.*
Mercy of God, manifested in the institution of the Universal Church, *we trust in Thee.*
Mercy of God, contained in the institution of the Holy Sacraments, *we trust in Thee.*
Mercy of God, anticipating us with graces, *we trust in Thee.*
Mercy of God, peace of the dying, *we trust in Thee.*
Mercy of God, refreshment and relief of the souls in Purgatory, *we trust in Thee.*
Mercy of God, heavenly delight of the blessed, *we trust in Thee.*
Mercy of God, crown of all the saints, *we trust in Thee.*
Mercy of God, inexhaustible source of miracles, *we trust in Thee.*

Lamb of God, Who didst show us Thy greatest mercy in redeeming the world on the cross, *spare us, O Lord.*
Lamb of God, Who dost mercifully offer Thyself for us in every Holy Mass, *graciously hear us, O Lord.*
Lamb of God, Who takest away the sins of the world, through Thy inexhaustible Mercy, *have mercy on us.*

V. The tender mercies of the Lord are over all His works.
R. *The Mercies of the Lord I will sing forever.*

LET US PRAY:

O God, Whose Mercy is infinite and Whose treasures of pity are inexhaustible, graciously look down upon us and increase in us Thy Mercy so that we may never, even in the greatest trials, give way to despair, but may always trustfully conform ourselves to Thy Holy Will, which is Mercy itself. Through Our Lord Jesus Christ, the King of Mercy, Who with Thee and the Holy Spirit shows us Mercy for ever and ever. *Amen.*

Litany of Our Lady of La Salette (Message of September 18, 1985)

Lord, have Mercy on us. *Christ, have Mercy on us.* Lord, have Mercy on us. Christ, hear us. *Christ, graciously hear us.* God, the Father of Heaven, *have Mercy on us.* God, the Son, Redeemer of the world, *have Mercy on us.* God, the Holy Ghost, *have Mercy on us.* Holy Trinity, One God, *have Mercy on us.*

Our Lady of La Salette, Mother of God, *pray for us.*
Our Lady of La Salette, Queen and Mother of men, *pray for us.*
Our Lady of La Salette, Messenger of Divine Mercy, *pray for us.*
Our Lady of La Salette, all-powerful suppliant, *pray for us.*
Thou who restrainest the arm of the Lord angered against us, *pray for us.*
Thou who sheddest so many tears on account of our sins and misfortunes, *pray for us.*
Thou who carest so much for us, in spite of all our ingratitude, *pray for us.*
Thou who dost so lovingly invite us to have recourse to thee, *pray for us.*
Thou who dost reproach us with our violation of Sunday and with blasphemy, pray for us.
Thou who dost complain so sorrowfully of the profanation of holy things, *pray for us.*
Thou who dost so strongly recommend prayer, and especially morning and evening prayer, *pray for us.*
Thou who dost condemn so severely our lusts and the shameful pleasures of the world, *pray for us.*
Thou who dost remind us so touchingly of the Passion of Jesus, *pray for us.*
Thou whose apparition is a source of salvation for poor sinners, *pray for us.*
Thou who dost invite so pressingly the just to redouble their fervor, *pray for us.*
Thou whose threatening prophecies have so justly alarmed the world, *pray for us.*
Thou who dost promise so many blessings if we become converted, *pray for us.*
Thou who didst cause to spring up at Thy feet a fountain of miraculous water, *pray for us.*
Thou who, after the example of Jesus, dost heal every infirmity, *pray for us.*
Thou who dost desire to be honored and invoked throughout the world, *pray for us.*
Thou who didst cause so many works of reparation to be undertaken and to prosper, *pray for us.*
Our Lady of La Salette, living example of charity, *pray for us.*
Victim of penance and expiation, *pray for us.*
Model of modesty and simplicity, *pray for us.*
Standard of obedience and submission, *pray for us.*
Source of burning zeal and of the apostleship, *pray for us.*
Loving Mother of the poor and of children, *pray for us*
Light of the blind and of the ignorant, *pray for us.*
Consolation of the sick and of the afflicted, *pray for us.*
Hope of the despairing, *pray for us.*
Help of the Church militant, *pray for us.*
Advocate of the Church suffering, *pray for us.*
Glory of the Church triumphant, *pray for us.*
By thy bitter complaints of men's sinfulness, *render us docile to the law of thy Divine Son, O Mary!*
By thy abundant tears, *obtain for us the grace to weep over our sins, O Mary!*
By thy motherly sufferings, *obtain for us resignation in all our trials, O Mary!*
By thy apparitions and thy miracles, *revive the faith of thy people, O Mary!*
By thy mysterious looks towards Rome, *make us more and more devoted to the Holy See, O Mary!*
By thy incomparable tenderness, *make us love thee more and more, O Mary!*
By thy ravishing beauty, *make us sigh after Heaven, O Mary!*
By thy new assumption, *draw us after thee, O Mary!*

LET US PRAY: Lord Jesus Christ, who, in Thy infinite mercy, didst send to us on the mountain of La Salette Thy ever glorious Mother in order to remind us of our Christian duties, grant that, moved by Her tears and docile to Her warnings, we may appease in this life Thy just anger by a sincere repentance, and that we may merit by our good works the grace to enjoy Thee eternally in Heaven. Thou who livest and reignest world without end. *Amen.*

Litany of the Miraculous Infant (Message of September 28, 1985)
(For private devotion only)

Lord, have Mercy on us. *Christ, have Mercy on us.* Lord, have Mercy on us. Christ, hear us.
Christ, graciously hear us. God, the Father of Heaven, *have Mercy on us.* God, the Son,
Redeemer of the world, *have Mercy on us.* God, the Holy Ghost, *have Mercy on us.*
Holy Trinity, One God, *have Mercy on us.*

O miraculous Infant Jesus, *have mercy on us.*
Infant Jesus, true God and Lord, *have mercy on us.*
Infant Jesus, whose omnipotence is manifested in a wonderful manner, *have mercy on us.*
Infant Jesus, whose wisdom searches our hearts and minds, *have mercy on us.*
Infant Jesus, whose goodness continuously inclines to aid us, *have mercy on us.*
Infant Jesus, whose providence leads us to our last end and destiny, *have mercy on us.*
Infant Jesus, whose truth enlightens the darkness of our hearts, *have mercy on us.*
Infant Jesus, whose generosity enriches our poverty, *have mercy on us.*
Infant Jesus, whose friendship consoles the afflicted, *have mercy on us.*
Infant Jesus, whose mercy forgives our sins, *have mercy on us.*
Infant Jesus, whose strength invigorates us, have mercy on us.
Infant Jesus, whose power turns away all evils, *have mercy on us.*
Infant Jesus, whose justice deters us from sin, *have mercy on us.*
Infant Jesus, whose power conquers Hell, *have mercy on us.*
Infant Jesus, whose lovely countenance attracts our hearts, *have mercy on us.*
Infant Jesus, whose greatness holds the universe in its hand, *have mercy on us.*
Infant Jesus, whose love-inflamed Heart kindles our cold hearts, have mercy on us.
Infant Jesus, whose miraculous hand raised in benediction fills us with all blessings, *have mercy on us.*
Infant Jesus, whose sweet and holy Name rejoices the hearts of the faithful, *have mercy on us.*
Infant Jesus, whose glory fills the whole world, *have mercy on us.*
Be merciful. *Spare us, O Jesus.*
Be merciful. *Graciously hear us, O Jesus.*
From all evil, *deliver us, O Jesus*
From all sin, *deliver us, O Jesus*
From all distrust of Your infinite goodness, *deliver us, O Jesus*
From all doubts in Your power of miracles, *deliver us, O Jesus*
From all lukewarmness in Your veneration, *deliver us, O Jesus*
From all trials and misfortunes, *deliver us, O Jesus*

Through the mysteries of Your holy childhood, *deliver us, O Jesus*
Through the intercession of Mary, Your Virgin Mother, and St. Joseph, Your foster father, *we beseech You, hear us.*
That You would pardon us, *we beseech You, hear us.*
That You would bring us to true repentance, *we beseech You, hear us.*
That You would preserve and increase in us love and devotion to Your sacred infancy, *we beseech You, hear us.*
That You would never withdraw Your miraculous hand from us, *we beseech You, hear us.*
That You would keep us mindful of your numberless benefits, *we beseech You, hear us.*
That You would inflame us more and more with love for Your Sacred Heart, *we beseech You, hear us.*
That You would graciously hear all who call upon You with confidence, *we beseech You, hear us.*
That You would preserve our country in peace, *we beseech You, hear us.*
That You would free us from all impending evils, *we beseech You, hear us.*
That You would give eternal life to all who act generously toward You, *we beseech You, hear us.*
That You would pronounce a merciful sentence on us at the judgment, *we beseech You, hear us.*
That You would in Your miraculous image remain our consoling refuge, *we beseech You, hear us.*
Jesus, Son of God and of Mary, *we beseech You, hear us.*

Lamb of God, who takes away the sins of the world, *spare us, O Jesus.*
Lamb of God, who takes away the sins of the world, *graciously hear us, O Jesus.*
Lamb of God, who takes away the sins of the world, *have mercy on us*

V. Infant Jesus, hear us. *R. Infant Jesus, graciously hear us.*

Our Father, etc.

LET US PRAY:

O Miraculous Infant Jesus, prostrate before Your sacred image, we beseech You to cast a merciful look on our troubled hearts. Let Your tender Heart, so inclined to pity, be softened at our prayers, and grant us that Grace for which we ardently implore You. Take from us all affliction and despair, all trials and misfortunes with which we are laden. For Your sacred Infancy's sake hear our prayers and send us consolation and aid, that we may praise You, with the Father and the Holy Spirit, forever and ever. *Amen.*

Prayer to St. Benedict (Message of December 7, 1985)

"O glorious St. Benedict, sublime model of all virtues, pure vessel of God's grace! Behold me, humbly kneeling at thy feet. I implore thy loving heart to pray for me before the throne of God. To thee I have recourse in all the dangers which daily surround me. Shield me against my enemies, inspire me to imitate thee in all things. May thy blessing be with me always, so that I may shun whatever God forbids and avoid the occasions of sin.

"Graciously obtain for me from God those favors and graces of which I stand so much in need, in the trials, miseries and afflictions of life. Thy heart was always so full of love, compassion, and mercy towards those who were afflicted or troubled in any way. Thou didst never dismiss without consolation and assistance anyone who had recourse to thee. I therefore invoke thy powerful intercession in the confident hope that thou wilt hear my prayers and obtain for me the special grace and favor I so earnestly implore (mention it), if it be for the greater glory of God and the welfare of my soul.

"Help me, O great St. Benedict, to live and die as a faithful child of God, to be ever submissive to His holy will, and to attain the eternal happiness of Heaven. Amen."

The Medal of St. Benedict is one of the Sacramentals of the Church, and as such it must be used. The value and power of the Medal must be ascribed to the merits of Christ Crucified, to the efficacious prayers of St. Benedict, to the blessing of the Church, and especially to the faith and holy disposition of the person using the Medal.

The following is a partial list of the many pious purposes of the Medal of St. Benedict.

1. It words off from both the soul and the body all dangers arising from the devil.
2. The Medal is powerful in obtaining for sinners the grace of conversion.
3. It obtains protection and aid for persons tormented by the evil spirit, and in temptations against holy purity.
4. It procures assistance in the hour of death.
5. It has often proved an efficacious remedy for bodily sufferings, and a means of protection against contagious diseases.
6. Expectant mothers have obtained special assistance for a safe delivery.
7. In time of storms, tempests and other dangers on land and sea it has been found to be a protection.
8. Even domestic animals have been visibly aided by it when infected with disease.

The power of St. Benedict is revealed in this small object that has been fostered by his spiritual sons many years. Marvelous is the aid which the St. Benedict Medal affords to its devout wearers in the manifold necessities of soul and body. On this account the Medal is well known and widely used throughout the Christian world; everywhere it is regarded as a highly favored object of devotion.

Origin and Explanation of the Medal

St. Benedict (born at Nursia, Italy, in 480 AD) had a profound veneration for the Holy Cross and for our Saviour Crucified. In virtue of the Sign of the Cross, he wrought many miracles and exercised great power over the spirits of darkness. In consequence of the great veneration in which St. Benedict was held from the early Middle Ages, it followed that a Medal was struck, one side of which represents St. Benedict holding the Cross in one hand and the Holy Rule in the other. Around the image of St. Benedict are these words in Latin:

"May his presence protect us in the hour of death."

St. Benedict has ever been the patron of the dying, because of the circumstances attending his own most glorious death, for he breathed forth his soul while standing in prayer before the Most Blessed Sacrament.

The reverse of the Medal shows the image of the Cross. Around the margin are the initials of Latin words which form verses supposed to have originated with the holy Father Benedict himself. The English translation is: "Be gone Satan! Suggest not to me thy vain things. The cup thou profferest me is evil; drink thou thy poison." In the angles formed by the arms of the Cross are the letters C.S.P.B., signifying "Cross of the holy Father Benedict." The letters on the Cross itself have this meaning: "May the holy Cross be my light; let not the dragon be my guide."

Use

No special way of carrying or applying the Medal is prescribed. It may be worn about the neck, attached to the scapular or the Rosary, or otherwise carried about one's person. Often it is placed in the fields, the foundations of buildings or attached to automobiles to call down God's blessing and the protection of St. Benedict. No particular prayer is prescribed, as the devout wearing itself is a continual silent prayer.

Litany of Our Lady, Queen of the Holy Innocents (Message of March 3, 1986)
(For private devotion only)

Lord, have Mercy on us. *Christ, have Mercy on us.* Lord, have Mercy on us. Christ, hear us. *Christ, graciously hear us.* God, the Father of Heaven, *have Mercy on us.* God, the Son, Redeemer of the world, *have Mercy on us.* God, the Holy Ghost, *have Mercy on us.* Holy Trinity, One God, *have Mercy on us.*

Mary, Queen of All Holy Innocents, *pray for us.*
Mother of the First Holy Innocent, Jesus, *pray for us.*
Mary, the protector of the Holy Innocents, *pray for us.*
Mary, who cares for all the Holy Innocents, *pray for us.*
Mary, the guardian of All the Holy Innocents, *pray for us.*
Mary, the refuge of all little children who are the Holy Innocents, *pray for us.*
Mary, teacher of purity for the Holy Innocents, *pray for us.*
Mary, the source of consolation for the Holy Innocents, *pray for us.*
Mary's Immaculate Heart, the joy of Jesus and the Holy Innocents, *pray for us.*
Mary, the Mother of all unwanted Holy Innocents, *pray for us.*
Mary, the beacon of Light for the Holy Innocents, *pray for us.*
Mary, the Love of the Holy Ghost and lover of the Holy Innocents, *pray for us.*
Mary, the way to Peace for the Holy Innocents, *pray for us.*
Mary, the guide to bring back all Holy Innocents, *pray for us.*
Mary, Queen of the elect who are the Holy Innocents, *pray for us.*
Mary; Lily of help in temptation for the Holy Innocents, *pray for us.*
Mary, the hope of all the Holy Innocents, *pray for us.*

Lamb of God, Who takes away the sins of the world, *spare us, O Lord.*
Lamb of God, Who loves all the Holy Innocents, *graciously hear us, O Lord.*
Lamb of God, who takes away the sins of the world, *have mercy on us.*

LET US PRAY:

Oh Mother of the Holy Innocents, give all women the courage to bear their Holy Innocents into the World, so that they can do the Mission they were born to do for the Glory of Jesus and the Eternal Father in the Kingdom of Light. Our Lady, Queen of the Holy Innocents, *pray for us. Amen.*

Litany of the Holy Angels (Message of March 22, 1986)

Lord, have mercy. *Christ, have mercy.* Lord, have mercy. Christ, hear us. *Christ, graciously hear us.*
God the Father, Creator of the Angels, *have mercy on us.*
God the Son, Lord of the Angels, *have mercy on us.*
God the Holy Spirit, Life of the Angels, *have mercy on us.*
Holy Trinity, delight of all the Angels, *have mercy on us.*

Holy Mary, *pray for us.*
Queen of Angels, *pray for us.*
All you Choirs of Angels, *pray for us.*
Holy Seraphim, *pray for us.*
Holy Cherubim, *pray for us.*
Holy Thrones, *pray for us.*
Holy Angels of Adoration, *pray for us.*
Holy Virtues, *pray for us.*
Holy Dominations, *pray for us.*
Holy Principalities, *pray for us.*
Holy Powers, *pray for us.*

Holy Archangel Michael, *pray for us.*
Conqueror of Lucifer, *pray for us.*
Angel of-Faith and humility, *pray for us.*
Guardian of the Anointing of the Sick, *pray for us.*
Patron of the Dying, *pray for us.*
Prince of the Heavenly hosts, *pray for us.*
Guide of souls to the judgment seat of God, *pray for us.*

Holy Archangel Gabriel, *pray for us.*
Angel of the Incarnation, *pray for us.*
Faithful Messenger of God, *pray for us.*
Angel of hope and peace, *pray for us.*
Protector of all servants and handmaids of God, *pray for us.*
Guardian of Baptism, *pray for us.*
Patron of Priests, *pray for us.*

Holy Archangel Raphael, *pray for us.*
Angel of divine love, *pray for us.*

Conqueror of the hellish fiend, *pray for us.*
Helper in great distress, *pray for us.*
Angel of suffering and healing, *pray for us.*
Patron of physicians, wanderers and travelers, *pray for us.*
All holy Archangels, *pray for us.*
Angels of service before the throne of God, *pray for us.*
Angels of service for mankind, *pray for us.*
Holy Guardian Angels, *pray for us.*
Helpers in all our needs, *pray for us.*
Light in all darkness, *pray for us.*
Support in all danger, *pray for us.*
Advisers of our consciences, *pray for us.*
Intercessors before the throne of God, *pray for us.*
Shield or defense against evil spirits, *pray for us.*
Our constant companions, *pray for us.*
Our safest Guides, *pray for us.*
Our truest Friends, Our wisest Counselors, *pray for us.*
Our models of prompt obedience, *pray for us.*
Comforters in abandonment, *pray for us.*
Mirrors of humility and sincerity, *pray for us.*
Angels of our families, *pray for us.*
Angels of our priests and pastors, *pray for us.*
Angels of our children, *pray for us.*
Angels of our home and country, *pray for us.*
Angels of Holy Church, *pray for us.*
All you holy Angels, *pray for us.*
During life, *assist us.*
In death, *assist us.*
In Heaven, *we shall be grateful to you.*

Lamb of God, you who takes away the sins of the world, *spare us, O Lord.*
Lamb of God, you who takes away the sins of the world, *graciously hear us, O Lord.*
Lamb of God, you who takes away the sins of the world, *have mercy on us.*

Christ, hear us. *Christ, graciously hear us.* God has given His Angel charge over You *to guard You in all your ways.*

LET US PRAY:

Almighty, eternal God, grant us the help of your Heavenly Hosts that we may be preserved from the terrible assaults of the evil one by the Precious Blood of our Lord Jesus Christ and the intercession of the most Blessed and Immaculate Virgin Mary, so that free from all adversity we may serve you again in peace. Through Christ our Lord. *Amen.*

(With ecct, approbation Apostolic Administration Innsbruck, 2/14/51)

Litany of St. Philomena (Message of June 1, 1986)

Lord, have Mercy on us. *Christ, have Mercy on us.* Lord, have Mercy on us. Christ, hear us. *Christ, graciously hear us.* God, the Father of Heaven, *have Mercy on us.* God, the Son, Redeemer of the world, *have Mercy on us.* God, the Holy Ghost, *have Mercy on us.* Holy Trinity, One God, *have Mercy on us.*

Holy Mary, Queen of Virgins, *pray for us.*

St. Philomena, filled with abundant graces from the cradle, *pray for us.*
St. Philomena, model of virgins, *pray for us.*
St. Philomena, temple of the most perfect humility, *pray for us.*
St. Philomena, victim of the Love of Christ, *pray for us.*
St. Philomena, example of strength and perseverance, *pray for us.*
St. Philomena, invincible athlete of chastity, *pray for us.*
St. Philomena, mirror of most heroic virtues, *pray for us.*
St. Philomena, firm and intrepid before torments, *pray for us.*
St. Philomena, scourged like thy Divine Spouse, *pray for us.*
St. Philomena, pierced by a shower of arrows, *pray for us.*
St. Philomena, consoled, in chains, by the Mother of God, *pray for us.*
St. Philomena, miraculously cured in prison, *pray for us.*
St. Philomena, sustained by Angels in the midst of tortures, *pray for us.*
St. Philomena, who preferred humiliation and death to the splendor of a throne, *pray for us.*
St. Philomena, who converted the witnesses by her martyrdom, *pray for us.*
St. Philomena, who wore out the fury of thy executioners, *pray for us.*
St. Philomena, patroness of the innocent, *pray for us.*
St. Philomena, patroness of youth, *pray for us.*
St. Philomena, refuge of the unfortunate, *pray for us.*
St. Philomena, health of the sick and infirm, *pray for us.*
St. Philomena, new light of the Church Militant, *pray for us.*
St. Philomena, who confounds the impiety of our age, *pray for us.*
St. Philomena, who re-animates the Faith and courage of the faithful, *pray for us.*
St. Philomena, whose name is glorious in Heaven, and terrible in Hell, *pray for us.*
St. Philomena, illustrious by the most splendid miracles, *pray for us.*
St. Philomena, powerful with God, *pray for us.*
St. Philomena, who reigns in Glory, *pray for us.*

Lamb of God, Who takes away the sins of the world, *spare us, O Lord.*
Lamb of God, Who loves all the Holy Innocents, *graciously hear us, O Lord.*
Lamb of God, who takes away the sins of the world, *have mercy on us.*

V. Pray for us, St. Philomena.
R. That we may be made worthy of the promises of Christ.

LET US PRAY:

We beg Thee, O Lord, to grant us the pardon our sins by the intercession of St. Philomena, virgin and martyr, who was always pleasing in thy sight by her eminent chastity and the profession of every virtue. *Amen.*

Litany of the Three Patrons (Message of August 27, 1986)

Lord, have Mercy on us. *Christ have Mercy on us.* Lord have Mercy on us. Christ hear us. *Christ graciously hear us.* God, the Father of Heaven, *have Mercy on us.* God, the Son, Redeemer of the World, *have Mercy on us.* God, the Holy Ghost, *have Mercy on us.* Holy Trinity, One God, *have Mercy on us.*

Mary our Mother and the Mother of Jesus, *pray for us.*
Mary, our Mother of Consolation, *pray for us.*
Mary, the refuge of sinners, *pray for us.*
Mary, the guiding star of our lives, *pray for us.*
Mary, source of strength in our weakness, *pray for us.*
Mary, source of light in our darkness, *pray for us.*
Mary, source of consolation in our sorrows, *pray for us.*
Mary, source of victory in our temptations, *pray for us.*
Mary, who leads us to Jesus, *pray for us.*
Mary, who keeps us with Jesus, *pray for us.*
Mary, who redeems us through Jesus, *pray for us.*
Mary, Mother of consolation, our Patroness, *pray for us.*

St. Augustine, triumph of divine grace, *pray for us.*
St. Augustine, so faithful to grace, *pray for us.*
St. Augustine, glowing with pure Love of God, *pray for us.*
St. Augustine, filled with zeal for God's glory, *pray for us.*
St. Augustine, bright star in the firmament of the Church, *pray for us.*
St. Augustine, so great and so humble, *pray for us.*
St. Augustine, dauntless defender of the Faith, *pray for us.*
St. Augustine, vanquisher of heresy, *pray for us.*
St. Augustine, Prince of bishops and doctors, *pray for us.*

St. Monica, devout mother of St. Augustine, *pray for us.*
St. Monica, whose prayers won Augustine from sin, *pray for us.*
St. Monica, whose prayers gave Augustine to God, *pray for us.*
St. Monica, pattern for wives, *pray for us.*
St. Monica, model of mothers and mother of Saints, *pray for us.*
St. Monica, exemplar of widows, *pray for us.*
St. Monica, devoted to prayer, *pray for us.*
St. Monica, so patient in trials, *pray for us.*
St. Monica, so resigned in sorrow, *pray for us.*
St. Monica, so happy in death, *pray for us.*
St. Monica, devoted child of Mary, *pray for us.*
St. Monica, mother of Consolation, *pray for us.*

Lamb of God Who takest away the sins of the world, *spare us, O Lord.*
Lamb of God Who takest away the sins of the world, *graciously hear us, O Lord.*
Lamb of God Who takest away the sins of the world, *have mercy on us, O Lord.*

V. Pray for us, O Holy Mother of Consolation.
R. That we may be made worthy of the Promises of Christ.
V. Pray for us, O holy mother, St. Monica,
R. That we may be made worthy of the Promises of Christ.

LET US PRAY:

O Lord, Jesus Christ, Father of Mercies and God of all consolation, grant propitiously to Thy servants, that joyfully venerating Thy most pure Mother Mary as Our Lady of Consolation, we may be consoled by Her in our sorrows, fortified in our trials through life, and in dying, may merit the ineffable consolations of Heaven for all Eternity. *Amen.*

Litany of the Saints (Message of November 1, 1986)

Lord, have Mercy on us. *Christ, have Mercy on us.* Lord, have Mercy on us. Christ, hear us. *Christ, graciously hear us.* God, the Father of Heaven, *have Mercy on us.* God, the Son, Redeemer of the world, *have Mercy on us.* God, the Holy Ghost, *have Mercy on us.* Holy Trinity, One God, *have Mercy on us.*

Holy Mary, *pray for us.*
Holy Mother of God, *pray for us.*
Holy Virgin of Virgins, *pray for us.*
St. Michael, *pray for us.*
St. Gabriel, *pray for us.*
St. Raphael, pray for us.
All ye holy Angels and Archangels, *pray for us.*
All ye holy orders of blessed spirits, *pray for us.*
St. John Baptist, *pray for us.*
St. Joseph, *pray for us.*
All ye holy Patriarchs and Prophets, *pray for us.*
St. Peter, *pray for us.*
St. Paul, *pray for us.*
St. Andrew, *pray for us.*
St. James, *pray for us.*
St. John, *pray for us.*
St. Thomas, *pray for us.*
St. James, *pray for us.*
St. Philip, *pray for us.*
St. Bartholomew, *pray for us.*
St. Matthew, *pray for us.*
St. Simon, *pray for us.*
St. Thaddeus, *pray for us.*
St. Matthias, *pray for us.*
St. Barnabas, *pray for us.*
St. Luke, *pray for us.*
St. Mark, *pray for us.*
All ye holy apostles and evangelists, *pray for us.*
All ye holy disciples of Our Lord, *pray for us*
All ye holy innocents, *pray for us.*
St. Stephen, *pray for us.*
St. Lawrence, *pray for us.*
St. Vincent, *pray for us.*
SS. Fabian and Sebastian, *pray for us.*
SS. John and Paul, *pray for us.*
SS. Cosmas and Damian, *pray for us.*
SS. Gervase and Protuse, *pray for us.*
All ye holy Martyrs, *pray for us.*
St. Sylvester, *pray for us.*
St. Gregory, *pray for us.*
St. Ambrose, *pray for us.*
St. Augustine, *pray for us.*
St. Jerome, *pray for us.*
St. Martin, *pray for us.*
St. Nicholas, *pray for us.*
All ye holy Bishops and Confessors, *pray for us.*
All ye holy Doctors, *pray for us.*
St. Anthony, *pray for us.*
St. Benedict, *pray for us.*
St. Bernard, *pray for us.*
St. Dominic, *pray for us.*
St. Francis, *pray for us.*
All ye holy Priests and Levites, *pray for us.*
All ye holy Monks and Hermits, *pray for us.*
St. Mary Magdalen, *pray for us.*
St. Agatha, *pray for us.*
St. Lucy, *pray for us.*
St. Agnes, *pray for us.*
St. Cecilia, *pray for us.*
St. Catharine, *pray for us.*
St. Anastasia, *pray for us.*
All ye holy Virgins and Widows, *pray for us.*
All ye men and women, saints of God, *pray for us.*
Make intercession for us.

Be merciful, *spare us, O Lord.*
Be merciful, *graciously hear us, O Lord.*
From all evil, *O Lord, deliver us.*
From all sin, *O Lord, deliver us.*
From Thy wrath, *O Lord, deliver us.*
From a sudden and unprovided death, *O Lord, deliver us.*
From the deceits of the devil, *O Lord, deliver us.*
From anger, hatred, and all ill will, *O Lord, deliver us.*
From the spirit of fornication, *O Lord, deliver us.*
From lightning and tempest *O Lord, deliver us.*
From the scourge of earthquake, *O Lord, deliver us.*
From pestilence, famine, and war, *O Lord, deliver us.*
From everlasting death, *O Lord, deliver us.*
Through the mystery of Thy holy Incarnation, *O Lord, deliver us.*
Through Thy coming, *O Lord, deliver us.*
Through Thy nativity, *O Lord, deliver us.*
Through Thy baptism and holy fasting, O Lord, deliver us.
Through Thy cross and passion, *O Lord, deliver us.*
Through Thy death and burial, *O Lord, deliver us.*
Through Thy holy resurrection, *O Lord, deliver us.*
Through Thy admirable ascension, *O Lord, deliver us.*
Through the coming of the Holy Ghost, the Paraclete, *O Lord, deliver us.*

In the Day of Judgment, *we sinners beseech Thee, hear us.*
That Thou wouldst spare us, *we beseech Thee, hear us.*
That Thou wouldst pardon us, *we beseech Thee, hear us.*
That Thou wouldst vouchsafe to bring us to true penance, *we beseech Thee, hear us.*
That Thou wouldst vouchsafe to govern and preserve Thy holy Church, *we beseech Thee, hear us.*
That thou wouldst vouchsafe to preserve our Apostolic Prelate and all ecclesiastical Orders in holy religion, *we beseech Thee, hear us.*
That Thou wouldst vouchsafe to humble the enemies of Thy holy Church, *we beseech Thee, hear us.*
That Thou wouldst vouchsafe to give peace and true concord to Christian kings and princes, *we beseech Thee, hear us.*
That Thou wouldst vouchsafe to grant peace and unity to all Christian people, *we beseech Thee, hear us.*
That Thou wouldst vouchsafe to confirm and preserve us in Thy holy service, *we beseech Thee, hear us.*
That Thou wouldst lift up our minds to Heavenly desires, we beseech Thee, hear us.
That Thou wouldst tender eternal good things to all our benefactors, *we beseech Thee, hear us.*
That Thou wouldst deliver our souls and those of our brethren, kinsfolk, and benefactors from eternal damnation, *we beseech Thee, hear us.*
That Thou wouldst vouchsafe to give and preserve the fruits of the earth, *we beseech Thee, hear us.*
That Thou wouldst vouchsafe to give eternal rest to all the faithful departed, *we beseech Thee, hear us.*
That Thou wouldst vouchsafe graciously to hear us, Son of God, *we beseech Thee, hear us.*

Lamb of God, Who takest away the sins of .the world, *spare us, O Lord.*
Lamb of God, Who takest away the sins of the world, *hear us, O Lord.*
Lamb of God, Who takest away the sins of the world, *have mercy upon us, O Lord.*

Christ, hear us. *Christ, graciously hear us.* Lord, have mercy upon us.
Christ, have mercy upon us. Lord, have mercy upon us.

Our Father, etc. (In secret.)

V. And lead us not into temptation
R. But deliver us from evil. Amen.

Glory be to the Father, etc.

V. Save Thy servants,
R. Trusting in Thee, O my God.
V. Be unto us, O Lord, a tower of strength,
R. From the face of the enemy.
V. Let not the enemy prevail against us,
R. Nor the son of iniquity have power to hurt us.
V. O Lord, deal not with us according to our sins,
R. Neither reward us according to our iniquities.
V. Let us pray for our chief bishop.
R. The Lord preserve him, and give him life, and make him blessed upon earth, and deliver him not to the will of his enemies.
V. Let us pray for our benefactors.
R. Vouchsafe, O Lord, for Thy name's sake, to reward with eternal life all those who have done us good.
V. Let us pray for the faithful departed.
R. Eternal rest give to them, O Lord, and let perpetual light shine upon them.
V. May they rest in peace.
R. Amen.
V. For our absent brethren.
R. O my God, save Thy servants trusting in Thee.
V. Send them help, O Lord, from Thy holy place.
R. And from Sion protect them.
V. O Lord hear my prayer,
R. And let my cry come unto Thee.

LET US PRAY;

O God, Whose property it is always to have mercy and to spare, receive our petitions, that we, and all Thy servants who are hound by the chain of sin, may, by the compassion of Thy goodness, mercifully be absolved.

Hear, we beseech Thee, O Lord, the prayer of Thy suppliants, and pardon the sins of those who confess to Thee, that, of Thy bounty, Thou mayest grant us pardon and peace. *Amen.*

Litany of Our Lady of Mount Carmel (Message of December 7, 1986)

Lord, have Mercy on us. *Christ, have Mercy on us.* Lord, have Mercy on us. Christ, hear us. *Christ, graciously hear us.* God, the Father of Heaven, *have Mercy on us.* God, the Son, Redeemer of the world, *have Mercy on us.* God, the Holy Ghost, *have Mercy on us.* Holy Trinity, One God, *have Mercy on us.*

Our Lady of Mount Carmel, Queen of Heaven, *pray for us sinners.*
Our Lady of Mount Carmel, vanquisher of Satan, *pray for us sinners.*
Our Lady of Mount Carmel, most dutiful daughter, pray for us sinners.
Our Lady of Mount Carmel, most pure Virgin, pray *for us sinners.*
Our Lady of Mount Carmel, most devoted Spouse, *pray for us sinners.*
Our Lady of Mount Carmel, most tender mother, *pray for us sinners.*
Our Lady of Mount Carmel, perfect Model of Virtue, *pray for us sinners.*
Our Lady of Mount Carmel, sure anchor of Hope, *pray for us sinners.*
Our Lady of Mount Carmel, refuge in affliction, *pray for us sinners.*
Our Lady of Mount Carmel, dispenser of God's gifts, *pray for us sinners.*
Our Lady of Mount Carmel, tower of strength against our foes, *pray for us sinners.*
Our Lady of Mount Carmel, our aid in danger, *pray for us sinners.*
Our Lady of Mount Carmel, road leading to Jesus, *pray for us sinners.*
Our Lady of Mount Carmel, our Light in darkness, *pray for us sinners.*
Our Lady of Mount Carmel, our consolation at the hour of death, *pray for us sinners.*
Our Lady of Mount Carmel, advocate of the most abandoned sinners, *pray for us sinners.*

For those who grieve Thy Son, *with confidence we come to Thee, O Lady of Mount Carmel.*
For those who neglect to pray, *with confidence we come to Thee, O Lady of Mount Carmel.*
For those who are in their agony, *with confidence we come to Thee, O Lady of Mount Carmel.*
For those who delay their conversion, *with confidence we come to Thee, O Lady of Mount Carmel.*
For those suffering in Purgatory, *with confidence we come to Thee, O Lady of Mount Carmel.*
For those who know Thee not, *with confidence we come to Thee, O Lady of Mount Carmel.*

Lamb of God, Who takest away the sins of the world, *spare us, O Lord.*
Lamb of God, Who takest away the sins of the world, *hear us, O Lord.*
Lamb of God, Who takest away the sins of the world, *have mercy upon us, O Lord.*

V. Our Lady of Mount Carmel, hope of the despairing,
R. Intercede for us with Thy Divine Son.

LET US PRAY:

Our Lady of Mount Carmel, glorious Queen of Angels, Channel of God's tenderest Mercy to man, refuge and advocate of sinners, with confidence I prostrate myself before Thee, beseech Thee to obtain for me (pause to mention request silently). In return I solemnly promise to have recourse to Thee in all my trials, sufferings and temptations, and I shall do all in my power to induce others to love and reverence Thee and to invoke Thee in all their needs. I thank Thee for the numberless blessings which I have received from Thy Mercy and powerful intercession. Continue to be my shield in danger, my guide in life, and my consolation at the hour of death. *Amen.*

Litany of the Holy Childhood of Jesus (Message of December 24, 1986)

Lord have Mercy on us. *Christ have Mercy on us.* Lord have Mercy on us; Christ hear us. *Christ graciously hear us.* God, the Father of Heaven, *have Mercy on us.* God, the Son, Redeemer of the world, *have Mercy on us.* God, the Holy Spirit, *have Mercy on us.* Holy Trinity, One God, *have Mercy on us.*

O Divine Infant Jesus, sent to Earth from Heaven, *have mercy on us.*
O Divine Infant Jesus, born of Mary in Bethlehem, have *mercy on us.*
O Divine Infant Jesus, wrapped in swaddling clothes, *have mercy on us.*
O Divine Infant Jesus, placed in the crib, *have mercy on us.*
O Divine Infant Jesus, praised by the Angels, *have mercy on us.*
O Divine Infant Jesus, adored by the Shepherds, *have mercy on us.*
O Divine Infant Jesus, proclaimed as savior through Thy Adorable name, *have mercy on us.*
O Divine Infant Jesus, anointed by a star, *have mercy on us.*
O Divine Infant Jesus, worshiped by the Magi with symbolic Gifts, *have mercy on us.*
O Divine Infant Jesus, presented in the Temple by the Virgin, *have mercy on us.*
O Divine Infant Jesus, embraced by the Aged Simeon, *have mercy on us.*
O Divine Infant Jesus, revealed in the Temple by the Prophetess Anna, *have mercy on us.*
O Divine Infant Jesus, persecuted by King Herod, *have mercy on us.*
O Divine Infant Jesus, fleeing into exile in Egypt, *have mercy on us.*
O Divine Infant Jesus, crowning with Martyrdom the infants of Bethlehem, *have mercy on us.*
O Divine Infant Jesus, rejoicing the Heart of Mary with Thy, words, *have mercy on us.*
O Divine Infant Jesus, learning to take Thy first steps in exile, *have mercy on us.*
O Divine Infant Jesus, returning from Egypt to be reared in Nazareth, *have mercy on us.*
O Divine Infant Jesus, loved by all as a Shining example of obedience, *have mercy on us.*
O Divine Infant Jesus, brought to the Temple at the age of twelve, *have mercy on us.*
O Divine Infant Jesus, lost by Mary and Joseph on their return home, *have mercy on us.*
O Divine Infant Jesus, sought for three days, with great sorrow, *have mercy on us.*
O Divine Infant Jesus, found with great delight, *have mercy on us.*

Be Merciful, O Jesus.
Be Merciful, *hear us, O Jesus.*
From all evil, deliver us O Jesus.
From all sin, *deliver us, O Jesus*
From misconduct in the Church, *deliver us O Jesus.*
From quarrels and anger, *deliver us O Jesus.*
From lies and thievery, *deliver us O Jesus.*
From evil talk and bad example, *deliver us O Jesus.*
From bad habits, *deliver us O Jesus.*
By Thine Incarnation, *deliver us O Jesus.*
By Thy birth, *deliver us O Jesus.*
By Thy most bitter poverty, *deliver us, O Jesus.*
By thy persecution and suffering, *deliver us O Jesus.*
Through the intercession of Thy Most Holy Mother, *deliver us O Jesus.*
Through the intercession of Thy Holy Foster Father, *deliver us O Jesus.*
Through the intercession of the Holy Innocents, *deliver us O Jesus.*
Through the intercession of all the angels and saints, *deliver us O Jesus.*

We, Thy sinful children, *beseech Thee to hear us.*
Hear our prayer for the salvation of the unfortunate heathen, *we beseech Thee to hear us.*
With pity, *we beseech Thee to hear us.*
That Thou wouldst look kindly upon our small gifts, *we beseech Thee to hear us.*
That Thou wouldst number the men of God among Thy saints, *we beseech Thee to hear us.*
That Thou wouldst richly bless their apostolic works, *we beseech Thee to hear us.*
That all the world may kneel before Thee, *we beseech Thee to hear us.*
That we may be zealous to convert all unbelievers in the name of Thy Holy Childhood, *we beseech Thee to hear us.*
That we may keep our Baptismal Vows faithfully, *we beseech Thee to hear us.*
That we may rejoice to be children of Thy Father in Heaven, *we beseech Thee to hear us.*
That we may pray as Christian children, freely and devoutly, *we beseech Thee to hear us.*
That we may ever honor and love our Father in Heaven, *we beseech Thee to hear us.*
That we may willingly obey Thy Commandments, *we beseech Thee hear us.*
That we may inscribe in our hearts the Fourth Commandment "Honor Thy Father and Thy Mother," *we beseech Thee to hear us.*
That we may grow in wisdom and virtue as we grow in years, *we beseech Thee to hear us.*
That Thou will keep us innocent, *we beseech Thee to hear us.*
That Thou wilt deliver us from temptation, *we beseech Thee to hear us.*

That Thou wilt instill in us great love and devotion for Thy Mother Mary, *we beseech Thee to hear us.*
That we may never make an unworthy Confession, *we beseech thee to hear us.*
That we may receive Holy Communion with sincerity, *we beseech Thee to hear us.*
That Thou wilt grant our parents a long life, *we beseech Thee to hear us.*
That Thou will grant them Thy best gifts, *we beseech Thee to hear us.*
That Thou wilt enlighten our pastors and give them strength, *we beseech Thee to hear us.*
That Thou wilt repay our benefactors with Eternal gifts, *we beseech Thee to hear us.*
That Thou wilt have mercy upon the poor souls in Purgatory, *we beseech Thee to hear us.*

Lamb of God, Who takest away the sins of the world, *spare us, O Lord.*
Lamb of God, Who takest away the sins of the world, *hear our prayer, O Lord*
Lamb of God, Who takest away the sins of the world, *have mercy on us, O Lord.*

V. Christ hear us.
R. Christ graciously hear us.

Our Father Who art in Heaven, etc.

LET US PRAY:

We pray to Thee, Heavenly Father, Who for the Infant Jesus' sake, adopted us as Thy children, and as heirs of Heaven, look kindly upon the children not of the Faith and let them participate in our unearned and priceless Fortune. We ask this through the Infant Jesus Christ, Thy Son, Our Lord, Who liveth and reigneth with Thee and the Holy Spirit, forever and ever. *Amen.*

Litany of the Holy Spirit (Message of April 19, 1987)

Lord, have Mercy on us. *Christ, have Mercy on us.* Lord, have Mercy on us.
Father All Powerful, *have Mercy on us.* Jesus, Eternal Son of the
Father, Redeemer of the world, *save us.* Spirit of the Father and the
Son, boundless life of both, *sanctify us.* Holy Trinity, *hear us.*

Holy Spirit, Who proceedest from the Father and the Son, *enter our Hearts.*
Holy Spirit, Who art equal to the Father and the Son, *enter our hearts.*
Promise of God the Father, *have mercy on us.*
Ray of Heavenly Light, *have mercy on us.*
Author of All Good, *have mercy on us.*
Source of Heavenly Water, *have mercy on us.*
Consuming Fire, *have mercy on us.*
Ardent Charity, *have mercy on us.*
Spiritual Unction, *have mercy on us.*
Spirit of Love and Truth, *have mercy on us.*
Spirit of Wisdom and understanding, *have mercy on us.*
Spirit of Counsel and fortitude, *have mercy on us.*
Spirit of Knowledge & piety, *have mercy on us.*
Spirit of the Fear of the Lord, *have mercy on us.*
Spirit of Grace and prayer, *have mercy on us.*
Spirit of Peace and meekness, *have mercy on us.*
Spirit of modesty and innocence, *have mercy on us.*
Holy Spirit, the comforter, *have mercy on us.*
Holy Spirit, the Sanctifier, *have mercy on us.*
Holy Spirit Who governest the Church, *have mercy on us.*
Gift of God The Most High, *have mercy on us.*
Spirit Who fillest the Universe, *have mercy on us.*
Spirit of adoption of the children of God, *have mercy on us.*

Holy Spirit, inspire us with horror of sin.
Holy Spirit, come and renew the face of the Earth.
Holy Spirit shed Thy light into our souls.
Holy Spirit engrave Thy Law in our hearts.
Holy Spirit inflame us with the flame of Thy love.
Holy Spirit open to us the Treasures of Thy Graces.
Holy Spirt teach us to pray well.
Holy Spirit, enlighten us with Thy Heavenly inspirations.
Holy Spirit, lead us in the way of Salvation.
Holy Spirit, grant us the only necessary Knowledge.
Holy Spirit, inspire in us the practice of good.
Holy Spirit, grant us the merits of all virtues.
Holy Spirit, make us persevere in justice.
Holy Spirit, be our everlasting reward.

Lamb of God, Who takest away the sins of the world, *send us Thy Holy Spirit.*
Lamb of God, Who takest away the sins of the world, *pour down into our souls the Gifts of the Holy Spirit.*
Lamb of God, Who takest away the sins of the world, *grant us the Spirit of wisdom and piety.* \

V. Come Holy Spirit! Fill the hearts of Thy faithful,
R. *And enkindle in them the Fire of Thy Love.*

LET US PRAY:

Grant, O Merciful Father, that Thy Divine Spirit may enlighten, inflame, and purify us, that He may penetrate us with His Heavenly dew and make us fruitful in good works, through Our Lord Jesus Christ, thy Son, Who with thee in the Unity of the Same spirit, liveth and reigneth forever and ever. Amen.

Litany of Our Lady of Sorrows (Message of March 31, 1988)

Lord, have Mercy on us. *Christ, have Mercy on us.* Lord, have mercy on us. Christ, Hear us. *Christ, graciously hear us.* God the Father of Heaven, *have Mercy on us.* God, the Son, Redeemer of the World, *have Mercy on us.* God, the Holy Spirit, *have Mercy on us.* Holy Trinity, One God, *have Mercy on us.*

Holy Mary, Mother of God, *pray for us.*
Holy Virgin of virgins, *pray for us.*
Mother of the crucified, *pray for us.*
Mother most sorrowful, *pray for us.*
Mother most tearful, *pray for us.*
Mother afflicted, *pray for us.*
Mother forsaken, *pray for us.*
Mother bereft of Thy Child, *pray for us.*
Mother transfixed with the sword, *pray for us.*
Mother consumed with grief, *pray for us.*
Mother filled with anguish, *pray for us.*
Mother crucified in Heart, *pray for us.*
Mother most sad, *pray for us.*
Fountain of tears, *pray for us.*
Abyss of suffering, *pray for us.*
Mirror of patience, *pray for us.*
Rock of constancy, *pray for us.*
Joy of the afflicted, *pray for us.*
Ark of the desolate, *pray for us.*
Anchor of confidence, *pray for us.*
Refuge of the forsaken, *pray for us.*
Shield of the oppressed, *pray for us.*
Conqueror of the incredulous, *pray for us.*
Comfort of the wretched, *pray for us.*
Medicine of the sick, *pray for us.*
Strength of the weak, *pray for us.*
Haven of the shipwrecked, *pray for us.*
Calmer of tempests, *pray for us.*
Resource of mourners, *pray for us.*
Terror of the treacherous, *pray for us.*
Treasure of the faithful, *pray for us.*
Theme of Prophets, *pray for us.*
Staff of the Apostles, *pray for us.*
Queen of the Martyrs, *pray for us.*
Light of confessors, *pray for us.*
Pearl of virgins, *pray for us.*
Consolation of widows, *pray for us.*
Joy of all Saints, *pray for us.*

Lamb of God, Who takest away the sins of the world, *spare us, O Jesus.*
Lamb of God, Who takest away the sins of the world, *graciously hear us, O Jesus.*
Lamb of God, Who takest away the sins of the world, *have mercy on us. Amen.*

Look down upon us, deliver us, and save us from all trouble, in the Power of Jesus Christ. Amen.

LET US PRAY:

Imprint, O Lady, Thy wounds upon my heart that I may read there, in sorrow and love: sorrow to endure every sorrow for Thee; love to despise every love but Thine. Amen.

(Conclude with Apostles' Creed, Hail Holy Queen, and three Hail Mary's in honor of the Most Holy Heart of Mary.)

Litany of Our Lady of Good Counsel (Message of June 18, 1988)

Lord, have Mercy on us. *Christ, have Mercy on us.* Lord, have mercy on us. Christ Hear us. *Christ, graciously hear us.* God the Father of Heaven, *have Mercy on us.* God, the Son, Redeemer of the World, *have Mercy on us.* God, the Holy Spirit, *have Mercy on us.* Holy Trinity, One God, *have Mercy on us.*

Holy Mary, *pray for us.*
Holy Mother of God, *pray for us.*
Holy Virgin of virgins, *pray for us.*
Mother of Good Council, *pray for us.*
Daughter of the Heavenly Father, *pray for us.*
Mother of the Divine Son, *pray for us.*
Spouse of the Holy Ghost, *pray for us.*
Temple of the most Holy Trinity, *pray for us.*
Dispenser of Graces, *pray for us.*
Gate of Heaven, *pray for us.*
Queen of Angels *pray for us.*
Honor of Patriarchs, *pray for us.*
Glory of Prophets, *pray for us.*
Counsellor of Apostles, *pray for us.*
Counsellor of Martyrs, *pray for us.*
Counsellor of Confessors, *pray for us.*
Counsellor of Virgins, *pray for us.*
Counsellor of all Saints, *pray for us.*
Counsellor of the Afflicted, *pray for us.*
Counsellor of Widows and Orphans, *pray for us.*
Counsellor of the Sick, *pray for us.*
Counsellor of the Sorrowful and of Prisoners, *pray for us.*
Counsellor of the Poor, *pray for us.*
Counsellor of the Needy, *pray for us.*
Counselor in all Dangers, *pray for us.*
Counsellor in all Temptations, *pray for us.*
Counsellor of penitent Sinners, *pray for us.*
Counsellor of the Dying, *pray for us.*

In all affairs and necessities, *give us good counsel.*
In all doubts and perplexities, *give us good counsel.*
In all afflictions and adversities, *give us good counsel.*
In all dangers and misfortunes, *give us good counsel.*
In all undertakings and concerns, *give us good counsel.*
In all our needs, *give us good counsel.*
In all crosses and sufferings, *give us good counsel.*
In all temptations and snares, *give us good counsel.*
In persecution and calumny, *give us good counsel.*
In all wrong suffered, *give us good counsel.*
In all dangers of soul and body, *give us good counsel.*
In all the events of our life, *give us good counsel.*
In all sickness and infirmity, *give us good counsel.*
In the hour of death, *give us good counsel.*

Lamb of God, Who takest away the sins of the world, *spare us, O Lord.*
Lamb of God, Who takest away the sins of the world, *graciously hear us, O Lord.*
Lamb of God, Who takest away the sins of the world, *have mercy on us. Amen.*

Our Father…

V. In all anxiety and trouble
R. *Bring us to good counsel, O Blessed Virgin Mary.*

LET US PRAY:

O God, the Giver of all good and perfect gifts, let us, who seek refuge with Mary obtain in all our wants, troubles and affairs good counsel, help, and assistance for the sake of Jesus Christ, thy Son.

(With ecclesiastical approbation, Bishop F.J. Klein, National Director CWL)

Litany for the Souls in Purgatory (Message of December 7, 1988)
(For private use only)

Lord, have mercy on us. *Christ, have mercy on us.* Lord, have mercy on us. Christ, hear us.
Christ, graciously hear us. God the Father of Heaven, *have mercy on the souls of the faithful departed.*
God the Son, Redeemer of the world, *have mercy on the souls of the faithful departed.*
God the Holy Spirit, *Have mercy on the souls of the faithful departed.*
Holy Trinity, One God, *Have mercy on the souls of the faithful departed.*

Holy Mary, *pray for the souls of the faithful departed.*
Holy Mother of God, *pray for the souls of the faithful departed.*
Saint Michael, *pray for the souls of the faithful departed.*
Saint Gabriel, *pray for the souls of the faithful departed.*
All ye holy Angels and Archangels, *pray for the souls of the faithful departed.*
Saint John the Baptist, *pray for the souls of the faithful departed.*
Saint Joseph, *pray for the souls of the faithful departed.*
All ye holy Patriarchs and Prophets, *pray for the souls of the faithful departed.*
Saint Peter, *pray for the souls of the faithful departed.*
Saint Paul, *pray for the souls of the faithful departed.*
Saint John, *pray for the souls of the faithful departed.*
All ye holy Apostles and Evangelists, *pray for the souls of the faithful departed.*
Saint Stephen, *pray for the souls of the faithful departed.*
Saint Lawrence, *pray for the souls of the faithful departed.*
All ye holy Martyrs, *pray for the souls of the faithful departed.*
Saint Gregory, *pray for the souls of the faithful departed.*
Saint Ambrose, *pray for the souls of the faithful departed.*
All ye holy Bishops and Confessors, *pray for the souls of the faithful departed.*
Saint Mary Magdalen, *pray for the souls of the faithful departed.*
Saint Catherine, *pray for the souls of the faithful departed.*
All ye holy Virgins and Widows, *pray for the souls of the faithful departed.*
All ye Saints of God, *make intercession for the souls of the faithful departed.*

Be merciful, *Spare them, O Lord.*
Be merciful, *Hear them, O Lord.*

From all evil, *O Lord, deliver them.*
From Thy wrath, *O Lord, deliver them.*
From the flame of fire, *O Lord, deliver them.*
From the region of the shadow of death, *O Lord, deliver them.*
Through Thine Immaculate Conception, *O Lord, deliver them.*
Through Thy Nativity, *O Lord, deliver them.*
Through Thy Most Holy Name, *O Lord, deliver them.*
Through the multitude of Thy tender mercies, *O Lord, deliver them.*
Through Thy most bitter Passion, *O Lord, deliver them.*
Through Thy most Sacred Wounds, *O Lord, deliver them.*
Through Thy most Precious Blood, *O Lord, deliver them.*
Through Thine ignominious death, by which
Thou hast destroyed our death, *O Lord, deliver them.*

We sinners, *we beseech Thee, hear us.*
O Thou Who didst absolve the sinner woman and hear the prayer of the good thief, *we beseech Thee, hear us.*
That thou wouldst release our deceased parents, relations and benefactors from the bonds of their sins and the punishment for them, *we beseech Thee, hear us.*
That Thou wouldst hasten the day of visiting Thy faithful detained in the receptacles of sorrow, and wouldst transport them to the city of eternal peace, *we beseech Thee, hear us.*
That Thou wouldst shorten the time of expiation for their sins and graciously admit them into the holy sanctuary, into which no unclean thing can enter, *we beseech Thee, hear us.*
That through the prayers and alms of Thy Church, and especially by the inestimable Sacrifice of Thy Holy Altar, Thou wouldst receive them into the tabernacle of rest and crown their longing hopes with everlasting fruition, *we beseech Thee, hear us.*
Son of God, *we beseech Thee, hear us.*

Lamb of God, Who takest away the sins of the world, *grant them eternal rest.*
Lamb of God, Who takest away the sins of the world, *grant them eternal rest.*
Lamb of God, Who takest away the sins of the world, *grant them eternal rest.*

Christ, hear us. *Christ, graciously hear us.*

Lord, have mercy on us. *Christ, have mercy on us.*
Lord, have mercy on us.

Our Father, Who art in Heaven, etc.
V. And lead us not into temptation,
R. But deliver us from all evil. Amen.

V. From the gates of Hell,
R. Deliver their Souls, O Lord.
V. May they rest in peace.
R. Amen.
V. O Lord, hear my prayer,
R. And let my cry come unto Thee.

LET US PRAY:

O God, Creator and Redeemer of all the faithful, grant to the Souls of Thy departed servants the remission of all their sins, that through our pious supplications they may obtain the pardon which they have always desired. Through Jesus Christ Our Lord. *Amen.*

O God, the Giver of pardon and the Lover of the salvation of men, we beg Thy clemency on behalf of our brethren, kinsfolk and benefactors who have departed this life, that by the intercession of the Blessed Virgin Mary and of all the Saints, Thou wouldst receive them into the joys of Thine everlasting kingdom. Through Christ Our Lord. *Amen.*

O God, to Whom it belongs always to have mercy and to spare, be favorably propitious to the Souls of Thy servants and grant them the remission of all their sins, that being delivered from the bonds of this mortal life, they may be admitted to life everlasting. Through Jesus Christ Our Lord. *Amen.*

Short Litany for the Souls in Purgatory (Message of December 15, 1988)

(For private use only)

The just shall be in everlasting remembrance; *He shall not fear the evil hearing,*

V. Absolve, O Lord, the souls of the faithful departed from every bond of sin,
R. And by the help of Thy *grace may they be enabled to escape the avenging judgment, and to enjoy the happiness of eternal life.*

Because in Thy mercy are deposited the souls that departed in an inferior degree of grace, *Lord, have mercy.*
Because their present suffering is greatest in the knowledge of the pain that their separation from Thee is causing Thee, *Lord, have mercy.*
Because of their present inability to add to Thy accidental glory, *Lord, have mercy.*
Not for our consolation, O Lord; not for their release from purgative pain, O God; but for Thy joy and the greater accidental honor of Thy throne, O Christ the King, *Lord, have mercy.*

For the souls of our departed friends, relations and benefactors, *grant light and peace, O Lord.*
For those of our family who have fallen asleep in Thy bosom, O Jesus, *grant light and peace, O Lord.*
For those who have gone to prepare our place, *grant light and peace, O Lord.*
For those who were our brothers (or sisters) in Religion, *grant light and peace, O Lord.*
For priests who were our spiritual directors, *grant light and peace, O Lord.*
For men or women who were our teachers in school, *grant light and peace, O Lord.*
For those who were our employers or employees, *grant light and peace, O Lord.*
For those who were our associates in daily toil, *grant light and peace, O Lord.*
For any soul whom we ever offended, *grant light and peace, O Lord.*
For our enemies now departed, *grant light and peace, O Lord.*
For those souls who have none to pray for them, *grant light and peace, O Lord.*
For those forgotten by their friends and kin, *grant light and peace, O Lord.*
For those now suffering the most, *grant light and peace, O Lord.*
For those who have acquired the most merit, *grant light and peace, O Lord.*
For the souls next to be released from Purgatory, *grant light and peace, O Lord.*
For those who, while on earth, were most devoted to God the Holy Ghost, to Jesus in the Most Blessed Sacrament, to the holy Mother of God, *grant light and peace, O Lord.*
For all deceased popes and prelates, *grant light and peace, O Lord.*
For all deceased priests, seminarians and religious, *grant light and peace, O Lord.*
For all our brethren in the Faith everywhere, *grant light and peace, O Lord.*
For all our separated brethren who deeply loved Thee, and would have come into Thy household had they known the truth, *grant light and peace, O Lord.*
For those souls who need, or in life asked our prayers, *grant light and peace, O Lord.*
For those, closer to Thee than we are, whose prayers we need, *grant light and peace, O Lord.*

That those may be happy with Thee forever, who on earth were true exemplars of the Catholic Faith, *grant them eternal rest, O Lord.*
That those may be admitted to Thine unveiled Presence, who as far as we know never committed mortal sin, *grant them eternal rest, O Lord.*
That those may be housed in glory, who lived always in recollection and prayer, *grant them eternal rest, O Lord.*
That those may be given the celestial joy of beholding Thee, who lived lives of mortification and self-denial and penance, *grant them eternal rest, O Lord.*
That those may be flooded with Thy love, who denied themselves even Thy favors of indulgence and who made the heroic act for the souls who had gone before them, *grant them eternal rest, O Lord.*
That those may be drawn up to the Beatific Vision, who never put obstacles in the way of sanctifying grace and who ever drew closer in mystical union with Thee, *grant them eternal rest, O Lord.*

V. Eternal rest give unto them, O Lord,
R. And let perpetual light shine upon them.

LET US PRAY:

Be mindful, O Lord, of Thy servants and handmaids, *N.* and *N.*, who are gone before us with the sign of faith and repose in the sleep of grace. To these, O Lord, and to all who rest in Christ, grant, we beseech Thee, a place of refreshment, light and peace, through the same Christ Our Lord. *R. Amen.*

Litany for the Faithful Departed (Message of July 26, 1989)

Lord, have mercy. *Christ, have mercy.* Lord, have mercy. Christ, hear us.
Christ, graciously hear us. God, the Father of Heaven, *have mercy on the souls of the faithful departed.*
God, the Son, Redeemer of the world, *have mercy on the souls of the faithful departed.*
God, the Holy Spirit, *have mercy on the souls of the faithful departed.*
Holy Trinity, one God, *have mercy on the souls of the faithful departed.*

Holy Mary, *pray for the souls of the faithful departed.*
Holy Mother of God, *pray for the souls of the faithful departed.*
Holy Virgin of virgins, *pray for the souls of the faithful departed.*
St. Michael, *pray for the souls of the faithful departed.*
All holy Angels and Archangels, *pray for the souls of the faithful departed.*
All choirs of celestial Spirits, *pray for the souls of the faithful departed.*
St. John the Baptist, *pray for the souls of the faithful departed.*
St. Joseph, *pray for the souls of the faithful departed.*
All holy Patriarchs and Prophets, *pray for the souls of the faithful departed.*
St. Peter, *pray for the souls of the faithful departed.*
St. Paul, *pray for the souls of the faithful departed.*
St. John, *pray for the souls of the faithful departed.*
All holy Apostles and Evangelists, *pray for the souls of the faithful departed.*
St. Stephen, *pray for the souls of the faithful departed.*
St. Lawrence, *pray for the souls of the faithful departed.*
All holy Martyrs, *pray for the souls of the faithful departed.*
St. Gregory, *pray for the souls of the faithful departed.*
St. Ambrose, *pray for the souls of the faithful departed.*
St. Augustine, *pray for the souls of the faithful departed.*
St. Jerome, *pray for the souls of the faithful departed.*
All holy Pontiffs and Confessors, *pray for the souls of the faithful departed.*
All holy Doctors, *pray for the souls of the faithful departed.*
All holy Priests and Levites, *pray for the souls of the faithful departed.*
All holy Monks and Hermits, *pray for the souls of the faithful departed.*
St. Mary Magdalen, *pray for the souls of the faithful departed.*
St. Catherine, *pray for the souls of the faithful departed.*
St. Barbara, *pray for the souls of the faithful departed.*
All holy Virgins and Widows, *pray for the souls of the faithful departed.*
All Saints of God, *pray for the souls of the faithful departed.*

Be merciful to them. *Spare them, O Lord.*
Be merciful to them. *Graciously hear us, O Lord.*

From all suffering, *O Lord, deliver them.*
From all delay, *O Lord, deliver them.*
From fearful darkness, *O Lord, deliver them.*
From their mourning and tears, *O Lord, deliver them.*
By your Incarnation, *O Lord, deliver them.*
By your Nativity, *O Lord, deliver them.*
By your Baptism and holy fasting, *O Lord, deliver them.*
By your most profound humility, *O Lord, deliver them.*
By your perfect submission, *O Lord, deliver them*
By your infinite love, *O Lord, deliver them.*
By your anguish and torment, *O Lord, deliver them.*
By your sacred Wounds, *O Lord, deliver them.*
By your Cross and bitter Passion, *O Lord, deliver them.*
By your ignominious Death, *O Lord, deliver them.*
By your glorious Resurrection, *O Lord, deliver them.*
By your admirable Ascension, *O Lord, deliver them.*
By the coming of the Paraclete, *O Lord, deliver them.*

Lamb of God, you take away the sins of the world, *give them rest.*
Lamb of God, you take away the sins of the world, *give them rest.*
Lamb of God, you take away the sins of the world, *give them eternal rest.*

Jesus Christ, hear us. *Jesus Christ, graciously hear us.*
Lord, have mercy, *Christ, have mercy.* Lord, have mercy.

Our Father, etc.

V. From the fate of Hell,
R. O Lord, you have delivered them.

LET US PRAY:

O Lord, the Creator and Redeemer of all the faithful, grant to the souls of your departed servants the remission of all their sins; that by the humble supplications of your Church, they may obtain that pardon which they have always desired of your mercy. Grant this through our Lord Jesus Christ, Your Son, who lives and reigns with you and the Holy Spirit, one God, for ever and ever. *Amen.*

Short Prayers

Prayer to St. Michael (Message of December 24, 1983)

St Michael, the Archangel, defend us in battle. Be our defense against the wickedness and snares of the devil. May God rebuke him, we humbly pray; and do thou, O Prince of the Heavenly Host, by the Divine Power of God, thrust into Hell Satan, and all the evil spirits who wander throughout the world, seeking the ruin of souls. Amen.

Prayer to St. Gabriel (Message of December 24, 1983)

O Blessed Archangel St. Gabriel, we beseech thee, do thou intercede for us at the Throne of Divine Mercy in our present necessities, that as Thou didst announce to Mary the Mystery of the Incarnation, so though Thy prayers and patronage in Heaven, we may obtain the benefits of the same, and sing the praise of God, forever in the land of the living. Amen.

Prayer for Removal of Those Returned to Life through Witchery (Message of January 13, 1984)

If the walking 'dead' (zombies) are encountered, and the prayer is read, be not surprised if the zombie-spirit vanishes and takes the body with it back to Hell. Prayer is more powerful than an exorcism against undead souls (those who died, yet still walk due to Voodoo.)

"I tell you, in the Name of Jesus Christ, Be Gone, if thou are a Disciple of Satan! I am to tell you, in God's name to Be Gone, for there is only One God, the Lord, High God in Heaven, You will return to Hell and tell him these exact words that I have told you."

"In the Name of the Father, and of the Son, and of the Holy Ghost. Amen."

(You must say 'Holy Ghost' not 'Holy Spirit' for the prayer to work.)

Miraculous St. Joseph Prayer (Message of January 13, 1984)

(Protects from death by fire, by poison, by war, or suddenly.)

"O St. Joseph, whose protection is so great, so strong, so prompt, before the Throne of God, I place in you all my interests and desires.

O St. Joseph, do assist me by your Powerful Intercession and obtain for me, from your Divine Son all Spiritual Blessings, through Jesus Christ Our Lord, so that having engaged here below your Heavenly Power, I may offer my thanksgiving and homage to the Most Loving of Fathers.

O St. Joseph, I never weary of contemplating you, and Jesus asleep in your arms. I dare not approach while He reposes near your heart. Press him, in my name, and kiss His fine head for me. Ask Him to return the kiss when I draw my dying breath.

St. Joseph, Patron of Departing Souls, Pray for us. Amen.

Prayer to obtain the Glorification of Padre Pio (Message of December 7, 1985)

O Jesus, full of grace and charity, victim for sinners, so impelled by love for us that you willed to die on the Cross, I humbly beseech you to glorify in Heaven and on earth the Servant of God, Padre Pia of Pietrelcina, who generously participated in your sufferings, who loved you so much and laboured so faithfully for the glory of your Heavenly Father and for the good of souls.

With confidence I beseech you to grant me, through his intercession, the grace of ... which I ardently desire.

Glory be to the Father...(three times).

Imprimatur - Manfredonia, 12-3-1971 + **Valentino Vallat**, *Archbishop*

Prayer for Parents (Message of March 3, 1986)

O Father, may you grant to all parents the Gift of Your Grace, touching their hearts and minds. May they be open to Love You alone are. May Your Love burn in their breasts till they are able to share it with Family, Friends, and even with their worst Enemies.

Next, say:
Four: Our Father's;   Seven: Hail Mary's;   One: Glory Be...   One: Apostle's Creed
Four: Jesus, Mary, Joseph, I love you, save souls!

The Our Father (Message of April 17, 1987)

Our Father, Who art in Heaven, hallowed be thy Name. Thy Kingdom come; Thy Will be done on earth as it is in Heaven. Give us this day our daily bread; and forgive us our trespasses against us: and lead us not into temptation, but deliver us from evil. Amen.

The Hail Mary (Message of April 17, 1987)

Hail Mary, full of Grace. The Lord is with you; blessed is the fruit of your womb, Jesus. Holy Mary, Mother of God, pray for us now and at the hour of our death. Amen.

The Glory Be to the Father (Message of April 17, 1987)

Glory be to the Father, and to the Son, and to the Holy Spirit, as it was in the beginning, is now, and ever shall be, world without end. Amen.

www.ingramcontent.com/pod-product-compliance
Lightning Source LLC
Chambersburg PA
CBHW081323040426
42453CB00013B/2282